The Collected Poems of E. J. Pratt second edition

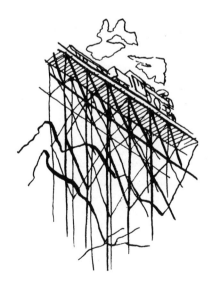

Published by the Macmillan Company of Canada Limited, Toronto

The Collected

Edited with an introduction by Northrop Frye

Second edition

Poems of E. J. Pratt

Printed and bound in Canada
by McCorquodale & Blades Printers Limited

Designed and illustrated
by Frank Davies, M.T.D.C.

Set in Baskerville type ten point on twelve point body

The handwriting of E. J. Pratt is reproduced
on the front and back covers of this book's case.

Reprinted 1970

To Viola my wife
and to Claire my daughter
this book
is lovingly dedicated

CONTENTS

MANY MOODS (1932)

CONTINUED

PART TWO: NARRATIVE POEMS

EDITOR'S PREFACE

This second edition of the *Collected Poems* of E. J. Pratt comprises all the poems that the author is willing to reprint, along with *Behind the Log, Towards the Last Spike,* and a group classified as "Later Poems", which have been written since the appearance of the first edition in 1944. As compared with the first edition, "Carlo" and "A Dirge", from *Newfoundland Verse,* "Putting Winter to Bed" from *Many Moods,* and "The Mirage" and "The Illusion" (formerly called "The Drowning") from *The Fable of the Goats and Other Poems* have been added. "A Reverie on a Dog" and "The Fable of the Goats", not included here, may be found in the first edition.

If the reader is wondering, as he easily may, why this poet should need either an editor or an introduction, I should explain that my very simple editorial duties have been assumed purely as an act of personal homage to the poet in his seventy-fifth year.

N. F.

The purpose of this introduction is not to speak for a poet who can speak quite well for himself. Its purpose is to encourage the reader to commit himself to the poet. If he is unfamiliar with Pratt, this is the right book for him to start with. Pratt cannot be sampled in anthologies: he must be read in bulk or not at all. If he is familiar with only part of Pratt's work, this book will give him the poet's whole scope and range. If he has certain preconceived ideas about Pratt, he will be able to compare them with the poems. If he knows Pratt thoroughly, he still has a rich and complex poetic experience awaiting him. Pratt has genuine simplicity, but, as William Blake wrote, there is a wide gulf between the simple and the insipid. Simplicity is difficult, not easy; it destroys laziness and prejudice, it does not confirm them.

Pratt's life has been outwardly quiet, but he has been one of those creators Henry James spoke of, who do not need to search for experience because they are the kind of people on whom nothing is lost. Born in Newfoundland in 1883, his first impressions were of Newfoundland fishing villages, where, in the words of one of their folk songs, "fish is low and flour is high", and where men fought for their food at the risk of their lives. More than once his father, who was a clergyman, had to inform a fisherman's wife that her husband would not return from the sea. Newfoundland was followed by Victoria College, where he was graduated in 1911, and by graduate work in theology and psychology. In Methodism at that time the battle of "higher criticism" had been won, Biblical archaeology (see "The Epigrapher") was opening up, there was general enthusiasm for such new world-pictures as "evolution", *Angst* and *Existenz* were unheard of, and there was no difficulty—certainly the poet has never found any—in being Christian and liberal at the same time. Psychology was concerned largely with experiments in sensory response to signals, with colour wheels that turned grey when revolved, an apparatus that made the poet long for a more entertaining type of spinner:

Fled was the class-room's puny space—
His eye saw but a whirling disk.

("IN ABSENTIA")

Finally he became a teacher of English literature at Victoria College, and remained there until his retirement as Professor Emeritus in 1953. Each of these strata of experience can be easily traced in his work. As a student of literature he struck his roots directly into Shakespeare and the major Romantics—poets great enough to allow him to find his own mode of poetic speech for himself. He has never followed or started any particular "trend" in poetry, never learned or imposed any particular mannerisms of expression. The record of the rest of his life, from *Newfoundland Verse* in 1923 onwards, is the substance of this book.

It is interesting to compare the original *Newfoundland Verse* with what the author has been willing to reprint of it here. Always contemptuous of what he calls "O thouing", he has tried to cut away two things: the intrusion of the poet on his reader, and the detachment of the poet from his surroundings. He is already well aware that writing narrative poetry is no job for an egocentric poet. For narrative, the poet must have a story worth telling, and then get out of its way. Thus, in the final quatrain of "The Ice-Floes":

Of twenty thousand seals that were killed
  To help to lower the price of bread;
Of the muffled beat . . . of a drum . . . that filled
  A nave . . . at our count of sixty dead.

The dots are not put there just to look impressive; they are there to slow down the end of a beautifully paced narrative. There is no attempt to pack in Higher Significance, no bluster about red-blooded heroes, no underlining of the irony, no comment on the tragedy. The poet knows that a good story cannot be pumped up by fine writing, and that a fable that is any good contains its own moral.

It is a law of poetic creation that the poet who is willing to lose his personality in his work finds it again. Out of his self-effacing concern with the poetic object, Pratt developed a flexible, unpretentious speaking style which is amazingly versatile, yet always unmistakably his. A slight turn in one direction, and this style goes into broad burlesque, with comic rhymes and anticlimaxes in the tradition of *Hudibras* and *Don Juan*:

A walrus' heart and pancreas,
A blind Auk from the coast of Java,
A bull moose that had died from gas
While eating toadstools near Ungava.

(THE WITCHES' BREW)

A slight turn in another direction, and it becomes delicate and fanciful, as in this description of Cassiopeia:

For high above the table head
Shall sway a candelabrum where,
According to the legend, dwelt a
Lady seated in a chair
With Alpha, Beta, Gamma, Delta,
Busy braiding up her hair.

("THE DEPRESSION ENDS")

It can dramatize a poker game or a whale hunt, summarize history or expound science, swivel easily from the colloquial to the eloquent. In a tragic context, the same style can achieve the peculiar virtue of narrative, of being able to communicate the most deeply impressive moments in a bald, flat statement, as in the account of Lalemant's martyrdom in *Brébeuf*:

*Lalemant died in the morning at nine, in the
    flame
Of the pitch-belts.*

"Ther is namore to seye," as Chaucer, who ought
to have known something about narrative, so
often remarks.

The patient scholarship and research that has
gone into the major poems is another self-effacing quality that has made for distinctiveness.
One would expect such research in *Brébeuf* or
Towards the Last Spike, but the poet also understands that aspect of erudition which is irresist-
ibly comic. In fact, he did not really find himself as a narrative poet until the knowledge
painfully acquired in a decade of study began
to strike him as having a funny side. Before
The Witches' Brew, according to his own account, he had composed and burnt a portentous
epic named *Clay,* which apparently contained a
good deal of metrically organized information.
The wit and exuberance of *The Great Feud* depend on the plethora of unusual technical terms,
and *The Witches' Brew* itself, in the energy of
its defiance of an environment of Methodism and
prohibition, sweeps in an encyclopaedic survey of
brands of liquor, to the great confusion of its
original reviewers.

In all his poetry Pratt's language bristles with
the concrete and the definite. He has always
understood that the imagination has to realize
its whole area, not bits and pieces of it, and he
has the swift selective eye—or rather ear—for the
relevant detail that distinguishes the scholar
from the pedant. In search of a monosyllable
that would convey the hardness of rock, he ransacked a department of geology until he extracted the word "schist". While he was working on
Behind the Log, anyone in a naval uniform he
met would be backed into a corner and forced
to reveal what he knew (or, much more fre-
quently, did not know) about the anatomy of a

ship. For the band in *The Titanic,* he asked me for a term in music denoting a moderate rate of speed—four syllables, main accent on the third. I gave him his choice of andantino, moderato, and allegretto. He chose andantino, but as the line "The allegretto strains in human tears" occurs in a poem published many years later, he had clearly not forgotten the alternatives.

Another feature already present in *Newfoundland Verse* is the unifying of the poet with his society, and of that society with nature. The rhythm that drives the sea against the rocks drives the blood through the human body; even when in bed inside a cottage the spirit is aware of its kinship with the wind outside. It is against this background of identity that man fights nature in his tiny open boats, his work gangs, his hunting and clearing of land. The struggle for life is an enmity which has a kind of innocence about it, because it is an enmity without hatred:

The hour had called for argument more rife
With the gambler's sacrificial bids for life,
The final manner native to the breed
Of men forging decision into deed—
Of getting down again into the sea,
And testing rowlocks in an open boat,
Of grappling with the storm-king bodily,
And placing Northern fingers on his throat.

(THE ROOSEVELT AND THE ANTINOE)

The reader will notice that Pratt's moral standards have few surprises: he is much more of a spokesman than a critic of public opinion and generally accepted social reactions. The reason—or one reason—is that he is almost always dealing with a society in a state of emergency: a Newfoundland fishing village depending on the next catch; a nation at war anxiously scanning the headlines; a band of missionaries surrounded by hostile Indians; sailors or railway workers trying to finish a dangerous quest on schedule. Such societies are engaged, and those who go out to meet the engagement are quite obviously

xvii

heroes: there is no time to analyse motives or question values.

The conception of heroism in Pratt is of the kind that belongs to our age, and to an industrial democracy. It is the whole group engaged in the quest that is the hero. When Pratt names an individual hero, like Brébeuf, he thinks of the heroism as like that of a soldier who has received a medal for valour—as representative rather than isolated. The cowards and slackers who desert the quest are usually ignored. In the story of the *Titanic* there are many obvious things to consider: the "hap" or mysterious fate that attracted Hardy, the outrage at the incompetence of those in charge that brought some blistering essays from Conrad, the vainglorious confidence that the ship was unsinkable which seems, in retrospect, to have almost deliberately aimed at the iceberg. But Pratt pays little attention to any of this. His chief interest is in the society of the first-class lounge, with the luxurious food, the music, the gossip, and the brilliantly described poker game. It is a brittle society, without much human point to it—until disaster strikes. Then it becomes the beleaguered group that the poet so well understands, and its genuine humanity suddenly becomes the focus of the poem, and the key to its meaning.

Not only is the individual hero apt to be anonymous, but, especially in the later narratives, even the crucial heroic *act* is not definitely pointed out: it is merely diffused through the poem. Nothing is truer to the spirit of modern heroism than the story told in *Behind the Log*: but where is the thrilling moment, the wild death-defying charge, the cops-and-robbers race, the cliff-hanging suspense? The genuine heroic act takes place unconsciously, in the midst of preoccupation; it has been done before even the doer is aware of having done it. Further, it takes place in time, and an instant later has vanished forever into the dark. What the group as a whole accomplishes—the railway, the martyr's shrine, the terms of a victorious peace—may last longer, but that too is temporal. The story of the *Titanic* is only one of several studies in Pratt (see "The Ritual", "The Sea-Cathedral", "A Prairie Sunset") of a tremendous glittering achievement that does nothing but disappear.

In this world of unconscious or preoccupied action, communication takes place very largely on unconscious levels too. The communication of loyalty and comradeship which makes heroism possible is mostly unconscious; the communication of enmity is even more primitive, like the squid's awareness of the whale in *The Cachalot* as:

. . . a deep consonant that rides
Below the measured beat of tides
With that vast, undulating rhythm
A sounding sperm whale carries with him.

Such unconscious communication takes many forms. There is correspondence, the feeling in "The Ground Swell" of the identity of man and nature, already mentioned. There is the answering sign, as when in "Come Away, Death" modern man looks into the face of death with the same "hieroglyph" of horror as his caveman ancestor. There is repetition on different levels, as when in "Erosion" the sea carves the rocks, then, after wrecking a boat, carves the lines of agony on a widow's face. On a conscious level Pratt is fascinated by the intricate machinery of signals and response, of radar and asdic in *Behind the Log,* of wireless messages in *The Titanic,* of electric charges bounced off an unresponsive whale or an unromantic moon.

Of all conscious signals the most important is the human word, especially the word of command that starts the social achievement going. But what is the origin of the word of command? Pratt observed how in the Second World War the cause of tyranny depended on Hitler's screaming

"Baritone", and the cause of freedom on the measured cadences of Churchill. His sense of the immense moral force in rhetoric can be seen all through the later poems. In *Towards the Last Spike* he takes the anonymity of heroism for granted, to an extent that startled some of his readers:

As individuals
The men lost their identity; as groups,
As gangs, they massed, divided, subdivided,
Like numerals only.

"Where are the coolies in your poem, Ned?" protests another poet, F. R. Scott. Twenty years earlier there would probably have been more about the coolies. At this stage the poet is interested rather in the power of the word, and in the source of its power. He finds it in the Parliamentary debates, with Macdonald's "from sea to sea" countering Blake's "to build a road over that sea of mountains". Both phrases are Biblical, with Biblical promises lurking in one and Biblical warnings in the other. The source of the word of command, as far as this poem is concerned, is a battle of metaphors, a conflict of rival visions. And if rhetoric is so important in controlling the movement of society, poetry is by implication even more so. In "Myth and Fact" the poet shows us how much of our life is involved in realizing and giving substance to the dreams of childhood, and the myths which are the dreams of man's childhood.

The sense of the identity of man and nature, and of man as a rebellious child of nature, led Pratt naturally to the theme of evolution, the sense of the eons of ferocity that lie behind human hatred and warfare. This is the theme of some of his best known poems, of "Silences", of "The Prize Cat", of "From Stone to Steel":

The snarl Neanderthal is worn
Close to the smiling Aryan lips,

The civil polish of the horn
Gleams from our praying finger tips.

This is normally a pessimistic conception, but the pessimism for Pratt has an important qualification. When we look from the outside on one of Pratt's heroic exploits, we see people suffering, dying, and finally vanishing into the awful annihilation of the past. When we look from the outside at evolution, we see only an endless struggle to survive which has been practically all pain and cruelty. But when we shift the view to the inside, we see an exuberant, unquenchable force of life, which fights to maintain itself certainly, but can find its fulfilment also in defeat and death. Sometimes this shift to the inside in Pratt is unexpectedly literal, as when he takes us on that wonderful voyage through the interior of the cachalot whale, or places us within a Scotchman's stomach to watch the metamorphosis of oatmeal into obstinacy. But it is this transfer of attention from the external nature, red in tooth and claw, to the internal life force, swarming and exulting and devouring itself in other forms, that gives to that magnificent fantasy *The Great Feud* its logical coherence.

It is consistent with his interest in evolving life that the poet should admire size, health, strength and energy. His sympathies are normally on the side of "The Big Fellow". "Breed" is a favourite word of his: it has no racial connotations, but means that the poet likes things to be fully developed examples of what they are. It pleases him when a rock is hard, when a whale is huge, when a Scotchman is named Sandy MacTavish. But "evolution" is much too simplified a picture of reality by itself. There is a pull of inertia backwards as well as development forwards. The ferocity of Tom the Cat from Zanzibar, in *The Witches' Brew*, is explained by such a retrograde movement:

His stock were traitors to the sea,

Had somehow learned the ways of earth,
The need of air, the mystery
Of things warm-blooded, and of birth.

In a more serious context in "The Highway",
brief but one of Pratt's definitive poems, he
speaks of the development of life from the star
through the rose to, not man, but to Christ as
the fulfilment of man. In the last stanza he
speaks of the misstep or falling away which is so
much older a conception than evolution, and
still seems an essential one:

But what made our feet miss the road that
  brought
The world to such a golden trove,
In our so brief a span?
How may we grasp again the hand that wrought
Such light, such fragrance, and such love,
O star! O rose! O Son of Man?

The first great product of the evolutionary force
is mechanism, the intricate machinery of the revolving stars, the automatic movements of matter,
the wonderful complex precision of animal
bodies. Pratt recurs over and over to the ana-
logy between the machine and the animal: in
"The Submarine", in "The Dying Eagle", in
"The Man and the Machine":

The man whose hands were on the wheel
Could trace his kinship through her steel,
Between his body warped and bent
In every bone and ligament,
And this "eight-cylinder" stream-lined,
The finest model yet designed.

Several poets, including Hart Crane, have as-
serted that the modern poet ought to be able
to make an unforced and spontaneous use of
mechanical imagery: Pratt is one of the few poets
who have done so. It is particularly in warfare
that he notices the reappearance of mechanical
forms and rhythms in human life, of how insect

forms, like the locusts in the Apocalypse, take on
the outlines of conscious malignity:

It is these that the rearguards are facing—
Creatures of conveyer belts,
Of precision tools and schedules.
They breathe through carburetted lungs;
If pierced, they do not feel the cut,
And if they die, they do not suffer death.

(DUNKIRK)

The Tartars and Mongols who swept over Asia,
the Nazis who polluted modern Europe, the
Iroquois who tortured Brébeuf, all derive their
ferocity from the mechanical energy of life, like
the bonitoes and barracudas in "Silences". But
they are evil, not innocent, because they are
also actively resisting the pull forward of their
real human nature into love. "The Highway" of
the human race is a path that "lies through
Gethsemane". In the dialectic of love and ferocity the reason may take either side: if it chooses
ferocity we have that strange phenomenon of
the modern age, the reasoning mechanism, the
destroying angel that the pitiful rabble of free
men at Dunkirk wrestled with and held until
daybreak:

No tolerance befogged the reason—
The reason with its clear-swept halls,
Its brilliant corridors . . .
The straightedge ruled out errors,
The tremors in the sensory nerves,
Pity and the wayward impulses,
The liberal imbecilities.

If the reason joins forces with love, on the other
hand, it can see, to return to the last stanza of
"The Highway", that the Son of Man is ident-
ical with the star and the rose, and includes
them, and that the divinity of man is not an
ideal to be reached in the future, but a presence
confronting him now.

Pratt's religious views are never obtrusive, but
they organize all his poetry. Considering that

xxiii

he has a degree in theology, it is not surprising that they should be consciously held—he can hardly have acquired his Christian archetypes in the way that a sleeping camper acquires mosquito bites, involuntarily and in the dark. They come out most clearly in two extraordinary poems, "The Truant" and "The Depression Ends", modestly included with the "Extravaganzas" in the first edition of this book.

"The Truant" presents us with the figure of a "Great Panjandrum", a prince of the power of the air, who talks as though he were God, who obviously thinks he is God, but who is no more God than Blake's Urizen, Shelley's Jupiter, Byron's Arimanes, or Hardy's President of the Immortals. He is the mechanical power of the universe: he controls the stars, the movement of matter, the automatic instincts of living things, even reason and consciousness. It infuriates him that something in the human soul should elude him, and as he screams at man in the "shrillest tenor" which is the voice of tyranny, he gradually takes on the outlines of Satan the accuser. What he has to accuse man of is his mortality. As far as we can see, everything man does, however heroic, vanishes and leaves not a rack behind. The Panjandrum should know, for he was in the "grey shape with the paleolithic face" that sank the *Titanic,* in the mechanical mantrap sprung at Dunkirk, even in the "leopards full of okra pods" in *The Great Feud.* He was certainly in the Iroquois torturing Brébeuf, knowing that they could kill anything that could die, driven by a demonic curiosity to find somewhere in Brébeuf's body the source of his strength, the origin of the word of command that had driven him into the wilderness. Brébeuf represented a more advanced civilization than the Iroquois, but that was not why he was there: his origin was not in France

But in the sound of invisible trumpets blowing
Around two slabs of board, right-angled, ham-
  mered
By Roman nails and hung on a Jewish hill.

Similarly the "genus homo" in "The Truant"
taunts the Panjandrum with his lack of real
intelligence, but the real source of his strength is
his knowledge that for him there can be no God
who has not also been a human being, suffered
with the beleaguered society which is Pratt's
hero, yielded to the power of death, and yet
conquered it too. His language toward the
Panjandrum is humorous, erudite, arrogant, but
behind all his brilliance is his awareness of "A
dying thirst within a Galilean valley".

"The Depression Ends" is the poem that most
vividly summons up, for those who know him,
the personality of Ned Pratt: his kindness and
his genius for friendship, his epic generosity and
hospitality. No one who has ever encountered
his limitless good will can doubt that he would,
if he could, give an "apocalyptic dinner". But
as the poem goes on, the significance of this ad-
jective begins to sink in. This is no stag party:
this is Pratt's beleaguered society on the march.
All the oppressed and hungry and neglected in
human history, all the lame and halt and blind,
all the slaves and the poor, all the invisible pro-
letariat who are the people of God, are shuffling
raggedly and dazedly into a splendid feasting-
hall. The hall turns out to be the starry heavens,
their original birthright and their dwelling-place,
as the emptiness of outer space and the empty
inner spaces of hungry stomachs are simultane-
ously filled. At one pole of human life is a cross,
at the other is a last supper; and these two
poles give position and meaning to everything
that occurs between them.

The prevailing idiom in Canadian poetry when
Pratt began to write was that of the romantic
lyric as practised by Carman, Roberts, D. C.
Scott and Marjorie Pickthall. It was an idiom

that was most successful in evocative nostalgia, as in Carman's "Low Tide on Grand Pré", in fairylike fantasy, as in Scott's "Piper of Arll", in wistful charm, as in Marjorie Pickthall's "Little Sister of the Prophet". The noises that exploded in *Newfoundland Verse*, the pounding of surf, the screaming of wind, the crash of ships on rocks, rudely shattered these moods. Yet if we look back to earlier Canadian poetry, we can see that the effort to convey something of the size and variety of the country through narrative, often realistic narrative, was much more deeply rooted in Canadian literature. There are no Canadian lyrics of any account before about 1880, but there are several quite striking ninteenth-century experiments in narrative, which in their various moods and themes— bleakness in Heavysege, fantasy in Duvar, mythopoeia in Isabella Crawford—not only anticipate Pratt but indicate how sure Pratt's technical instincts were.

It is because his imagination has been so concrete, so devoted to realizing the Canadian environment directly in front of him, that Pratt's career has been so odd a mixture of the popular and the unfashionable. When everybody was writing subtle and complex lyrics, Pratt developed a technique of straightforward narrative; when everybody was experimenting with free verse, Pratt was finding new possibilities in blank verse and octosyllabic couplets. He had the typical mark of originality: the power to make something poetic out of what everybody had just decided could no longer be poetic material. He worked unperturbed while the bright young men of the twenties, the scolding young men of the thirties, the funky young men of the forties, and the angry young men of the fifties, were, like Leacock's famous hero, riding off rapidly in all directions. Meanwhile he was reaching an increasingly large public in Canada, and by 1940, when *Brébeuf* appeared, he was established in Canada as one of the few good popular poets of the twentieth century. He has never been afraid to be topical, is in fact rather impatient with poets of "still life", and he has accepted both the responsibilities and the risks that go with being a kind of unofficial laureate.

Many popular poets are either deliberately bad poets, or, if good ones like Burns or Kipling, are admired for bad reasons, as anti-intellectual rallying-points. Pratt has never been what we ordinarily think of as an "intellectual". He is not a poet of verbal jig-saw puzzles, of ambiguities or dense textures or erudite allusions, nor has he ever built himself a religio-political Eiffel Tower from which to look down on the human situation. His moral and social values are where those of most sensible people are, and where the heart usually is in the body, a little left of centre. But he has never been anti-intellectual either, a feat which requires a good deal of integrity in this age. He is a scholar and university teacher, with graduate degrees in several disciplines, who works with the whole weight of poetic tradition behind him, and has never talked as through he undervalued culture or intelligence. Yet he has been able to introduce poetry to thousands of readers, including high-school children, with little if any previous experience of it. Meanwhile the cycle of fashion has come full circle, and Pratt looks much more modern and contemporary, if that is a virtue, in 1958 than he did in 1938.

His work now, of course, has a stature and an authority that reaches beyond Canada. But he will always have a special place in the affections of Canadian readers (I am speaking by synecdoche of English Canada). His work began with Newfoundland, and his latest major narrative ends in British Columbia. On his seventy-fifth birthday the CBC recorded tributes to him from all over Canada, some of the most eloquent being from the province of the ice-floes and from the province of the last spike. It was a sign that the work he had helped to do had been, not of course done, but well begun. In defiance of every geographical and economic law, Canada has made itself not simply a nation but an environment. It is only now emerging from its beginning as a shambling, awkward, absurd country, groping and thrusting its way through incredible distances into the west and north, plundered by profiteers, interrupted by European wars, divided by language, and bedevilled by climate, yet slowly and inexorably bringing a culture to life. And as long as that culture can remember its origin, there will be a central place in its memory for the poet in whom it found its tongue.

Victoria College   N.F.
September, 1958

Part One

POEMS CHIEFLY LYRICAL

NEWFOUNDLAND VERSE
(1923)

To my mother

NEWFOUNDLAND

Here the tides flow,
And here they ebb;
Not with that dull, unsinewed tread of waters
Held under bonds to move
Around unpeopled shores—
Moon-driven through a timeless circuit
Of invasion and retreat;
But with a lusty stroke of life
Pounding at stubborn gates,
That they might run
Within the sluices of men's hearts,
Leap under throb of pulse and nerve,
And teach the sea's strong voice
To learn the harmonies of new floods,
The peal of cataract,
And the soft wash of currents
Against resilient banks,
Or the broken rhythms from old chords
Along dark passages
That once were pathways of authentic fires.

Red is the sea-kelp on the beach,
Red as the heart's blood,
Nor is there power in tide or sun
To bleach its stain.
It lies there piled thick
Above the gulch-line.
It is rooted in the joints of rocks,
It is tangled around a spar,
It covers a broken rudder,
It is red as the heart's blood,
And salt as tears.

Here the winds blow,
And here they die,
Not with that wild, exotic rage
That vainly sweeps untrodden shores,
But with familiar breath
Holding a partnership with life,
Resonant with the hopes of spring,
Pungent with the airs of harvest.

2

They call with the silver fifes of the sea,
They breathe with the lungs of men,
They are one with the tides of the sea,
They are one with the tides of the heart,
They blow with the rising octaves of dawn,
They die with the largo of dusk,
Their hands are full to the overflow,
In their right is the bread of life,
In their left are the waters of death.

Scattered on boom
And rudder and weed
Are tangles of shells;
Some with backs of crusted bronze,
And faces of porcelain blue,
Some crushed by the beach stones
To chips of jade;
And some are spiral-cleft
Spreading their tracery on the sand
In the rich veining of an agate's heart;
And others remain unscarred,
To babble of the passing of the winds.

Here the crags
Meet with winds and tides—
Not with that blind interchange
Of blow for blow
That spills the thunder of insentient seas;
But with the mind that reads assault
In crouch and leap and the quick stealth,
Stiffening the muscles of the waves.
Here they flank the harbours,
Keeping watch
On thresholds, altars and the fires of home,
Or, like mastiffs,
Over-zealous,
Guard too well.

Tide and wind and crag,
Sea-weed and sea-shell
And broken rudder—
And the story is told
Of human veins and pulses,
Of eternal pathways of fire,

Of dreams that survive the night,
Of doors held ajar in storms.

THE TOLL OF THE BELLS

I   We gave them at the harbour every token—
    The ritual of the guns, and at the mast
    The flag half-high, and as the cortege passed,
All that remained by our dumb hearts unspoken.
And what within the band's low requiem,
    In footfall or in head uncovered fails
    Of final tribute, shall at altar-rails
Around a chancel soon be offered them.

And now a throbbing organ-prelude dwells
    On the eternal story of the sea;
    Following in undertone, the Litany
Ends like a sobbing wave; and now begins
A tale of life's fore-shortened days; now swells
The tidal triumph of Corinthians.

II   But neither trumpet-blast, nor the hoarse din
    Of guns, nor the drooped signals from those mute
    Banners, could find a language to salute
The frozen bodies that the ship brought in.
To-day the vaunt is with the grave. Sorrow
    Has raked up faith and burned it like a pile
    Of driftwood, scattering the ashes while
Cathedral voices anthemed God's To-morrow.

Out from the belfries of the town there swung
    Great notes that held the winds and the pagan roll
    Of open seas within their measured toll,
Only the bells' slow ocean tones, that rose
And hushed upon the air, knew how to tongue
That Iliad of Death upon the floes.

THE GROUND SWELL

Three times we heard it calling with a low,
    Insistent note; at ebb-tide on the noon;
    And at the hour of dusk, when the red moon
  Was rising and the tide was on the flow;
  Then, at the hour of midnight once again,
    Though we had entered in and shut the door
    And drawn the blinds, it crept up from the shore
  And smote upon a bedroom window-pane;
Then passed away as some dull pang that grew
Out of the void before Eternity
    Had fashioned out an edge for human grief;
  Before the winds of God had learned to strew
  His harvest-sweepings on a winter sea
    To feed the primal hungers of a reef.

THE SHARK

He seemed to know the harbour,
So leisurely he swam;
His fin,
Like a piece of sheet-iron,
Three-cornered,
And with knife-edge,
Stirred not a bubble
As it moved
With its base-line on the water.

His body was tubular
And tapered
And smoke-blue,
And as he passed the wharf
He turned,
And snapped at a flat-fish
That was dead and floating.
And I saw the flash of a white throat,
And a double row of white teeth,
And eyes of metallic grey,
Hard and narrow and slit.

5

Then out of the harbour,
With that three-cornered fin
Shearing without a bubble the water
Lithely,
Leisurely,
He swam—
That strange fish,
Tubular, tapered, smoke-blue,
Part vulture, part wolf,
Part neither—for his blood was cold.

THE FOG

It stole in on us like a foot-pad,
Somewhere out of the sea and air,
Heavy with rifling Polaris
And the Seven Stars.
It left our eyes untouched,
But took our sight,
And then,
Silently,
It drew the song from our throats,
And the supple bend from our ash-blades;
For the bandit,
With occult fingering,
Had tangled up
The four threads of the compass,
And fouled the snarl around our dory.

THE BIG FELLOW

A huge six-footer,
Eyes bay blue,
And as deep;
Lower jaw like a cliff,

6

Tongue silent,
As hard and strong as a husky.

A little man,
In a pressed suit,
Standing before him,
Had dug a name out of the past,
And flung it at him
Under cover of law.

The big fellow
Leaned over him,
Like a steel girder,
Just for a moment,
Then swung around on his heel
Without striking.

And I thought of the big Newfoundland
I saw, asleep by a rock
The day before,
That was galvanized by a challenge,
But eyeing a cur,
He turned,
Yawned,
Closed one eye,
Then the other,
And slept.

IN ABSENTIA

Erect and motionless he stood,
    His face a hieroglyph of stone,
Stopped was his pulse, chilled was his blood,
    And stiff each sinew, nerve and bone.

The spell an instant held him, when
    His veins were swept by tidal power,
And then life's threescore years and ten
    Were measured by a single hour.

The world lay there beneath his eye;
    The sun had left the heavens to float

A hand-breadth from him, and the sky
   Was but an anchor for his boat.

Fled was the class-room's puny space—
   His eye saw but a whirling disk;
His old and language-weathered face
   Shone like a glowing asterisk!

What chance had he now to remember
   The year held months so saturnine
As ill-starred May and blank September,
   With that brute tugging at his line?

THE FLOOD-TIDE

He paused a moment by the sea,
   Then stooped, and with a leisured hand
He wrote in casual tracery
   Her name upon the flux of sand.

The waves beat up and swiftly spun
   A silver web at every stride;
He watched their long, thin fingers run
   The letters back into the tide.

But she had written where the tide
   Could never its grey waters fling;
She watched the longest wave subside
   Ere it could touch the lettering.

IN LANTERN LIGHT

I could not paint, nor could I draw
   The look that searched the night;
The bleak refinement of the face I saw
   In lantern light.

A cunning hand might seize the crag,
  Or stay the flight of a gull,
Or the rocket's flash; or more—the lightning jag
  That lit the hull.

But as a man born blind must steal
  His colours from the night
By hand, I had to touch that face to feel
  It marble white.

THE DROWNING

The rust of hours,
    Through a year of days,
Has dulled the edge of the pain;
    But at night
    A wheel in my sleep
Grinds it smooth and keen.

    By day I remember
    A face that was lit
With the softness of human pattern;
    But at night
    It is changed in my sleep
To a bygone carved in chalk.

    A cottage inland
    Through a year of days
Has latched its doors on the sea;
    But at night
    I return in my sleep
To the cold, green lure of the waters.

CARLO

*"The dog that saved the lives of more than
ninety persons in that recent wreck, by swimming
with a line from the sinking vessel to the shore,*

9

*well understood the importance as well as the
risk of his mission."—Extract from a Newfoundland paper.*

I see no use in not confessing—
To trace your breed would keep me guessing;
It would indeed an expert puzzle
To match such legs with a jet-black muzzle.
To make a mongrel, as you know,
It takes some fifty types or so,
And nothing in your height or length,
In stand or colour, speed or strength,
Could make me see how any strain
Could come from mastiff, bull, or Dane.
But, were I given to speculating
On pedigrees in canine rating,
I'd wager this—not from your size,
Not merely from your human eyes,
But from the way you held that cable
Within those gleaming jaws of sable,
Leaped from the taffrail of the wreck
With ninety souls upon its deck,
And with your cunning dog-stroke tore
Your path unerring to the shore—
Yes, stake my life, the way you swam,
That somewhere in your line a dam,
Shaped to this hour by God's own hand,
Had mated with a Newfoundland.

They tell me, Carlo, that your kind
Has neither conscience, soul, nor mind;
That reason is a thing unknown
To such as dogs; to man alone
The spark divine—he may aspire
To climb to heaven or even higher;
But God has tied around the dog
The symbol of his fate, the clog.
Thus, I have heard some preachers say—
Wise men and good, in a sort o' way—
Proclaiming from the sacred box
(Quoting from Butler and John Knox)

How freedom and the moral law
God gave to man, because He saw
A way to draw a line at root
Between the human and the brute.
And you were classed with things like bats,
Parrots and sand-flies and dock-rats,
Serpents and toads that dwell in mud,
And other creatures with cold blood
That sightless crawl in slime, and sink.
Gadsooks! It makes me sick to think
That man must so exalt his race
By giving dogs a servile place;
Prate of his transcendentalism,
While you save men by mechanism.
And when I told them how you fought
The demons of the storm, and brought
That life-line from the wreck to shore,
And saved those ninety souls or more,
They argued with such confidence—
'Twas instinct, nature, or blind sense.
A *man* could know when he would do it;
You did it and never knew it.

And so, old chap, by what they say,
You live and die and have your day,
Like any cat or mouse or weevil
That has no sense of good and evil
   (Though sheep and goats, when they have died,
The Good Book says are classified);
But you, being neuter, go to—well,
Neither to heaven nor to hell.

I'll not believe it, Carlo; I
Will fetch you with me when I die,
And, standing up at Peter's wicket,
Will urge sound reasons for your ticket;
I'll show him your life-saving label
And tell him all about that cable,
The storm along the shore, the wreck,
The ninety souls upon the deck;
How one by one they came along,
The young and old, the weak and strong—
Pale women sick and tempest-tossed,
With children given up for lost;

11

I'd tell him more, if he would ask it—
How they tied a baby in a basket,
While a young sailor, picked and able,
Moved out to steady it on the cable;
And if he needed more recital
To admit a mongrel without title,
I'd get down low upon my knees,
And swear before the Holy Keys,
That, judging by the way you swam,
Somewhere within your line, a dam
Formed for the job by God's own hand,
Had littered for a Newfoundland.

I feel quite sure that if I made him
Give ear to that, I could persuade him
To open up the Golden Gate
And let you in; but should he state
That from your legs and height and speed
He still had doubts about your breed,
And called my story of the cable
"A cunningly devised fable",
Like other rumours that you've seen
In Second Peter, one, sixteen,
I'd tell him (saving his high station)
The devil take his legislation,
And, where life, love, and death atone,
I'd move your case up to the Throne.

OVERHEARD BY A STREAM

Here is the pool, and there the waterfall;
This is the bank; keep out of sight, and crawl
Along the side to where that alder clump
Juts out. 'Twas there I saw a salmon jump,
A full eight feet, not fifteen minutes past.
Bend low a bit! or else the sun will cast
Your shadow on the stream. Still farther; stop!
Now joint your rod; reel out your line, and drop

Your leader with the "silver doctor" on it,
Behind that rock that's got the log upon it.

There's nothing here; the water is too quiet;
You need a pool with rapids flowing by it;
Plenty of rush and motion, heave and roar,
To turn their thoughts from things upon the shore;
The day's too calm—I told you that before.
Just mind your line! I tell you that he's there.
I saw him spring up ten feet in the air—
Twelve pounder, if an ounce! Great Mackinaw!
Look! Quick! He's on! The "doctor" in his jaw...

Snapped! Gone! You big fool: worse than any fool!
What did you think to find here in this pool—
A minnow or a shiner—that you tried
With such a jerk to land him on the side
Of this high bank? That was a salmon—fool!
The biggest one that swam within this pool;
The one I saw that jumped twelve feet—not lower;
Would tip the scales at fourteen pounds or more.
Lost—near that rock that's got the log upon it,
Gone—with the leader and the "doctor" on it.

THE HISTORY OF JOHN JONES

The sun never shone,
The rain could not fall
On a steadier man than John.
A holy man was John,
And honest withal.
His mates had never heard
Drop from his guarded lip
An idle word,
But twice—first, while on board his ship,
When he had lost his pipe, he swore,
Just a mild damn, and nothing more;
And once he cursed
The government; but then he reckoned
The Lord forgave him for the first,
And justified the second.

13

And he was temperate in all his ways,
Was John;
He never drank, but when Thanksgiving days
Came on;
Never in summer on a fishing trip
Would he allow the smell on board his ship;
Only in winter or in autumn,
When a cramp or something caught him,
Would he take it, for he prized it,
Not for its depraved abuses,
But for its discreeter uses,
As his Church had authorized it.
The sun had never shone
On a kinder man than John,
Nor upon
A better Christian than was John.
He was good to his dog, he was good to his cat,
And his love went out to his horse;
He loved the Lord and his Church, of course,
For righteous was he in thought and act;
And his neighbours knew, in addition to that,
He loved his wife, as a matter of fact.

Now, one fine day it occurred to John,
That his last great cramp was on;
For nothing that the doctor wrote
Could stop that rattle in his throat.
He had broken his back upon the oar,
He had dried his last boat-load of cod,
And nothing was left for John any more,
But to drift in his boat to the port of God.

THE EPIGRAPHER

His head was like his lore—antique,
His face was thin and sallow-sick,
With god-like accent he could speak
Of Egypt's reeds or Babylon's brick
Or sheep-skin codes in Arabic.

14

To justify the ways divine,
He had travelled Southern Asia through—
Gezir down in Palestine,
Lagash, Ur and Eridu,
The banks of Nile and Tigris too.

And every occult Hebrew tale
He could expound with learned ease,
From Aaron's rod to Jonah's whale.
He had held the skull of Rameses—
The one who died from boils and fleas.

Could tell how—saving Israel's peace—
The mighty Gabriel of the Lord
Put sand within the axle-grease
Of Pharaoh's chariots; and his horde
O'erwhelmed with water, fire and sword.

And he had tried Behistun Rock,
That Persian peak, and nearly *clomb* it;
His head had suffered from the shock
Of somersaulting from its summit—
Nor had he quite recovered from it.

From that time onward to the end,
His mind had had a touch of gloom;
His hours with jars and coins he'd spend,
And ashes looted from a tomb,—
Within his spare and narrow room.

His day's work done, with the last rune
Of a Hammurabi fragment read,
He took some water spiced with prune
And soda, which imbibed, he said
A Syrian prayer, and went to bed.

* * * * * *

And thus he trod life's narrow way,—
His soul as peaceful as a river—
His understanding heart all day
Kept faithful to a stagnant liver.

15

L'ENVOI
When at last his stomach went by default,
His graduate students bore him afar
To the East where the Dead Sea waters are,
And pickled his bones in Eternal Salt.

GREAT TIDES

Great Tides! You filled the reaches up
   Under the North's wild blow;
Yet could not spare this smaller cup
   Its salter overflow.

Huge hands! You rear our bulwarks up
   With power to none akin;
Yet cannot lift a door-latch up
   That a lad may enter in.

ON THE SHORE

Come home! the year has left you old;
   Leave those grey stones; wrap close this shawl
Around you for the night is cold;
   Come home! he will not hear your call.

No sign awaits you here but the beat
   Of tides upon the strand,
The crag's gaunt shadow with gull's feet
   Imprinted on the sand,
And spars and sea-weed strewn
   Under a pale moon.

Come home! he will not hear your call;
Only the night winds answer as they fall
    Along the shore,
    And evermore
Only the sea-shells

On the grey stones singing,
And the white foam-bells
Of the North Sea ringing.

COME NOT THE SEASONS HERE

Comes not the springtime here,
  Though the snowdrop came,
And the time of the cowslip is near,
  For a yellow flame
Was found in a tuft of green;
  And the joyous shout
  Of a child rang out
That a cuckoo's eggs were seen.

Comes not the summer here,
  Though the cowslip be gone,
Though the wild rose blow as the year
  Draws faithfully on;
Though the face of the poppy be red
  In the morning light,
  And the ground be white
With the bloom of the locust shed.

Comes not the autumn here,
  Though someone said
He found a leaf in the sere
  By an aster dead;
And knew that the summer was done,
  For a herdsman cried
That his pastures were brown in the sun,
  And his wells were dried.

Nor shall the winter come,
  Though the elm be bare,
And every voice be dumb
  On the frozen air;
But the flap of a waterfowl
  In the marsh alone,
Or the hoot of a horned owl
  On a glacial stone.

BEFORE AN ALTAR

(After Gueudecourt)

Break we the bread once more,
   The cup we pass around—
No, rather let us pour
   This wine upon the ground;

And on the salver lay
   The bread—there to remain.
Perhaps, some other day,
   Shrovetide will come again.

Blurred is the rubric now,
   And shadowy the token,
When blood is on the brow,
   And the frail body broken.

A DIRGE

Now let the earth take
   Into its care,
All that it travailed for,
   All that it bare.

Leaves of the forest,
   Yellow and red,
The drifting and scattered,
   The dying and dead;

Grass of the hill-slopes,
   Sickled and dried,
Vines that over-night
   Blasted and died;

Blossoms and flowers
   Nipped with the cold,
Trees that have fallen
   A century old;

Moths of the candle-flame,
  Gnats from the stream,
Wraiths from the moonlight,
  Spectres of dream;

All that the earth gave,
  All that it bare—
With all its far kindred
  Of water and air.

And in those rutted acres
  Which the heart's red blood has sown,
Soon shall the bramble flourish
  Where the gentian had grown;
And wherever ran the myrtle,
  Let the dust of thistles be shed,
For these, with nightshade and burdock,
  Shall fast cover the dead.

THE ICE-FLOES

Dawn from the Foretop! Dawn from the Barrel!
  A scurry of feet with a roar overhead;
The master-watch wildly pointing to Northward,
  Where the herd in front of *The Eagle* was spread!

Steel-planked and sheathed like a battleship's nose,
She battered her path through the drifting floes;
Past slob and growler we drove, and rammed her
Into the heart of the patch and jammed her.
There were hundreds of thousands of seals, I'd swear,
In the stretch of that field—"white harps" to spare
For a dozen such fleets as had left that spring
To share in the general harvesting.
The first of the line, we had struck the main herd;
The day was ours, and our pulses stirred
In that brisk, live hour before the sun,
At the thought of the load and the sweepstake won.

We stood on the deck as the morning outrolled
On the fields its tissue of orange and gold,

And lit up the ice to the north in the sharp,
Clear air; each mother-seal and its "harp"
Lay side by side; and as far as the range
Of the patch ran out we saw that strange,
And unimaginable thing
That sealers talk of every spring—
The "bobbing-holes" within the floes
That neither wind nor frost could close;
Through every hole a seal could dive,
And search, to keep her brood alive,
A hundred miles it well might be,
For food beneath that frozen sea.
Round sunken reef and cape she would rove,
And though the wind and current drove
The ice-fields many leagues that day,
We knew she would turn and find her way
Back to the hole, without the help
Of compass or log, to suckle her whelp—
Back to that hole in the distant floes,
And smash her way up with her teeth and nose.
But we flung those thoughts aside when the shout
Of command from the master-watch rang out.

Assigned to our places in watches of four—
    Over the rails in a wild carouse,
    Two from the port and starboard bows,
Two from the broadsides—off we tore,
In the breathless rush for the day's attack,
With the speed of hounds on a caribou's track.
With the rise of the sun we started to kill,
A seal for each blow from the iron bill
Of our gaffs. From the nose to the tail we ripped them,
    And laid their quivering carcasses flat
On the ice; then with our knives we stripped them
    For the sake of the pelt and its lining of fat.
With three fathoms of rope we laced them fast,
    With their skins to the ice to be easy to drag,
With our shoulders galled we drew them, and cast
    Them in thousands around the watch's flag.
Then, with our bodies begrimed with the reek
    Of grease and sweat from the toil of the day,
    We made for *The Eagle*, two miles away,

At the signal that flew from her mizzen peak.
And through the night, as inch by inch
   She reached the pans with the "harps" piled high,
   We hoisted them up as the hours filed by
To the sleepy growl of the donkey-winch.

Over the bulwarks again we were gone,
With the first faint streaks of a misty dawn;
Fast as our arms could swing we slew them,
Ripped them, "sculped" them, roped and drew them
To the pans where the seals in pyramids rose
Around the flags on the central floes,
Till we reckoned we had nine thousand dead
By the time the afternoon had fled;
And that an added thousand or more
Would beat the count of the day before.
So back again to the patch we went
To haul, before the day was spent,
Another load of four "harps" a man,
To make the last the record pan.
And not one of us saw, as we gaffed, and skinned,
And took them in tow, that the north-east wind
Had veered off-shore; that the air was colder;
   That the signs of recall were there to the south,
The flag of *The Eagle*, and the long, thin smoulder
   That drifted away from her funnel's mouth.
Not one of us thought of the speed of the storm
   That hounded our tracks in the day's last chase
(For the slaughter was swift, and the blood was warm),
   Till we felt the first sting of the snow in our face.
We looked south-east, where, an hour ago,
   Like a smudge on the sky-line, someone had seen
The Eagle, and thought he had heard her blow
   A note like a warning from her sirene.
We gathered in knots, each man within call
   Of his mate, and slipping our ropes, we sped,
Plunging our way through a thickening wall
   Of snow that the gale was driving ahead.
We ran with the wind on our shoulder; we knew
That the night had left us this only clue
Of the track before us, though with each wail
That grew to the pang of a shriek from the gale,
Some of us swore that *The Eagle* screamed

Right off to the east; to others it seemed
On the southern quarter and near, while the rest
  Cried out with every report that rose
  From the strain and the rend of the wind on the floes
That *The Eagle* was firing her guns to the west.
And some of them turned to the west, though to go
  Was madness—we knew it and roared, but the notes
Of our warning were lost as a fierce gust of snow
  Eddied, and strangled the words in our throats.
Then we felt in our hearts that the night had swallowed
  All signals, the whistle, the flare, and the smoke
To the south; and like sheep in a storm we followed
  Each other; like sheep we huddled and broke.
Here one would fall as hunger took hold
Of his step; here one would sleep as the cold
Crept into his blood, and another would kneel
Athwart the body of some dead seal,
And with knife and nails would tear it apart,
To flesh his teeth in its frozen heart.
And another dreamed that the storm was past,
  And raved of his bunk and brandy and food,
And *The Eagle* near, though in that blast
  The mother was fully as blind as her brood.
Then we saw, what we feared from the first—dark places
Here and there to the left of us, wide, yawning spaces
Of water; the fissures and cracks had increased
  Till the outer pans were afloat, and we knew,
As they drifted along in the night to the east,
  By the cries we heard, that some of our crew
Were borne to the sea on those pans and were lost.
  And we turned with the wind in our faces again,
  And took the snow with its lancing pain,
Till our eye-balls cracked with the salt and the frost;
Till only iron and fire that night
  Survived on the ice as we stumbled on;
As we fell and rose and plunged—till the light
  In the south and east disclosed the dawn,
And the sea heaving with floes—and then,
The Eagle in wild pursuit of her men.

And the rest is as a story told,
  Or a dream that belonged to a dim, mad past,

Of a March night and a north wind's cold,
   Of a voyage home with a flag half-mast;
Of twenty thousand seals that were killed
   To help to lower the price of bread;
Of the muffled beat . . . of a drum . . . that filled
   A nave . . . at our count of sixty dead.

THE IRON DOOR

An Ode

(1927)

To some very dear memories

THE IRON DOOR

(An Ode)

Its features half-revealed in passing gleams
Which had no origin in earthly light,
Half-buried in a shifting mass of gloom
Which had no kinship with the face of night,
It had its station in the cliffs to stand
Against the clamour of eternal storm.
A giant hand
Had wrought it cruciform,
And placed deep shadows on the sunken panels,
Then in ironic jest,
Had carven out the crest
Of death upon the lintel.
Out of some Plutonian cave
It had been brought, and hung
Within its granite architrave.
I saw no latch or knocker on the door;
It seemed the smith designed it to be swung
But once, then closed forevermore.

The noise as of stubborn waters
Came in from a distant tide
To the beat of Time with slow,
Immeasurable stride.
From an uncharted quarter,
A wind began to blow,
And clouds to rise,
And underneath I saw the forms of mortals
Come and go,
And heard their cries,—
Fragments of speech, bewildered pleas,
That rose upon the pauses of the wind,
To hush upon the thunder of great seas.
And I thought what vain credulities
Should lure those human souls before
This vast inexorable door.

A music which the earth has only known
In the drab hours of its emptiness,
Or in the crisis of a fiery stress
Fell on my ear

In broken chord and troubled undertone.
For in this scale were tragic dreams
Awaiting unfulfilled decrees,
Some brighter than the purest gleams
Of seraphic ecstasies;
And some with hopes and fears
Which ran their paling way
Beyond the boundaries of availing prayer,
To dim-illumined reaches where the frore,
Dumb faces of despair
Gazed at their natural mirror in the door.
Then with the intermittent lull
Of wind and the dull
Break of transitory light,
Where rents in the shawl of the darkness
Revealed star-bursts and clouds in flight,
The cries were winged into language,
And forms which were featureless grew
Into the shapes of persons I knew
Who had tasted of life and had died.

Standing, anxious-eyed,
So small against the drift of space,
Enveloped by the gloom,
A boy searched for his father's face,
With that unvoiced appeal,
Which I remember, when he brought
A water-spaniel home one day,
Crushed beneath an engine-wheel;
And could not, by a rational way,
Be fully made to understand
That the mending of a lifeless body lay
Beyond the surgery of his father's hand.

A master mariner
Stood looking at the dull
Outline of a basalt spur,
Which in the fall and lift of fog,
Took on the shape of a gigantic hull.
He was old and travel-stained,
And his face grained
With rebel questionings
Urged with unsurrendered dignity;
For he had lost three sons at sea,

In a work of rescue known
To the high Atlantic records of that year.
Then as the crag took on the heaving motion
Of the fog, and the roar beat in his ear
Of surge afar off, he hallooed
The unknown admiral of the unknown ocean:—

Ahoy! The latitude and longitude?
Within these parts do the stars fail?
Is the sextant in default?
What signals and what codes prevail?
And is the taste of the water salt
About your reefs? Do you bury your dead
In the national folds?
Is the blood of your sailors red
When songs are sung
At the capstan bars? Are davits swung
At a call from the bridge when the night is dark,
And life like wine is spilled at a word to retrieve
The ravage of gales? Do courage and honour receive
On the wastes of your realm, their fair name and title?
As they do at our sea grey altars,—by your leave.

The fog closed in upon the spur,
The moving hull became a rock
Beneath the undulations, and the shock
Of winds from an unknown compass point cut short
The seaman's challenge till that sound again
From the hinter-sea broke through, and the swart
Impress on his face was stirred
By that insurgent flash
It once had known when after the report
Of his sons' loss on the High Seas, he had heard
With a throb of pride,
The authentic word
From the Captain's lips,
Of the way the lads had died.

Another form appeared,
One whom I knew so well,—endeared
To me by all the natural ties which birth
And life and much-enduring love impose.

There was no trace
Of doubt or consternation on her face,
Only a calm reliance that the door
Would open and disclose
Those who by swifter strides had gone ahead.
It was the same expression that she wore,
One evening, when with life-work done,
She went to bed,
In the serene belief that she could borrow
Sufficient strength out of the deep
Resources of a final sleep,
To overtake the others by the morrow.

A young man struck against the door
Demanding with his sanguine prime,
If the eternal steward registered
The unrecorded acts of time;
Not for himself insisting, but for one—
A stranger at his side—
For whom he had staked his life,
And on the daring odds had died.
No one had seen this young man go,
Or watched his plunge,
To save another whom he did not know.
Men only guessed the grimness of the struggle,
The body-tug, the valour of the deed,
For both were wrapped in the same green winding-
    sheet,
And blood-red was the colour of the weed
That lay around their feet.
Life for a life! The grim equivalent
Was vouched for by a sacred precedent;
But why the one who should have been redeemed
Should also pay the price
In the mutual sacrifice,
Was what he wished to know,
And urged upon the iron, blow by blow.

One who had sought for beauty all his days,
In form and colour, symphony and phrase,
Who had looked on gods made perfect by man's hand,
And Nature's glories on the sea and land,—
Now paused and wondered if the Creator's power,

Finding itself without a plan, was spent,
Leaving no relic at this vacant hour,
But a grave-stone and iron monument.

One who had sought for truth, but found the world
Outside the soul betray the one within,
Knew beacon signals but as casual fires,
And systems dead but for their power to spin,
Laid deeply to his heart his discipline,
Looked at the door where all the roadways closed,
And took it as the clench of evidence,
That the whole cosmic lie was predisposed,
Yet faced it with a fine indifference.

From somewhere near the threshold of the door,
A sharp insistent cry,
Above all other notes, arose,—
A miserere flung out to the sky,
Accompanied by a knocking
So importunate,
It might have been the great
Crescendo from the world of human souls,
Gathering strength to assail
The unhearing ears of God, or else to hail
His drowsy warders at the stellar poles.
Then through a rift
In a storm-cloud's eddying,
A greyness as of drift
Of winter snow in a belated spring,
Appeared upon a woman's face,
Eroded with much perishing.
The same dark burden under which the race
Reaches old age lay strapped upon her soul:—
That which collects in silence all the shame,
Through hidden passages of time and blood,
Then puts the open stigma of the blame
Upon a spotless name.

Why all the purchase of her pain,
And all her love could not atone
For that incalculable stain:
Why from that tortuous stream,—

Flesh of her flesh, bone of her bone,—
Should issue forth a Cain;
Were queries rained upon the iron plates.
'Twas not enough, it seemed, that her one gift
To life should be returned
To death, but that the Fates
Should so conspire
To have this one devoted offering burned
At such an altar, and by such a fire!
But what availed
A woman's cry against the arrest
Of hope when every rubric paled
Before the Theban mockery of the crest?

And at this darkest moment, as I dreamed,
The world with its dead weight of burdens seemed
To pause before the door, in drifts of sand,
And catacombs of rock and burial turf:
For every wind that raged upon the land
Had fled the nescient hollow of God's hand.
And all the music left upon its waters
Lay in the grey rotation of the surf,
With calls of seamen in great weariness
At their unanswered signals of distress;
And all the light remaining was bereft
Of colour and design in full eclipse;
No fragrance in the fields; no flowers left
But poppies with their charred autumnal lips.

Then with a suddenness beyond surprise,
When life was sinking in its cosmic trial,
And time was running down before my eyes,
New lights and shadows leaped upon the dial.

I have often heard it said that by some token,
As fragile as a shell,
Or a wish thrice-spoken,
The direst spell,
Though old and ringed of iron, might be broken;
That a fool's belief in the incredible,
Joined to the sounding magic of a name,
Makes up the stuff of miracle.
From such a source, it well might be,
Came this supreme authority.

It may have been the young man's claim
On life; or the old captain calling stormily
From sea to sea;
Or that root faith within a woman's heart;
Perhaps it was the white face of the child;
Or that last argument so wild
Of wing, of such tumultuous breath,
Its strange unreason might be made to prove
The case for life before the throne of death,
I do not know;
But in the dream the door began to move.

A light shot through the narrow cleft,
And shattered into hurrying gleams that rode
Upon the backs of clouds, and through deep hollows,
Like couriers with weird, prophetic code.
And as the door swung forward slowly,
A sound was heard, now like the beat
Of tides under the drive of winds,
Now like the swift deck-tread of feet,
Steadying to a drum
Which marshalled them to quarters, or the hum
Of multitudinous voices that would tell
Of the move of life invincible.

Then as the opening widened,
And the sound became more clear, I tried
With an insatiate hunger, to discover
The fountain of that light and life inside;
And with an exultation which outrode
The vaunt of raw untutored strength, I cried;—

Now shall be read
The faded symbols of the page which keeps
This hoary riddle of the dead.

But something heavy and as old as clay,
Which mires a human soul,
Laid hold upon the quest so that it fell,
Just baffled of its goal.
Beyond the threshold of the door,
I could not see; I only knew

That those who had been standing, waiting there,
Were passing through;
And while it was not given me to know
Whither their journey led, I had caught the sense
Of life with high auroras and the flow
Of wide majestic spaces;
Of light abundant; and of keen impassioned faces,
Transfigured underneath its vivid glow.

Then the door moved to its close with a loud,
Relentless swing, as backed by ocean power;
But neither gird of hinges, nor the feel of air
Returning with its drizzled weight of cloud,
Could cancel half the meaning of that hour,—
Not though the vision passed away,
And I was left alone, aware
Of blindness falling with terrestrial day
On sight enfeebled by the solar glare.

33

MANY MOODS

(1932)

To Viola and Claire

SEA-GULLS

For one carved instant as they flew,
The language had no simile—
Silver, crystal, ivory
Were tarnished. Etched upon the horizon blue.
The frieze must go unchallenged, for the lift
And carriage of the wings would stain the drift
Of stars against a tropic indigo
Or dull the parable of snow.

Now settling one by one
Within green hollows or where curled
Crests caught the spectrum from the sun,
A thousand wings are furled.
No clay-born lilies of the world
Could blow as free
As those wild orchids of the sea.

THE WAY OF CAPE RACE

Lion-hunger, tiger-leap!
The waves are bred no other way;
It was their way when the Norseman came,
It was the same in Cabot's day:
A thousand years will come again,
When a thousand years have passed away—
Galleon, frigate, liner, plane,
The muster of the slain.

They have placed the light, fog-horn and bell
Along the shore: the wardens keep
Their posts—they do not quell
The roar; they shorten not the leap.
The waves still ring the knell
Of ships that pass at night,
Of dreadnought and of cockle-shell:
They do not heed the light,
The fog-horn and the bell—
Lion-hunger, tiger-leap!

EROSION

It took the sea a thousand years,
A thousand years to trace
The granite features of this cliff,
In crag and scarp and base.

It took the sea an hour one night,
An hour of storm to place
The sculpture of these granite seams
Upon a woman's face.

THE SEA-CATHEDRAL

Vast and immaculate! No pilgrim bands,
In ecstasy before the Parian shrines,
Knew such a temple built by human hands,
With this transcendent rhythm in its lines;
Like an epic on the North Atlantic stream
It moved, and fairer than a Phidian dream.

Rich gifts unknown to kings were duly brought
At dawn and sunset and at cloudless noons,
Gifts from the sea-gods and the sun who wrought
Cascades and rainbows; flung them in festoons
Over the spires, with emerald, amethyst,
Sapphire and pearl out of their fiery mist.

And music followed when a litany,
Begun with the ring of foam bells and the purl
Of linguals as the edges cut the sea,
Crashed upon a rising storm with whirl
Of floes from far-off spaces where Death rides
The darkened belfries of his evening tides.

Within the sunlight, vast, immaculate!
Beyond all reach of earth in majesty,
It passed on southwards slowly to its fate—
To be drawn down by the inveterate sea
Without one chastening fire made to start
From altars built around its polar heart.

37

A PRAIRIE SUNSET

What alchemist could in one hour so drain
The rainbow of its colours, smelt the ore
From the September lodes of heaven, to pour
This Orient magic on a Western plain,
And build the miracle before our eyes
Of castellated heights and colonnades,
Carraran palaces, and cavalcades
Trooping through a city in the skies!
A northern cloud became a temple spire,
A southern reach showed argosies on fire,
And in the centre, with unhurried feet,
Came priests and paladins, soon to descend
To earth with swinging censers to attend
The god of harvests down amidst his wheat.

And scarcely less resplendent was the passing,
When with the night winds rising on the land,
The hosts were led by a Valkyrian hand
To their abodes, accompanied by the massing
Of amber clouds touched with armorial red,
By thrones dissolving, and by spirals hurled
From golden plinths, announcing to the world
That Day, for all its blazonry, was dead.
And when, like a belated funeral rite,
The last pale torch was smothered by the night,
The mind's horizon like the sky was stripped
Of all illusion but a fable told
Of gods that died, of suns and worlds grown cold,
In some extinct Promethean manuscript.

OUT OF STEP

(1931 A.D.)

When the celestial dance was planned
For star and constellation,
A mighty baton took command
Of perfect orchestration.

We praised the Master of the skies
For sun and moon and planet—
The ellipse was lovely to our eyes,
So gracefully he ran it.

But when the human dancers met,
This year—about two billion—
They fumbled with their minuet,
And CRASH went their pavilion!

THE MAN AND THE MACHINE

By right of fires that smelted ore
Which he had tended years before,
The man whose hands were on the wheel
Could trace his kinship through her steel,
Between his body warped and bent
In every bone and ligament,
And this "eight-cylinder" stream-lined,
The finest model yet designed.
He felt his lesioned pulses strum
Against the rhythm of her hum,
And found his nerves and sinews knot
With sharper spasm as she climbed
The steeper grades, so neatly timed
From storage tank to piston shot—
This creature with the cougar grace,
This man with slag upon his face.

THE PARABLE OF PUFFSKY

Puffsky knew not how to live,
But only how to sell,
And strange it is—this truth to tell—
That he was never known to give
And never known to buy.
Crack salesman of his time,
He kept financiers wondering why

He found such means to multiply
His wealth yet never parted with a dime.
He sold by night, he sold by day,
Sold long, sold short, sold anyway;
He'd sell his teeth, he'd sell his eyes; it made
No difference to his trade
No matter what he sold—
Bottles, gases, oils or foods—
The other fellow took the goods,
But Puffsky took the gold.

And yet alas!
One night it came to pass
That just the hour that Puffsky died,
He still assumed the bargain-rôle,
For, shambling up to God, he tried
To dicker with his soul.

And the good Lord sized him up and down,
And looked him through and through,
As he would a parvenu;
And then replied with darkening frown,
As Puffsky wedged his foot against the door.
"Sirrah—you may think it strange,
But on the floor
Of this Exchange
We neither barter, buy nor sell,
And neither dime nor rusty sou
Have we to offer you":
And whereupon the Lord adjusted well
A glittering monocle,
And said: "Hence—try thy game in hell."
So without further argument,
Thither Puffsky went.

Then Satan with a hoarse and bronchial laugh—
Amazed that such a spirit could exist—
Appointed a commission,
Composed of two professors on his staff,
A chemist and a pessimist,
To make report upon the apparition;
To estimate

Its size and weight,
Specific gravity,
And value in Gehenna currency.

And from the laboratory retort
Came back this joint report—
"Both size and weight
Are indeterminate.
It is a watered soul
That hath a swollen diaphragm,
Gaseous, but non-inflammable
When mixed with coal,
Therefore in hell
Not worth a current damn."

FROM STONE TO STEEL

From stone to bronze, from bronze to steel
Along the road-dust of the sun,
Two revolutions of the wheel
From Java to Geneva run.

The snarl Neanderthal is worn
Close to the smiling Aryan lips,
The civil polish of the horn
Gleams from our praying finger tips.

The evolution of desire
Has but matured a toxic wine,
Drunk long before its heady fire
Reddened Euphrates or the Rhine.

Between the temple and the cave
The boundary lies tissue-thin:
The yearlings still the altars crave
As satisfaction for a sin.

The road goes up, the road goes down—
Let Java or Geneva be—
But whether to the cross or crown,
The path lies through Gethsemane.

OLD AGE

So poor again—with all that plunder taken;
Your mountain stride, your eagle vision—gone!
And the *All Hail* of your voice in a world forsaken
Of song and curving wings and the laughter of dawn.

So little is left; I cannot be persuaded
It is your hand that shakes; your step that falls;
Your will, once statured on the crags, now faded
To the round of a wheel chair and four dull walls.

And yet to-day as I watched your pale face yearning,
When the sun's warmth poured through the open door,
And something molten in your soul was burning
Memorial raptures life could not restore,

I knew, by some high trick of sight and hearing,
Your heart was lured beyond the window sills,
Adventuring where the valley mists were clearing,
And silver horns were blowing on the hills.

BLIND

It was your boast before the darkness fell,
That you could measure all your love, and chart
The return of mine so surely as to tell
Both boundary and trespass in my heart.

But when the dawn and the meridian
Entered their sudden fusion with the night;
When roses and anemones began
To grow as winter rushes in your sight;

I wondered by what navigator's sign,
By what vicarious starlight, you could trace
Horizons which were never yours nor mine,
Until your wistful fingers sought my face.

A LEGACY

The will she made contained no room for strife,
For twisted words concerning gold or lands,
For all the wealth that she had saved from life
Was such as lay within her folded hands.

She would have been less rich with other store,
And we the poorer if she had not willed
Only her heart, and then gone out the door,
Leaving that cupboard on the latch and filled.

THE DECISION

(To L.R., a college athlete who died May, 1923.)

You left the field and no one heard
A murmur from you. We,
With burning look and stubborn word,
Challenged the Referee—

Why he forbade you to complete
The run, hailing you back
Before your firm and eager feet
Were half-way round the track;

Unless he had contrived, instead,
To start you on a race,
With an immortal course ahead,
And daybreak on your face.

TO AN ENEMY

Some passionate hour before my own deep stripe
Has taken on its healing, I shall trace
Him out, and with clean linen I shall wipe
The stain from that raw cut upon his face;
And with the hand that smote him I shall turn

43

The audit strong against him, offering
Once more a wound for wound and burn for burn
Out of the heart's own codeless bargaining.

And he, with wound adjuring wound, shall draw
His equal measure to the sacrament
From an old well to which some mortals went
When, with their thirsts ablaze, they looked and saw
An Orient form uplifted in the skies,
And quenched their hate in his forgiving eyes.

THE HIGHWAY

What aeons passed without a count or name,
Before the cosmic seneschal,
Succeeding with a plan
Of weaving stellar patterns from a flame,
Announced at his high carnival
An orbit—with Aldebaran!

And when the drifting years had sighted land,
And hills and plains declared their birth
Amid volcanic throes,
What was the lapse before the marshal's hand
Had found a garden on the earth,
And led forth June with her first rose?

And what the gulf between that and the hour,
Late in the simian-human day,
When Nature kept her tryst
With the unfoldment of the star and flower—
When in her sacrificial way
Judaea blossomed with her Christ!

But what made *our* feet miss the road that brought
The world to such a golden trove,
In our so brief a span?
How may we grasp again the hand that wrought
Such light, such fragrance, and such love,
O star! O rose! O Son of Man?

44

PUTTING WINTER TO BED

Old Winter with an angry frown
Restationed on his head his crown,
And grew more obdurate,
As rumours every day had flown
From some officials near the throne
That he might abdicate.

Fixing his rivals with his eyes,
He thumped his chest and clapped his thighs,
And ground his Arctic heel,
Splintering the dais, just to show
That he was lord of ice and snow,
With sinews of wrought steel.

His patience had been sorely tried
By a recent blow dealt to his pride,
When March, the stripling, dared
To jeer at him with callow yells,
And shake the hoary icicles
From off the royal beard.

Then at a most indecent time,
The lusty youngster nearing prime,
Gaining in reach and height,
Had called out Winter to his face
To meet him in a neutral place,
And join in single fight.

The gage accepted, Winter drew
First blood, then beat him black and blue
With Nordic thrust and swing,
Till March at last, the wily fox,
Clipped him on the equinox,
And bashed him round the ring;

And would have clearly had him down,
Captured his domain and crown,
When three parts through the bout,
Had not the king with a trick malign,
Cracked him on the nether sign,
And March was counted out.

45

So now, with an Alaskan ire,
He donned in full his white attire,
Lord of the Polar waste,
And claimed before those flabby-thewed
Contenders of a Southern brood,
He would not be displaced.

And yet before the week was passed,
Neuralgic headaches thick and fast
Were blinding him with tears;
Despite the boast, he needed rest
To stop that panting in his breast,
That buzzing in his ears.

He wandered to a frozen brook
Beneath dank willows where he took
His usual noon-day nap;
He heard dull subterranean calls,
Narcotic sounds from crystal falls,
The climbing of the sap.

He laid his head against a stump,
One arm reclined upon a clump
Of glaciated boulders;
The other held his side—he had
Pleuritic pains and very bad
Rheumatic hips and shoulders.

A sorry sight indeed he lay,
A god-like being in decay—
Dead leaves were all around him:
His favourite cave of ice was streaming,
And many a fallen trunk was steaming,
The day that April found him.

With one glance at his swollen feet,
Her diagnosis was complete,
That dropsy had set in:
She felt his pulse—"Lord, what a rate!
His heart is in a parlous state,
And colic roars within.

"O shame, that March should thus surprise him,
Without a thought to acclimatize him
Towards a mellow age;
I know another way benign
To lead him through an anodyne
Into his hermitage."

She spent the morning in the search
For twigs of alder and of birch
And shoots of pussy willow;
She wove these through a maze of fern,
Added some moss on her return,
And made the downiest pillow.

Then with a bath of rain and sleet,
She took the chilblains from his feet
With tender lubrication:
She poulticed out the angry spots,
The kinks and cramps and spinal knots,
And all discoloration.

So with her first aid rendered, she
Began her ancient sorcery,
Quietly to restore
His over-burdened mind to sleep,
Dreamless and passionless and deep,
Out of her wild-wood lore.

It took three days to get his throat
Clear of that wheezy guttural note,
His brain to vaporize;
She conjured him at last to rest,
Folded his hands across his breast
And sealed up both his eyes.

Then over his lank form she threw
The lightest coverlet she knew,
Brought from her deepest glades—
The whites and greys of quiet mood,
Pale pinks and yellows all subdued
With brown and purple shades;

The choicest of her tapestries,
Spring beauties and anemones
Plucked from the winter grass,

47

Wake-robins too: with these she took
Trout-lilies from a woodland brook
And cool hepaticas.

With one thing more, her task was done—
Something she found hid from the sun
Within a valley low;
"Just what he needs, dawn fresh and white—
The north wind brought it overnight—
A counterpane of snow.

"So now this makes his bed complete."
She doubled it across his feet,
And tucked it neatly in;
Then taking on a mood austere,
Kneeling, she whispered in his ear,
A word of discipline.

"Take heed! Before you enter sleep,
Swear by your honour you will keep
A vow which I propose:
Listen—an oath, which if you break,
'Twill carry for you in its wake
A multitude of woes.

"For eight months now, without demur,
You give your promise not to stir,
And not to roar or wail,
Or send your north wind with its snow,
Or yet the east whose vapours blow
Their shuddering sleet and hail.

"So help you then for evermore—
If you so much as cough or snore,
My seven younger sisters,
Who follow after me in turn,
Are under strict command to burn
Your body up with blisters.

"Of autumn, too, you must beware,
For if you rise to scent the air,
Our Indian-summer maid

Will plague you past what you endure,
Until you think your temperature
One hundred Centigrade.

"But if you keep this honest vow,
I pledge their virtue, here and now,
To rouse you in December;
Then you may come on Christmas Day
With furs and bells, reindeer and sleigh—
But, hand on heart—remember!"

And now, to make the pledge come true,
She walked around the king and drew
Three circles on his breast;
Murmured a charm, then bending down,
She graciously removed the crown,
And left him to his rest.

CHERRIES

"I'll never speak to Jamie again"—
Cried Jennie, "let alone wed,
No, not till blackbirds' wings grow white,
And crab-apple trees grow cherries for spite,
But I'll marry Percy instead."

But Jamie met her that self-same day,
Where crab-apple trees outspread,
And poured out his heart like a man insane,
And argued until he became profane,
That he never meant what he said.

Now strange as it seems, the truth must be told,
So wildly Jamie pled,
That cherries came out where the crab-apples grew,
And snow-winged blackbirds came down from the blue,
And feasted overhead.

A FELINE SILHOUETTE

They faced each other, taut and still;
Arched hickory, neck and spine;
Heads down, tails straight, with hair of quill,
The fence—the battleline.

The slits within their eyes describe
The nature of their feud;
Each came to represent a tribe
Which never was subdued.

One minute just before they fought,
Before their blood called—"Time",
One told the other what he thought
In words I cannot rhyme.

They hit each other in mid-air
In one terrific bound,
And even yet, as I'm aware,
They have not struck the ground.

THE CHILD AND THE WREN

(To Claire)

It took three weeks to make them friends—
The wren in fear the maid molest
Those six white eggs within the nest
She built up at the gable-ends.

What fearful language might be heard
(If only English she could speak)
On every day of the first week,
All from the throat of that small bird!

The scolding died away, and then
The fear was followed by surprise
At such sky-blue within the eyes,
That travelled from the girl to wren.

But that third week! I do not know—
It's neither yours to tell nor mine—
Some understanding glance or sign
Had passed between them to and fro;

For never was her face so flushed,
Never so brilliant blue her eye
At any gift that I could buy,
As at the news when in she rushed

To tell us that the wren had come,
With flutter and hop and gurgling sound,
From gable to tree, to shrub, to ground,
Right to her hand to get a crumb.

FROST

The frost moved up the window-pane
Against the sun's advance,
In line and pattern weaving there
Rich scenes of old romance—
Armies on the Russian snows,
Cockade, sword, and lance.

It spun a web more magical,
Each moment creeping higher,
For marble cities crowned the hills
With turret, fane and spire,
Till when it struck the flaming sash,
The Kremlin was on fire.

COMRADES

You—that could not stand the dust
Of a day's dry weather,
Nor in high winds
Shoulder a load together,
Without a faith that was broken,

And a love consumed
By the hot marl of words
That were spoken—

Do you not know that a hemlock root
Will enfold you together,
Though fair be the sky
Or foul be the weather?
To that same bed you shall come,
When the ear shall be deaf
And the lips be dumb;
Where under the turf,
Not a note shall be heard,
From the cry of a wren
To the thunder of surf.

ONE HOUR OF LIFE

This little face will never know
Cut of wind or bite of snow:
The sea will never wind its sheet
Around those pallid hands and feet.

Nor shall its sleeping heart, grown cold
After a pulse of life, unfold
That futile challenge on the face
Of one who with a last embrace

Could only cheat the earth to save
The plunder for another grave:
But in that hour of battle she
Forgot the patience of the sea.

TIME-WORN

What magic long ago was in your footstep,
That changed each night to day,

And swung high noon to midnight every hour
You went away.

How long the time—is now beyond my telling,
With days become as years,
And that last pledge of your returning—seasons
In arrears!

I only know my heart is beating slowly:
Come—and swift your feet!
Or else there will be neither noon nor midnight
When we meet.

TO ANGELINA, AN OLD NURSE

She lingers in our memory even yet,
Like an aroma or an anecdote,
Chipped from the 'nineties with her silhouette
Begemmed with buttons from the shoes to throat;
Her paper curls, her parlour pompadour,
Her leg-o'-mutton sleeves, the shawl she wore;
So trussed with cord and whalebone that she faced
The near annihilation of her waist.

Stark as a rampike under winter skies,
She brooded on us with her deep-set eyes
That never slept: mournful and thin was she,
Like something borrowed from eternity.
She never tucked us in our beds at night,
But feared we should not see the next day's light;
And when in course of time the morning broke,
She could not understand it that we woke.
She watched for every sneeze, for every whoop,
And even breadcrumbs in our throats was croup.
A lengthy spell of laughter was a fit,
And she could always put a stop to it.
Though healthy and as active as young beavers,
She always saw in us a soil for fevers.
When we were sound asleep within our cots,
She'd listen to our breathing, bending down
With many a murmur, many an anxious frown,

And turn us over on the search for spots,
Spots on the back and chest and diaphragm,
Spots on the tongue and throat *ad nauseam*—
It might have been a sunburn or the glow
Left over from a joy-ride in the snow,
But measles, chicken-pox or scarlatina
Was always present there to Angelina.
And when, our stomachs full, we went to bed,
Heavy with purloined cake instead of bread,
And gave a bilious scream within our sleep,
Or called her name—Lord, how her blood would creep!
This was delirium—her greatest fear,
The last of all the mortal ills that shocked her,
She knew that the eternal imps were near,
And sent at once for clergyman and doctor.

That town of ours had no apothecary,
And faith, for us he was not necessary.
For Angelina had the cupboards stacked
With every known and unknown medicine—
Hundreds of bottles, till the household smacked
Of things malodorous, day out, day in;
Powders and pills for every malady,
Goose oil and turkey rhubarb, turpentine,
And still more oil, pine syrup, senna tea,
Sulphur and blackstrap, tonics for the spring,
Liquids unnamed—acid and alkaline,
And all most pungent and disquieting.
She used not only standard remedies
By which all mothers classify the seasons:
She improvised for all emergencies
And filled us up for most fictitious reasons
Before the meals or after, on retiring,
Or any time when chilled or just perspiring;
The moment that we felt unduly merry,
It was our failing appetite, she said—
She touched our temples, charted out the head,
And reached at once for essence of wild cherry.

But then, her first and last line of defence,
The utmost limit of her confidence,
Was what she kept upon the highest board.

'Twas there her rancid Dead Sea salts were stored.
This saturated brine she daily poured
With senna down our throats in fixed routine.
What mattered it to her that we should go
At any time into the world unseen,
With spirits unprepared or hearts unclean;
It satisfied her conscience quite to know
That if we died, we died at least saline.

And yet, we know, that failing Angelina,
Our infancy and childhood would have been a
Most dull and unheroic sort of thing.
She gave to life its deepest flavouring,
She taught us tastes, improved our deglutition.
We loved her with a pale sardonic love—
The way she kept our thoughts on things above,
Etherialized our bodies by attrition,
The way she proved, despite our apprehensions,
That all she did was with the best intentions.

It's twenty-seven years ago today,
That sainted Angelina passed away,
Answering the summons of an evening bell.
Her soul or wraith or whatsoe'er it be,
That's left from her corporeality,
Spun out upon its voyage. Whither? Well,
It matters not: but this one thing we know,
That most unhappy would the old nurse be,
If somehow she were not allowed to go
Throughout the nurseries of the nebulae,
Stalking at will, administrative, grim,
With spoon or cup in hand full to the brim
With oil designed for the felicity
Of young and fever-spotted cherubim.

JOCK O' THE LINKS

Ah Jock! I'm sure that as a right
Good honest friend I ken ye,
And damned be he that would indite
A scornful word agen' ye:

A self-controlled God-fearin' Scot,
You fight with all that's evil,
But every time you top your shot
The odds are with the devil.

A softer heart in human breast
I do not know another,
And many a time, in many a test,
You've proved yourself a brother.
That man, I'll swear, is not alive
More temperate in speech,
But every time you fan your drive
I get beyond your reach.

That God is partial to the plaid,
Long-suffering, too, I've heard;
I hope He was the day I had
You stymied on the third;
I cannot vouch for rumour, but
One thing I trust is clear,
That when He saw you miss your putt,
He turned His one deaf ear.

I'm thankful, too, that when you dub
Your spoon, it's not on me
You break your new steel-shafted club,
But on your Highland knee.
And wise I have been to abstain
From comments on your stance,
With pibrochs crashing through your brain.
Culloden through your glance.

THE CONVICT HOLOCAUST

(Columbus, Ohio, 1930)

Waiting their turn to be identified,
After their fiery contact with the walls,
Three hundred pariahs ranged side by side
Upon the floors along the cattle stalls!

56

The fires consumed their numbers with their breath,
Charred out their names: though many of the dead
Gave proof of valour, just before their death,
That Caesar's legions might have coveted.

But these, still subject to the law's commands,
Received the last insignia of the cell:
The guards went through them, straightened out their hands,
And with the ink-brush got the thumb-prints well.

THE DRAG-IRONS

He who had learned for thirty years to ride
The seas and storms in punt and skiff and brig,
Would hardly scorn to take before he died
His final lap in Neptune's whirligig.

But with his Captain's blood he did resent,
With livid silence and with glassy look,
This fishy treatment when his years were spent—
To come up dead upon a grapnel hook.

THE LEE-SHORE

Her heart cried out,—"Come home, come home,"
When the storm beat in at the door,
When the window showed a spatter of foam,
And her ear rang with the roar
Of the reef; and she called again, "Come home,"
To the ship in reach of the shore.

"But not to-night," flashed the signal light
From the Cape that guarded the bay,
"No, not to-night," rang the foam where the white
Hard edge of the breakers lay;
"Keep away from the crash of the storm at its height,
Keep away from the land, keep away."

"Come home," her heart cried out again,
"For the edge of the reef is white."
But she pressed her face to the window-pane,
And read the flash of the signal light;
Then her voice called out when her heart was slain,
"Keep away, my love, to-night."

THE 6000

For creatures of this modern breed,
Reared from the element of flame,
Designed to match a storm for speed,
Ionia would have found a name,
Like Mercury or Bucephalus—
Some picturesque immortal label
That lifts a story into fable,
Out of the myths of Uranus;
Then changed its root to demonize
The nature of its strength and size
With fictions out of Tartarus.

Those giants of Vulcan, leather-skinned,
Whose frightful stare monocular
Made mad the coursers of the wind,
And chased the light of the morning star
Away from the Sicilian shore,
Would have been terror-blind before
This forehead which, had it been known
In Greek or Scandinavian lore,
Had turned the hierarchs to stone,
Had battered down the Martian walls,
Reduced to dust Jove's arsenals,
Or rammed the battlements of Thor.

His body black as Erebus
Accorded with the hue of night;
His central eye self-luminous
Threw out a cone of noon-day light,

Which split the gloom and then flashed back
The diamond levels of the track.
No ancient poet ever saw
Just such a monster as could draw
The Olympian tonnage of a load
Like this along an iron road;
Or ever thought that such a birth—
The issue of an inventor's dream—
With breath of fire and blood of steam,
Could find delivery on this earth.
In his vast belly was a pit,
Which even Homer would admit,
Or Dante, searching earth and hell,
Possessed no perfect parallel.
Evolved from no Plutonian forge,
The tender, like a slave, that followed,
Conveyed bitumen to his gorge,
Which on the instant it was swallowed
Ran black through crimson on to white.
Above the mass floated a swirl
Of crystal shapes, agate and pearl
And rose, like imps a-chase, and light
As thistledown, while the blast roared
With angry temperatures that soared
To seven hundred Fahrenheit.
Outside, the engine's dorsal plate,
Above the furnace door ajar,
Revealed the boiler's throbbing rate,
By dial fingers animate,
Like pulses at the jugular.

For every vital inch of steel,
A vibrant indicator read
Two hundred pounds plus twenty-five,
Waiting for the hour to drive
Their energy upon the wheel
In punches from the piston head.

And there another one supplied
The measure of the irrigation,
Whereby the lubricating tide,
Through linear runs and axle curves,
Made perfect his articulation.

And ramifying copper wire
Made up the system of his nerves,
In keeping with his lungs of fire.

Now with his armoured carapace
On head and belly, back and breast,
The Taurian prepared to face
The blurring stretches of the west.
To him it was of no concern
The evening gale was soon to turn
To the full stature of a storm
That would within an hour transform
The ranges for a thousand miles,
Close up all human thoroughfares,
Sweep down through canyons and defiles,
And drive the cougars to their lairs.

A lantern flashed out a command,
A bell was ringing as a hand
Clutched at a throttle, and the bull,
At once obedient to the pull,
Began with bellowing throat to lead
By slow accelerating speed
Six thousand tons of caravan
Out to the spaces—there to toss
The blizzard from his path across
The prairies of Saskatchewan.

THE RITUAL

I   She took her name beneath according skies,
With ringing harbour cheers, and in the lee
Of hills derived her birthright to the sea—
The adoration of a thousand eyes.
Each bulwark ran its way from stern to prow,
With the slim tracery of a sea-gull's wing,
And—happy augury for the christening—
The bottle broke in rainbows on her bow.

Beyond the port in roll and leap and curl,
In the rich hues of sunlight on the spray,
And in the march of tides—swept down the bay
The pageant of the morning, to the skirl
Of merry pipers as the rising gale
Sounded a challenge to her maiden sail.

II She left her name under revolted skies,
Before the break of day, upon a rock
Whose long and sunken ledge met the full shock
Of an Atlantic storm, and with the cries
Of the curlews issuing from dark caves,
Accompanied by the thud of wings from shags
That veered down from their nests upon the crags
To pounce on bulwarks shattered by the waves.

And the birthright that was granted for a brief,
Exultant hour with cheers and in the lee
Of hills was now restored unto the sea,
Amidst the grounded gutturals of the reef,
And with the grind of timbers on the sides
Of cliffs resounding with the march of tides.

THE DEPRESSION ENDS

If I could take within my hand
The rod of Prospero for an hour,
With space and speed at my command,
And astro-physics in my power,
Having no reason for my scheme
Beyond the logic of a dream
To change a world predestinate
From the eternal loom of fate,
I'd realize my mad chimera
By smashing distaff and the spinner,
And usher in the golden era
With an apocalyptic dinner.
I'd place a table in the skies
No earthly mind could visualize:
No instruments of earth could bound it—
'Twould take the light-years to go round it.

61

And to this feast I would invite
Only the faithful, the elect—
The shabby ones of earth's despite,
The victims of her rude neglect,
The most unkempt and motley throng
Ever described in tale or song.
All the good lads I've ever known
From the twelve winds of sea and land
Should hear my shattering bugle tone
And feel its summoning command.
No one should come who never knew
A famine day of rationed gruel,
Nor heard his stomach like a flue
Roaring with wind instead of fuel:
No self-made men who proudly claim
To be the architects of fame;
No profiteers whose double chins
Are battened on the Corn-Exchange,
While continental breadlines range
Before the dust of flour-bins.
These shall not enter, nor shall those
Who soured with the sun complain
Of all their manufactured woes,
Yet never had an honest pain:
Not these—the well-groomed and the sleeked,
But all the gaunt, the cavern-cheeked,
The waifs whose tightened belts declare
The thinness of their daily fare;
The ill-starred from their natal days,
The gaffers and the stowaways,
The road-tramps and the alley-bred
Who leap to scraps that others fling,
With luck less than the Tishbite's, fed
On manna from the raven's wing.

This dinner, now years overdue,
Shall centre in a barbecue.
Orion's club—no longer fable—
Shall fall upon the Taurus head.
No less than Centaurs shall be led
In roaring pairs forth from their stable

And harnessed to the Wain to pull
The mighty carcass of the bull
Across the tundras to the table,
Where he shall stretch from head to stern,
Roasted and basted to a turn.
I'd have the Pleiades prepare
Jugged Lepus (to the vulgar *hare*),
Galactic venison just done
From the corona of the sun,
Hoof jellies from Monoceros,
Planked tuna, shad, stewed terrapin,
And red-gut salmon captured in
The deltas of the Southern Cross.
Devilled shrimps, and scalloped clams,
Flamingoes, capons, luscious yams
And cherries from Hesperides;
And every man and every beast,
Known to the stars' directories
For speed of foot and strength of back,
Would be the couriers to this feast—
Mercury, Atlas, Hercules,
Each bearing a capacious pack.
I would conscript the Gemini,
Persuading Castor to compete
With Pollux on a heavy wager,
Buckboard against the sled, that he,
With Capricornus could not beat
His brother mushing Canis Major.
And on the journey there I'd hail
Aquarius with his nets and pail,
And Neptune with his prong to meet us
At some point on the shores of Cetus,
And bid them superintend a cargo
Of fresh sea-food upon the Argo—
Sturgeon and shell-fish that might serve
To fill the side-boards with *hors d'oeuvres*.

And worthy of the banquet spread
Within this royal court of night,
A curving canopy of light
Shall roof it myriad-diamonded.
For high above the table head
Shall sway a candelabrum where,

According to the legend, dwelt a
Lady seated in a chair
With Alpha, Beta, Gamma, Delta,
Busy braiding up her hair.
Sirius, the dog-star, shall be put
Immediately above the foot,
And central from the cupola
Shall hang the cluster—Auriga,
With that deep sapphire-hearted stella,
The loveliest of the lamps, Capella.

For all old men whose pilgrim feet
Were calloused with life's dust and heat,
Whose throats were arid with its thirst,
I'd smite Jove's taverns till they burst,
And punch the spigots of his vats,
Till flagons, kegs and barrels all
Were drained of their ambrosial
As dry as the Sahara flats.
For toothless, winded ladies who,
Timid and hesitating, fear
They might not stand the barbecue
 (Being so near their obsequies),
I'd serve purees fresh from the ear
Of Spica with a mild ragout—
To satisfy the calories—
Of breast of Cygnus stiffened by
The hind left leg of Aries,
As a last wind-up before they die.
And I would have no wardens there,
Searching the platters for a reason
To seize Diana and declare
That venison is out of season.
For all those children hunger-worn
From drought or flood and harvest failing,
Whether from Nile or Danube hailing,
Or Yangtze or the Volga born,
I'd communize the total yields
Of summer in the Elysian fields,
Gather the berries from the shrubs
To crown soufflés and syllabubs.

Dumplings and trifles and *éclaires*
And roly-polies shall be theirs;
Search as you may, you will not find
One dash of oil, one dish of prunes
To spoil the taste of the macaroons,
And I would have you bear in mind
No dietetic aunt-in-law,
With hook-nose and prognathic jaw,
Will try her vain reducing fads
Upon these wenches and these lads.
Now that these grand festivities
Might start with holy auspices,
I would select with Christian care,
To offer up the vesper prayer,
A padre of high blood—no white
Self-pinched, self-punished anchorite,
Who credits up against his dying
His boasted hours of mortifying,
Who thinks he hears a funeral bell
In dinner gongs on principle.
He shall be left to mourn this night,
Walled in his dim religious light:
Unto this feast he shall not come
To breathe his gloom. No! rather some
Sagacious and expansive friar,
Who beams good-will, who loves a briar,
Who, when he has his fellows with him
Around a board, can make a grace
Sonorous, full of liquid rhythm,
Boom from his lungs' majestic bass;
Who, when requested by his host
To do the honours to a toast,
Calls on the clan to rise and hold
Their glasses to the light a minute,
Just to observe the mellow gold
And the rare glint of autumn in it.

Now even at this hour he stands,
The benison upon his face,
In his white hair and moulded hands,
No less than in his spoken grace.
"We thank thee for this table spread
In such a hall, on such a night,

With such unusual stores of bread,
O Lord of love! O Lord of light!
We magnify thy name in praise
At what thy messengers have brought,
For not since Galilean days
Has such a miracle been wrought.
The guests whom thou hast bidden come,
The starved, the maimed, the deaf, and dumb,
Were misfits in a world of evil,
And ridden hard by man and devil.
The seven years they have passed through
Were leaner than what Israel knew.
Dear Lord, forgive my liberty,
In telling what thou mayst not know,
For it must seem so queer to thee,
What happens on our earth below:
The sheep graze on a thousand hills,
The cattle roam upon the plains,
The cotton waits upon the mills,
The stores are bursting with their grains,
And yet these ragged ones that kneel
To take thy grace before their meal
Are said to be thy chosen ones,
Lord of the planets and the suns!
Therefore let thy favours fall
In rich abundance on them all.
May not one stomach here to-night
Turn traitor on its appetite.
Take under thy peculiar care
The infants and the aged. Bestow
Upon all invalids a rare
Release of their digestive flow,
That they, with health returned, may know
A hunger equal to the fare,
And for these mercies, Lord, we'll praise
Thee to the limit of our days."

He ended. The salubrious feast
Began: with inundating mirth
It drowned all memories of earth:
It quenched the midnight chimes: nor ceased

It till the wand of Prospero,
Turning its magic on the east,
Broke on a master charm, when lo!
Answering the summons of her name,
Fresh from the surf of Neptune came
Aurora to the Portico.

THE FABLE OF THE GOATS

and other Poems

(1937)

To my sister Charlotte

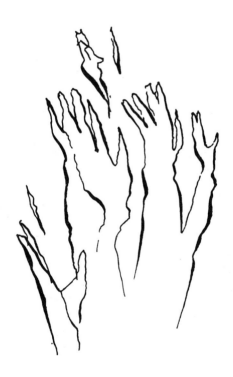

THE BARITONE

He ascended the rostrum after the fashion of the Caesars:
His arm, a baton raised oblique,
Answering the salute of the thunder,
Imposed a silence on the Square.
For three hours
A wind-theme swept his laryngeal reeds,
Pounded on the diaphragm of a microphone,
Entered, veered, ran round a coil,
Emerged, to storm the passes of the ether,
Until, impinging on a hundred million ear-drums,
It grew into the fugue of Europe.

Nickel, copper and steel rang their quotations to the skies,
And down through the diatonic scale
The mark hallooed the franc,
The franc bayed the lira,
With the three in full flight from the pound.
And while the diapasons were pulled
On the *Marseillaise,*
The *Giovanezza,*
And the *Deutschlandlied,*
A perfect stretto was performed
As the *Dead March* boomed its way
Through *God Save The King*
And the *Star Spangled Banner.*

Then the codetta of the clerics
(Chanting a ritual over the crosses of gold tossed into the
        crucibles to back the billion credit)
Was answered by
The clang of the North Sea against the bows of the destroyers,
The ripple of surf on the periscopes.
The grunt of the Mediterranean shouldering Gibraltar,
And the hum of the bombing squadrons in formation under
        Orion.

And the final section issued from the dials,
WHEN—
Opposed by contrapuntal blasts
From the Federated Polyphonic Leagues
Of Gynecologists,
Morticians.

And the Linen Manufacturers—
The great Baritone,
Soaring through the notes of the hymeneal register,
Called the brides and the grooms to the altar,
To be sent forth by the Recessional Bells
To replenish the earth,
And in due season to produce
Magnificent crops of grass on the battlefields.

FIRE

Wiser than thought, more intimate than breath,
More ancient than the plated rust of Mars,
Beyond the light geometry of stars,
Yet closer than our web of life and death—
This sergeant of the executing squads
Calls night from dawn no less than dawn from night;
This groom that teams the wolf and hare for flight
Is obstetrician at the birth of gods.
Around this crimson source of human fears,
Where rites and myths have built their scaffoldings,
With smoke of hecatombs upon her wings,
And chased by shadows of the coming years,
Our planet-moth tries blindly to survive
Her spinning vertigo as fugitive.

But stronger than its terror is the deep
Allurement, primary to our blood, which holds
Safety and warmth in unimpassioned folds,
Night and the candle-quietness of sleep;
With the day's bugles silent, when the will,
That feeds the tumult of our natures, rests
Along the broken arteries of its quests.
So, let the yellowing world revolve until
The old Sun's ultimate expatriate
On this exotic hearth leans forth to claim
Promethean virtue from a dying flame,
His fingers tapered—less to mitigate
The chilling accident of his sojourn
Than to invoke his ultimate return.

SEEN ON THE ROAD

The pundit lectured that the world was young
As ever, frisking like a spring-time colt
Around the sun, his mother. The class hung
Upon his words. I listened like a dolt,

And muttered that I saw the wastrel drawn
Along a road with many a pitch and bump
By spavined mules—this very day at dawn!
And heading for an ammunition dump.

The savant claimed I heckled him, but—Hell!
I saw the fellow in a tumbril there,
Tattered and planet-eyed and far from well,
With Winter roosting in his Alpine hair.

THE PRIZE CAT

Pure blood domestic, guaranteed,
Soft-mannered, musical in purr,
The ribbon had declared the breed,
Gentility was in the fur.

Such feline culture in the gads
No anger ever arched her back—
What distance since those velvet pads
Departed from the leopard's track!

And when I mused how Time had thinned
The jungle strains within the cells,
How human hands had disciplined
Those prowling optic parallels;

I saw the generations pass
Along the reflex of a spring,
A bird had rustled in the grass,
The tab had caught it on the wing:

Behind the leap so furtive-wild
Was such ignition in the gleam,
I thought an Abyssinian child
Had cried out in the whitethroat's scream

72

LIKE MOTHER, LIKE DAUGHTER

Helen, Deirdre, Héloïse,
Laura, Cleopatra, Eve!
The knight-at-arms is on his knees,
Still at your altars—by your leave.

The magic of your smiles and frowns
Had made you goddesses by right,
Divorced the monarchs from their crowns,
And changed world empires overnight.

You caught the *male* for good or ill,
And locked him in a golden cage,
Or let him out at your sweet will—
A prince or peasant, lord or page.

But do not preen your wings and claim
That when you passed away, the keys—
The symbols of your charm and fame—
Were buried with your effigies.

For, wild and lovely are your broods
That stole from you the ancient arts;
In tender or tempestuous moods,
They storm the barrens of our hearts.

Amy, Hilda, Wilhelmine,
Golden Marie and slim Suzette,
Viola, Claire and dark Eileen,
Brown-eyed Mary, blue-eyed Bett.

Daughters are ye of those days
When Troy and Rome and Carthage burned:
Ye cannot mend your mothers' ways
Or play a trick they hadn't learned.

But whether joy or whether woe—
Lure of lips or scorn of eyes—
We bless you either way we go,
In or out of Paradise.

THE OLD ORGANON (1225 A.D.)

When Genghis and his captains
Built their pyramids of skulls
Outside Bokhara and Herat,
And sacked Otrar and Samarcand,
There was no sophistry between the subject and the verb;
For what the Khan said, he meant.
Behind the dust were the hoofs of his cavalry,
Behind the smoke was his fire.
And when Mohammed and Jehal-ud-Din,
In their flight from the Indus to the Caspian,
Appealed to Allah for protection,
Even the Great God of Islam
Could find no escape for the faithful,
When he knew the flight was regimented
To the paces of a Mongol syllogism.

THE NEW (1937 A.D.)

Now when the delegates met around the tables
And lifted up their voices,
The subjects were their civilizing tasks,
The fulfilment of historic missions,
The redemption of the national honour,
And the emancipation of the slaves.
But flaws were hidden in the predicates,
And in the pips of the adverbials,
And the rhetorical adjectives
Assumed the protective colouring
Of the great cats against the jungle grass—
THEREFORE,
In all the wealth of their possessive pronouns,
Not a syllable was spared
For the oil reported in the foreign shales.

THE MYSTIC

Where do you bank such fires as can transmute
This granite-fact intransigence of life,

74

Such proud irenic faith as can refute
The upstart logic of this world of strife—
Its come-and-go of racial dust, its strum
Of windy discords from the seven seas,
Its scream of fifes and din of kettle-drum
That lead the march towards our futurities?
The *proof*, that slays the reason, has no power
To stem your will, corrode your soul—though lime
Conspire with earth and water to devour
The finest cultures from the lust of slime;
Though crumbled Tartar hordes break through their sod
To blow their grit into the eyes of God.

THE WEATHER GLASS

There is no refuge from this wind tonight,
Though sound the roof and double-latched the door,
And though I've trimmed the wick, there is no light,
Nor is there warmth although the tamaracks roar;
Nor will the battery of those surges keep
The hammering pulses silent in my sleep.

But one alone might quell this storm tonight,
And were he now this moment at the door,
His eyes would clear the shadows from this light,
His voice put laughter in the billets' roar,
And he would clasp me in his arms and keep
The wheeling gulls from screaming through my sleep.

THE EMPTY ROOM

I know that were my soul tonight
Strung to the silence of this room,
I'd hear remembered footfalls light
As wayward drift of lotus bloom.

Nor would it just be make-believe,
Were I to find her in this chair,

75

Or catch the rustle of her sleeve,
Or note the glint upon her hair.

Say, would you blame me if I knelt
To put faith to its enterprise?
So surely must her touch be felt
In liquid coolness on my eyes.

Now listen! If the veil should part
Within this holy ritual,
You'll hear a voice call to my heart
More lovely than a madrigal.

THE MIRAGE

Complete from glowing towers to golden base,
Without the lineage of toil it stood:
A crystal city fashioned out of space,
So calm and holy in its Sabbath mood,
It might constrain belief that any time
The altars would irradiate their fires,
And any moment now would start the chime
Of matins from the massed Cathedral spires.
Then this marmoreal structure of the dawn,
Built as by fiat of Apocalypse,
Was with the instancy of vision gone;
Nor did it die through shadow of eclipse,
Through clouds and vulgar effigies of night,
But through the darker irony of light.

THE ILLUSION

All patterns of the day were merged in one—
Clouds, wings and faces, dunes and harbour bars—
In a swift blur of vision as the sun
Went down at noon upon a drift of spars.

In such a lightless hour the sea had cleft
A heart, fumbling its way as through a strait,
Then passed, bequeathing to the common weft
No record but its arid distillate.

Though when night comes with sleep there still remains
Enough of daylight and of surf to trace
The artisan outside the storm-swept panes,
Refashioning the pallor of his face
To softer lines which thread my nescient mood
With the illusion of beatitude.

SILENCES

There is no silence upon the earth or under the earth like the
        silence under the sea;
No cries announcing birth,
No sounds declaring death.
There is silence when the milt is laid on the spawn in the
        weeds and fungus of the rock-clefts;
And silence in the growth and struggle for life.
The bonitoes pounce upon the mackerel,
And are themselves caught by the barracudas,
The sharks kill the barracudas
And the great molluscs rend the sharks,
And all noiselessly—
Though swift be the action and final the conflict,
The drama is silent.

There is no fury upon the earth like the fury under the sea.
For growl and cough and snarl are the tokens of spendthrifts
        who know not the ultimate economy of rage.
Moreover, the pace of the blood is too fast.
But under the waves the blood is sluggard and has the same
        temperature as that of the sea.

There is something pre-reptilian about a silent kill.

Two men may end their hostilities just with their battle-cries.
"The devil take you," says one.
"I'll see you in hell first," says the other.

And these introductory salutes followed by a hail of gutturals
and sibilants are often the beginning of friendship,
for who would not prefer to be lustily damned than
to be half-heartedly blessed?

No one need fear oaths that are properly enunciated, for they
belong to the inheritance of just men made perfect,
and, for all we know, of such may be the Kingdom of
Heaven.

But let silent hate be put away for it feeds upon the heart of
the hater.

Today I watched two pairs of eyes. One pair was black and the
other grey. And while the owners thereof, for the
space of five seconds, walked past each other, the grey
snapped at the black and the black riddled the grey.

One looked to say—"The cat,"

And the other—"The cur."

But no words were spoken;

Not so much as a hiss or a murmur came through the perfect
enamel of the teeth; not so much as a gesture of
enmity.

If the right upper lip curled over the canine, it went unnoticed.

The lashes veiled the eyes not for an instant in the passing.

And as between the two in respect to candour of intention or
eternity of wish, there was no choice, for the stare
was mutual and absolute.

A word would have dulled the exquisite edge of the feeling,

An oath would have flawed the crystallization of the hate.

For only such culture could grow in a climate of silence,—

Away back before the emergence of fur or feather, back to the
unvocal sea and down deep where the darkness spills
its wash on the threshold of light, where the lids never
close upon the eyes, where the inhabitants slay in
silence and are as silently slain.

STILL LIFE

and other Verse

(1943)

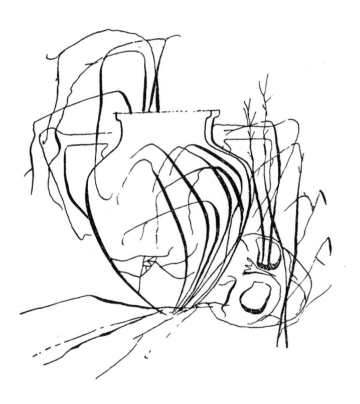

STILL LIFE

To the poets who have fled
To pools where little breezes dusk and shiver,
Who need still life to deliver
Their souls of their songs,
We offer roses blanched of red
In the Orient gardens,
With April lilies to limn
On the Japanese urns—
And time, be it said,
For a casual hymn
To be sung for the hundred thousand dead
In the mud of the Yellow River.

And if your metric paragraphs
Incline to Western epitaphs,
Be pleased to return to a plain
Where a million lie
Under a proletarian sky,
Waiting to trouble
Your lines on the scorched Ukrainian stubble.
On the veined marble of their snows
Indite a score to tether
The flight of your strain;
Or should you need a rougher grain
That will never corrode with weather,
Let us propose
A stone west of the bend where the Volga flows
To lick her cubs on the Stalingrad rubble.

Hasten, for time may pass you by,
Mildew the reed and rust the lyre;
Look—that Tunisian glow will die
As died the Carthaginian fire!
Today the autumn tints are on
The trampled grass at Marathon.
Here are the tales to be retold,
Here are the songs to be resung.
Go, find a cadence for that field-grey mould
Outcropping on the Parthenon.
Invoke, in other than the Latin tongue,
A Mediterranean Muse

To leave her pastoral loves—
The murmurs of her soft Theocritean fold,
Mimosa, oleander,
Dovecotes and olive groves,
And court the shadows where the night bedews
A Roman mausoleum hung
Upon the tides from Candia to Syracuse.

AUTOPSY ON A SADIST

(after Lidice)

The microscope was at a loss to tell
The composition of his brain and glands—
Why blood should be like catnip to his smell,
And paws be given him instead of hands.

What toxins in a mammal's milk could serve
To manufacture luxuries out of pains,
Anaesthetize the sympathetic nerve
Or turn to sleet the fluids of his veins?

Much less could it explain those pointed ears
That caught the raptures of a werewolf's howl,
The allegretto strains in human tears,
The hallelujahs in a tiger's growl.

THE STOICS

They were the oaks and beeches of our species.
Their roots struck down through acid loam
To weathered granite and took hold
Of flint and silica, or found their home
With red pyrites—fools' mistake for gold.
Their tunics, stoles and togas were like watersheds,
Splitting the storm, sloughing the rain.
Under such cloaks the morrow could not enter—
Their *gravitas* had seized a geologic centre
And triumphed over subcutaneous pain.

81

THE STOICS

Aurelius! What direction did you take
To find your hermitage?
We have tried but failed to make
That cool unflawed retreat
Where the pulses slow their beat
To an aspen-yellow age.
Today we cannot discipline
The ferments ratting underneath our skin.
Where is the formula to win
Composure from defeat?
And what specific can unmesh
The tangle of civilian flesh
From the traction of the panzers?
And when our children cry aloud
At screaming comets in the skies, what serves
The head that's bloody but unbowed?
What are the Stoic answers
To those who flag us at the danger curves
Along the quivering labyrinth of nerves?

FATHER TIME

Worry had crept into the old man's face.
Why did he have to tilt the hour-glass
So often? Strange, he thought, this hurried pace
Of the atoms as they strove to pass
From bulb to bulb, fighting their way
From life to death in an unexplained stampede.

He had measured many tempos in his season,
But never cared for speed.
He always liked the sanitary, slow,
Grave manner of the mountains.
He had seen them flow
In rivulets of crystal grains
Down through this very corridor
To the deltas of the ocean shore.
He had watched the plants and trees turn into coal;

The marks of the fronds were in the veins
Resembling those of his own hands and temples.
He remembered how he used to while
Away the aeons, pondering the roll
Of the Amazon and Nile.
The curve of the sand dunes of Sahara,
The depositions of the layers of gneiss,
The march of the granite boulders
Under the control
Of dynasties of ice.

He thought of the prehistoric file
Of the saurians, one long and leisured day,
On the crumbling bridges from Australia to Malay.
And now this new adventurer—
Which called itself a soul,
With its mélange of pride,
Courage, honour, suicide,
Pursuing an eternal goal—
Had come along to wreck
His cool pre-Cambrian sense of sequence.
He shot a last glance at the trek
Of the human granules through the bottleneck,
Then rose and smashed the glass, and with the dust
Christened the knoll—
SEBASTOPOL!

MISSING: BELIEVED DEAD: RETURNED

Steady, the heart!
Can you not see
You must not break
Incredulously?

The dead has come back,
He is here at the sill;
Try to believe
The miracle.
Give me more breath,
Or I may not withstand

83

The thrill of his voice
And the clasp of his hand.

Be quiet, my heart,
Can you not see
In the beat of my pulse
Mortality?

THE BRAWLER IN *WHO'S WHO*

The doctors claimed they never had
A case to handle quite so bad—
A record weight, abnormal girth,
And such disturbance at a birth.
The infant murdered his twin brother
And shortly after that his mother,
To celebrate his debut on the earth.

Defying pedagogic rules,
He made a Bedlam of his schools,
And wrecked them from the floor to rafter,
As one by one, with insane laughter,
Harrowed in soul and gaunt in feature,
His nurse, his father, and his teacher
Wasted, and passed into the great Hereafter.

Then came the War! and soon his name
Was but a synonym for fame;
The allied armies and their foes
Alike were stricken by his blows.
And, peace declared, he took the thanks
Of both; returned high in the ranks—
Lieutenant-Colonel with two D.S.O.s.

He married and his three young wives
In quick succession lost their lives—
A Gaul, a Teuton, and a Briton.
Just how those marital blooms were smitten,

The colonel never would confess:
They say the tale, now with the Press,
Remains by order of the Court unwritten.

Thence to a fortress—whereupon
He rounded up the garrison,
Heading that great historic riot
Concerning roaches in the diet.
A witness swore a brigadier
Gave him the bayonet from the rear
Which laid the brawler flat and strangely quiet.

For one whole day an undertaker
Worked hard upon this mischief-maker
To soften down the muscle twists,
Then called in two evangelists
Who managed somehow to erase
The indentations of his face
But failed to straighten out his knotted fists.

They buried him. That very night
With his left hook and lethal right
He put a dozen shades to rout.
The devil refereed the bout
And spread the rumour—so I'm told,
That Death failing to get him cold,
Had fouled him with a technical knock-out.

THE RADIO IN THE IVORY TOWER

(1937—Sept. 1939)

This is the castle of peace,
And this its quietest hour;
There isn't a cry from the gathering dusk,
There isn't a stir in the mist;
The fog has scarfed the moon and stars,
The curtains are drawn on the tides;
There isn't a wave at the curve of the shore;
A granite-grey silence covers the land,
And the gulls are asleep on a soundless swell.

85

Nor is there a sign that under this Rock,
At the heart of the earth, the volcanoes
Await the word of the Lord of Misrule
To renew their ancient carnival;
Nor is there a sign above the Rock
That the earth responds to the whip of the sun,
Directing its pace and its orbit.
This is the cloister of the world,
Reduced to a cell in the fortress of peace
In the midst of anonymous, infinite darkness.

A slight turn of a dial,
And night and space and the silence
Thronged and tongued with life—
As the hosts might swarm through a lens
From a blood drop
Or a spot of dust in the heavens.
Out of the void they came
To storm the base of the tower,
To hammer the walls of the cell
And tap at the mullioned panes.

Polaris, the scout of Orion,
Was frigidly, jealously
Watching a speck on the frontier.
Adjusting a monocle,
He focused a stare which had often congealed
The blood of explorers,
And frozen their hands to the sextants
Till their bodies starched on the parallels.
He flashed to his chief
That a pair of Muscovite eagles
Had taken his stare without blinking,
Had rifled the pole right under his nose,
And, southward advancing, had brushed with their wings
One-half the floor of the world.
Nor would it be long, he predicted,
Before complaints would come from the stars,
All the way from zenith to nadir,
That their eyes had been blinded by grit,

The moment those birds had swept
All the dust from the planet Tellurian
With one whiff of their insolent tails.

A civilized group from the west,
Lithe, sleek and genteel
And ambassadorial,
Silked from their speech to the rim of their cuffs,
Were joined by a rout from the east:
Battered, uncouth and down at the heel,
Reeking with smoke from Nanking,
Weathering typhoons off Shanghai and Burma,
They filled the night with their clamour,
And spattered the shirts of the Cabinet Ministers
With sludge from the bed of the Yangtze.

From the south, south-east and south-west
Came the ghosts of the master of rapture,
Invoked by their master executants.
Through larynx and fingers and lips,
From catgut and silver and brass,
They were harassed by spirits still in the flesh
Who strove through auditions
With tap-dance and croon, with yodel and bleat,
To grind out an art cacophonic.

And choirs arrayed in white robes
Who had heard of blood that redeemed,
Of fires that refined
And of glory that sanctified dying,
Were massed in their anthem formation
To peal forth their late Hallelujahs
To a sovereign of love, law and order.

Tenore robusto and coloratura,
Deep-chested contralto and basso profundo
Entered to sing of their balcony lovers,
Of jealousies, hates and neurotic farewells,
Of picadors, passionate gypsies,
Of damsels anaemic waiting at windows
For exiles that never returned.

*   *   *   *   *   *   *

The moon waxed and waned,
And came again to the full,

87

Till the sea arose to the equinox.
But only ferrets of sound
Came out of the fog
To worm themselves through the cracks in the cobbles.
The waters leaped at the splayed bastions—
The might of the waters
Against the weight of the concrete,
Against the strength of the steel—
But only the dull reverberation of their paws
Disturbed the insulation of the tower;
Only the faintest echoes seeped through the copper roof
As the gulls screamed around the weather-vane.

(September 1939)

The dial swung to the 69,
And with the sprint of light
On the last lap of the kilocycles
Blew in the great syllabic storm of the age.
Slow in the deep bass started the overture,
Heavy with guttural chords
And growling consonants that raked the cuspids
With timed explosions.
A crash of the dental mutes
Was followed by the pour of the open vowels
Along a huge Teutonic corridor.
And when the serried sibilants struck High G,
A child ran from the room of the tower,
An Alsatian bristled his neck,
A Dachshund slunk under a chair;
And the period ended with the frenzy
Of thirty thousand voices orchestrated
To reduce the Götterdämmerung
To a trundle lullaby.
O master mason! What was wrong with the mortar
That, built to withstand the siege of the sea,
Should crumble beneath the roar from a throat?

Another turn, and the static combined
With the music of march and the roll of drums,
To prelude the close of a civilized aeon.
With a new salute and macabre step,

Chaos came in at the call of the horns.
No longer did news pause to rest on the journey,
Relayed through the stations in story and comment,
To be combed and groomed by the censors
In the leisured light of the studios:
But straight from the rape of the liners,
From the listed decks of the cruisers,
From trenches and plants and fields,
Came the grind from the lurch of the life-boats,
The sputter of salt from the throats,
The caterpillar crunch of the tanks,
The cries that out-blared the burst of the shells,
And the wheeze from the lungs that followed the sirens
In the smother of black-outs that covered the world.

Then Time shedding his mask,
His lazy hour-glass, his rusty scythe,
And all his tattered mortalities
Curved over bowed decrepit shoulders,
Assumed the stature of a young Apollyon.
He rose to be the Paragon of power.
A set of golden keys
Closing all doors of life,
Fitting the wards of death,
Hung from a girdle at his waist;
And as he led his mad aerial legions
Around the turret,
What thunders tarried in his fists!
What voltage in the dark tips of his wings!

THE SUBMARINE

The young lieutenant in command
Of the famous submarine, the K-
148, had scanned
The sea circumference all day:
A thousand times or so his hand
Revolved the prism in the hope
That the image of the ship expected,
But overdue, might be reflected
Through the lenses of his periscope.

89

'Twas getting late, and not a mark
Had troubled the monotony
Of every slow expanding arc
Of the horizon. Suddenly
His grip froze to the handle! What
Was that amorphous yellow spot
To the north-east? Was it the lift
Of a wave, a curl of foam, a drift
Of cloud? Too slow for foam, too fast
For cloud. A minute more. At last
The drift was taking shape; his stroke
Of luck had fallen—it was SMOKE!

An hour of light in the western sky,
And thirty seconds for descent;
The quarry ten miles off. Stand-by!
The valves were opened—flood and vent—
And the water like a rumble of thunder
Entered the tanks. Two generators
Sparked her fins and drove her under
Down the ocean escalators.

No forebear of the whale or shark,
No saurian of the Pleiocene,
Piercing the sub-aquatic dark
Could rival this new submarine.
The evolution of the sea
Had brought forth many specimens
Conceived in horror—denizens
Whose vast inside economy
Not only reproduced their broods,
But having shot them from their wombs,
Devoured them in their family feuds
And passed them through their catacombs.
But was there one in all their race
Combined such terror with such grace,
As this disturber of the glooms,
This rapid sinuous oval form
Which knew unerringly the way
To sound and circumvent a storm
Or steal a march upon her prey?
No product she of Nature's dower,

No casual selection wrought her
Or gave her such mechanic power
To breathe above or under water.

In her thoracic cavities
One hundred tons of batteries
Were ready, on the dive, to start
The musculation of the heart.
And where outside a Ming museum
Could any antiquarian find
An assemblage such as here was shrined
Within the vault of her peritoneum?
Electric switches, indicators,
Diving alarm-horns, oscillators,
Rudder controls, and tubes and dials,
Yellow, white, magenta vials,
Pipes to force out battery gases,
Pressure gauges, polished brasses,
Surrounded human figures caught
At their positions, silent, taut,
Like statues in the tungsten light,
While just outside the cell was night
And a distant engine's monotone
Tapping at a telephone.
And now two hundred feet below
She held her bearings towards her foe,
While silence and the darkness flowed
Along an unnavigated road.

In half an hour she stopped and blew
The water ballast with her air,
Rose stealthily to surface where
Upon the mirror in full view,
Cutting an Atlantic swarth
The trail of smoke turned out to be
A fat mammalian of the sea,
Set on a course north-east by north,
And heavy with maternity.
Within her frame-work iron-walled
A thousand bodies were installed,
A snug and pre-lacteal brood
Drawing from her warmth and food,
Awaiting in two days or three
A European delivery.

91

Blood of tiger, blood of shark,
What a prey to stalk and strike
From an ambush in the dark
Thicket of the sea!

        Now like
The tiger-shark viviparous
Who with her young grown mutinous
Before the birth-hour with the smell
Of blood inside the mother, will expel
Them from her body to begin
At once the steerage of the fin,
The seizure of the jaw, the click
Of serried teeth fashioned so well
Pre-natally to turn the trick
Upon a shoal of mackerel—
So like the shark, the submarine
Ejected from her magazine
The first one of her foetal young.
It ran along the trolley, swung
Into a flooded tube and there
Under a jet of compressed air
It found the sea. A trip-latch in
The tube a second later sprung
A trigger, and the turbine power
Acting on the driving fin
Paced it at fifty miles per hour.

So huge and luscious was this feast,
The 148 released
Three others to offset the chance
Of some erratic circumstance
Of aim or speed or tide or weather.
And during this time nothing was seen
Except to an eye in the submarine
Of that bevy of sharks on the sea together,
So accurately spaced one after the other,
And driven by thirst derived from the mother.
Each seemed on the glass a tenuous feather
Of gold such as a curlew in flight

Would make with its nether wing skimming the swell;
Not a hint of a swerve to the left or right,
The gyros were holding the balance so well.

The rich-ripe mammal was swimming straight
On the course of her chart with unconcerned leisure,
Her steady keel and uniform rate
Combining so perfectly with the deep black
Of the hull—silhouette against the back-
Drop of the sunset to etch and measure
The target—when three of those shafts of foam
At the end of their amber stretch struck home.
The first one barely missed—to plough
A harmless path across her bow:
The next tore like a scimitar
Through flesh to rip the jugular;
Boilers and bulkheads broke apart
When the third torpedo struck the heart;
And with what logic did the fourth
Cancel the course north-east by north,
Hitting abaft the beam to rut
The exploding nitrates through her gut.

The young commander's time was short
To log the items for report.
Upon the mirror he descried
Three cavernous wounds in the mammal's side—
Three crumbled dykes through which the tide
Of a gluttonous Atlantic poured;
A heavy starboard list with banks
Of smoke fluted with steam which soared
From a scramble of pipes within her flanks;
Twin funnel-nostrils belching red,
A tilting stern, a plunging head,
The foundering angle in position,
And the sea's reach for a thousand souls
In the last throe of the parturition.

Now with her hyper-sensitive feel
Of her master's hands on the controls—
A pull of a switch, a turn of a wheel,
The submarine, like the deep-sea shark,
Went under cover, away from the light
And limn of the sunset, from the sight

Of the stars, to a native lair as dark
As a kraken's grave. She took her course
South-west by south—for what was the source
Of that hum to the port picked up by the oscillator?
A rhythm too rapid, too hectic for freighter
Or liner! This was her foe, not her prey:
Faster and louder, and heading her way!
Beyond the depth where the tanks could flood 'er,
She drove her nose down with the diving rudder,
Far from the storm of shells or thrust
Of the ram, away from the gear-wrenching zone
Of the depth-bomb, away from the scent and lust
Of a killer whose might was as great as her own.

THE INVADED FIELD

They brought their youth up on the lore
Of the Phoenix and the pyre,
Of birth from death and gold from fire
And the myth of the Aryan spore.

They measured life in metric tons,
Assessed both man and beast,
And with their patriot sweat they greased
The breechblocks of their guns.

They took their parables from mud—
How pure the crocus grows!
See how the fragrance of a rose
May spring from buried blood!

So, on the promise of this yield
The youth swung down the road,
Goose-stepping to their songs, and sowed
Their bodies on the field.

*   *   *   *   *   *   *

Now if a brier should here be born
In some ironic hour,
Let life infect both leaf and flower
But death preserve the thorn.

94

COME AWAY, DEATH

Willy-nilly, he comes or goes, with the clown's logic,
Comic in epitaph, tragic in epithalamium,
And unseduced by any mused rhyme.
However blow the winds over the pollen,
Whatever the course of the garden variables,
He remains the constant,
Ever flowering from the poppy seeds.

There was a time he came in formal dress,
Announced by Silence tapping at the panels
In deep apology.
A touch of chivalry in his approach,
He offered sacramental wine,
And with acanthus leaf
And petals of the hyacinth
He took the fever from the temples
And closed the eyelids,
Then led the way to his cool longitudes
In the dignity of the candles.

His mediaeval grace is gone—
Gone with the flame of the capitals
And the leisured turn of the thumb
Leafing the manuscripts,
Gone with the marbles
And the Venetian mosaics,
With the bend of the knee
Before the rose-strewn feet of the Virgin.
The *paternosters* of his priests,
Committing clay to clay,
Have rattled in their throats
Under the gride of his traction tread.

One night we heard his footfall—one September night—
In the outskirts of a village near the sea.
There was a moment when the storm
Delayed its fist, when the surf fell
Like velvet on the rocks—a moment only;
The strangest lull we ever knew!
A sudden truce among the oaks
Released their fratricidal arms;
The poplars straightened to attention

As the winds stopped to listen
To the sound of a motor drone—
And then the drone was still.
We heard the tick-tock on the shelf,
And the leak of valves in our hearts.
A calm condensed and lidded
As at the core of a cyclone ended breathing
This was the monologue of Silence
Grave and unequivocal.

What followed was a bolt
Outside the range and target of the thunder,
And human speech curved back upon itself
Through Druid runways and the Piltdown scarps,
Beyond the stammers of the Java caves,
To find its origins in hieroglyphs
On mouths and eyes and cheeks
Etched by a foreign stylus never used
On the outmoded page of the Apocalypse.

THE IMPATIENT EARTH

Back to the earth would we come
In the fullness of years,
As we return home at dusk
When our eyes are dim with day
And our feet tired with stubble.
We would come with slow step
Along the cool loam of lanes,
Home to your heart
With the mellow toll of bells in the west.

But not as today would we come
To the trumpet's unnatural summons,
With our loins girt for a longer race
And our faces set for a different goal,
With our feet strung to the measures of life,
To a riot of bells in the east.

This is the season for blood-root and bud-break,
For freshets and resinous airs,
For the mating migrations
Of swallows and whitethroats,
For the scaling of crags,
For the plangent call of the surf
Where ospreys are building their nests.

Then why should we come out of season
To take the long lease of your heart,
When the swift irresponsible trespass
Of our feet above ground
Is cut short by the halt of the sentry?—
There are months still to go for the autumn,
And months for the poppies to bloom,
Though hate and greed have grown to their harvest,
Though tolerance, forgiveness and love are forgotten
Like scars on the body of Christ—
Too soon in the morning for youth
To take the deep draught of your opiate!

THE DYING EAGLE

A light had gone out from his vanquished eyes;
His head was cupped within the hunch of his shoulders;
His feathers were dull and bedraggled; the tips
Of his wings sprawled down to the edge of his tail.
He was old, yet it was not his age
Which made him roost on the crags
Like a rain-drenched raven
On the branch of an oak in November.
Nor was it the night, for there was an hour
To go before sunset. An iron had entered
His soul which bereft him of pride and of realm,
Had struck him today; for up to noon
That crag had been his throne.
Space was his empire, bounded only
By forest and sky and the flowing horizons.
He had outfought, outlived all his rivals,
And the eagles that now were poised over glaciers

Or charting the coastal outlines of clouds
Were his by descent: they had been tumbled
Out of their rocky nests by his mate,
In the first trial of their fledgeling spins.

Only this morning the eyes of the monarch
Were held in arrest by a silver flash
Shining between two peaks of the ranges—
A sight which galvanized his back,
Bristled the feathers on his neck,
And shot little runnels of dust where his talons
Dug recesses in the granite.
Partridge? Heron? Falcon? Eagle?
Game or foe? He would reconnoitre.

Catapulting from the ledge,
He flew at first with rapid beat,
Level, direct; then with his grasp
Of spiral strategy in fight,
He climbed the orbit
With swift and easy undulations,
And reached position where he might
Survey the bird—for bird it was;
But such a bird as never flew
Between the heavens and the earth
Since pterodactyls, long before
The birth of condors, learned to kill
And drag their carrion up the Andes.

The eagle stared at the invader,
Marked the strange bat-like shadow moving
In leagues over the roofs of the world,
Across the passes and moraines,
Darkening the vitriol blue of the mountain lakes.
Was it a flying dragon? Head,
Body and wings, a tail fan-spread
And taut like his own before the strike;
And there in front two whirling eyes
That took unshuttered
The full blaze of the meridian.
The eagle never yet had known
A rival that he would not grapple,

But something in this fellow's length
Of back, his plated glistening shoulders,
Had given him pause. And did that thunder
Somewhere in his throat not argue
Lightning in his claws? And then
The speed—was it not double his own?
But what disturbed him most, angered
And disgraced him was the unconcern
With which this supercilious bird
Cut through the aquiline dominion,
Snubbing the ancient suzerain
With extra-territorial insolence,
And disappeared.

So evening found him on the crags again,
This time with sloven shoulders
And nerveless claws.
Dusk had outridden the sunset by an hour
To haunt his unhorizoned eyes.
And soon his flock flushed with the chase
Would be returning, threading their glorious curves
Up through the crimson archipelagoes
Only to find him there—
Deaf to the mighty symphony of wings,
And brooding
Over the lost empire of the peaks.

OLD HARRY

Along the coast the sailors tell
The superstition of its fame—
Of how the sea had faceted
The Rock into a human head
And given it the devil's name.

And much there was that would compel
A wife or mother of a seaman
To find a root in the belief
The rock that jutted from the reef
Was built to incarnate a demon.

But there's a story that might well
Receive a share of crediting,
And make the title fit the look
Of vacancy the boulder took
Under the ocean's battering.

Within that perforated shell
Of basalt worn by wave and keel
The demon ruler of the foam
One night upon returning home
Was changed into an imbecile,

Ordered to stay within his cell,
Clutch at the spectres in the air,
Listen to shrieks of drowning men,
And stare at phantom ribs and then
Listen again and clutch and stare.

So like a sea-crazed sentinel,
Weary of sailors and their ships,
Old Harry stands with salt weed spread
In matted locks around his head,
And foam forever on his lips.

THE TRUANT

"What have you there?" the great Panjandrum said
To the Master of the Revels who had led
A bucking truant with a stiff backbone
Close to the foot of the Almighty's throne.

"Right Reverend, most adored,
And forcibly acknowledged Lord
By the keen logic of your two-edged sword!
This creature has presumed to classify
Himself—a biped, rational, six feet high
And two feet wide; weighs fourteen stone;
Is guilty of a multitude of sins.
He has abjured his choric origins,

And like an undomesticated slattern,
Walks with tangential step unknown
Within the weave of the atomic pattern.
He has developed concepts, grins
Obscenely at your Royal bulletins,
Possesses what he calls a will
Which challenges your power to kill."

"What is his pedigree?"

"The base is guaranteed, your Majesty—
Calcium, carbon, phosphorus, vapour
And other fundamentals spun
From the umbilicus of the sun,
And yet he says he will not caper
Around your throne, nor toe the rules
For the ballet of the fiery molecules."
"His concepts and denials—scrap them, burn them—
To the chemists with them promptly."

                                                                "Sire,
The stuff is not amenable to fire.
Nothing but their own kind can overturn them.
The chemists have sent back the same old story—
'With our extreme gelatinous apology,
We beg to inform your Imperial Majesty,
Unto whom be dominion and power and glory,
There still remains that strange precipitate
Which has the quality to resist
Our oldest and most trusted catalyst.
It is a substance we cannot cremate
By temperatures known to our Laboratory.' "

And the great Panjandrum's face grew dark—
"I'll put those chemists to their annual purge,
And I myself shall be the thaumaturge
To find the nature of this fellow's spark.
Come, bring him nearer by yon halter rope:
I'll analyse him with the cosmoscope."

Pulled forward with his neck awry,
The little fellow six feet short,
Aware he was about to die,

Committed grave contempt of court
By answering with a flinchless stare
The Awful Presence seated there.

The ALL HIGH swore until his face was black.
He called him a coprophagite,
A genus *homo*, egomaniac,
Third cousin to the family of worms,
A sporozoan from the ooze of night,
Spawn of a spavined troglodyte:
He swore by all the catalogue of terms
Known since the slang of carboniferous Time.
He said that he could trace him back
To pollywogs and earwigs in the slime.
And in his shrillest tenor he began
Reciting his indictment of the man,
Until he closed upon this capital crime—
"You are accused of singing out of key,
(A foul unmitigated dissonance)
Of shuffling in the measures of the dance,
Then walking out with that defiant, free
Toss of your head, banging the doors,
Leaving a stench upon the jacinth floors.
You have fallen like a curse
On the mechanics of my Universe.

"Herewith I measure out your penalty—
Hearken while you hear, look while you see:
I send you now upon your homeward route
Where you shall find
Humiliation for your pride of mind.
I shall make deaf the ear, and dim the eye,
Put palsy in your touch, make mute
Your speech, intoxicate your cells and dry
Your blood and marrow, shoot
Arthritic needles through your cartilage,
And having parched you with old age,
I'll pass you wormwise through the mire;
And when your rebel will
Is mouldered, all desire
Shrivelled, all your concepts broken,

Backward in dust I'll blow you till
You join my spiral festival of fire.
Go, Master of the Revels—I have spoken."

And the little genus *homo*, six feet high,
Standing erect, countered with this reply—
"You dumb insouciant invertebrate,
You rule a lower than a feudal state—
A realm of flunkey decimals that run,
Return; return and run; again return,
Each group around its little sun,
And every sun a satellite.
There they go by day and night,
Nothing to do but run and burn,
Taking turn and turn about,
Light-year in and light-year out,
Dancing, dancing in quadrillions,
Never leaving their pavilions.

"Your astronomical conceit
Of bulk and power is anserine.
Your ignorance so thick,
You did not know your own arithmetic.
We flung the graphs about your flying feet;
We measured your diameter—
Merely a line
Of zeros prefaced by an integer.
Before we came
You had no name.
You did not know direction or your pace;
We taught you all you ever knew
Of motion, time and space.
We healed you of your vertigo
And put you in our kindergarten show,
Perambulated you through prisms, drew
Your mileage through the Milky Way,
Lassoed your comets when they ran astray,
Yoked Leo, Taurus, and your team of Bears
To pull our kiddy cars of inverse squares.

"Boast not about your harmony,
Your perfect curves, your rings
Of *pure and endless light*—'Twas we
Who pinned upon your Seraphim their wings,

103

And when your brassy heavens rang
With joy that morning while the planets sang
Their choruses of archangelic lore,
'Twas we who ordered the notes upon their score
Out of our winds and strings.
Yes! all your shapely forms
Are ours—parabolas of silver light,
Those blueprints of your spiral stairs
From nadir depth to zenith height,
Coronas, rainbows after storms,
Auroras on your eastern tapestries
And constellations over western seas.

"And when, one day, grown conscious of your age,
While pondering an eolith,
We turned a human page
And blotted out a cosmic myth
With all its baby symbols to explain
The sunlight in Apollo's eyes,
Our rising pulses and the birth of pain,
Fear, and that fern-and-fungus breath
Stalking our nostrils to our caves of death—
That day we learned how to anatomize
Your body, calibrate your size
And set a mirror up before your face
To show you what you really were—a rain
Of dull Lucretian atoms crowding space,
A series of concentric waves which any fool
Might make by dropping stones within a pool,
Or an exploding bomb forever in flight
Bursting like hell through Chaos and Old Night.

"You oldest of the hierarchs
Composed of electronic sparks,
We grant you speed,
We grant you power, and fire
That ends in ash, but we concede
To you no pain nor joy nor love nor hate,
No final tableau of desire,
No causes won or lost, no free
Adventure at the outposts—only
The degradation of your energy

When at some late
Slow number of your dance your sergeant-major **Fate**
Will catch you blind and groping and will send
You reeling on that long and lonely
Lockstep of your wave-lengths towards your end.

"We who have met
With stubborn calm the dawn's hot fusillades;
Who have seen the forehead sweat
Under the tug of pulleys on the joints,
Under the liquidating tally
Of the cat-and-truncheon bastinades;
Who have taught our souls to rally
To mountain horns and the sea's rockets
When the needle ran demented through the points;
We who have learned to clench
Our fists and raise our lightless sockets
To morning skies after the midnight raids,
Yet cocked our ears to bugles on the barricades,
And in cathedral rubble found a way to quench
A dying thirst within a Galilean valley—
No! by the Rood, we will not join your ballet."

LATER POEMS

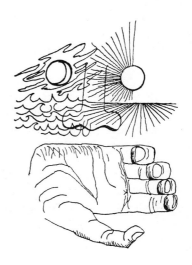

THE UNROMANTIC MOON

The radar pinged the moon one starlit night—
"Good evening!" the operator meant.
Less than "good evening" did the satellite
Reply—its echo quite indifferent.

Only the echo! Could it be that she
Had never trod the court of our conventions?
And learned the art in her simplicity
To ask—"My lord, just what are your intentions?"

Oho, ye lovers! Many centuries
Have written the inscriptions of your tender
Pledges—the cardiograms of your disease—
To that pale maiden with a neuter gender.

And so nocturnes might have been sung forever
By swains and courtiers equally dejected,
Had not a new Minerva chanted—"Never
Have lover-lunar orbits intersected."

Take up your lyres, but tune your orchard trills
To other ears than those of Heaven's queen:
Dead Letter Offices are crater sills
Surrendering to the prose of a machine.

THE GOOD EARTH

Let the mind rest awhile, lower the eyes,
Relieve the spirit of its Faustian clamour:
An atom holds more secrets than the skies;
Be patient with the earth and do not cram her

With seed beyond the wisdom of her soil.
She knows the foot and hoof of man and ox,
She learned the variations of their toil—
The ploughshare's sensitivity to rocks.

Gather the stones for field and garden walls,
Build cellars for your vegetable stores,

Forgo the architecture of your halls,
Until your hands have fashioned stable doors.

She likes the smell of nitrates from the stalls,
She hates a disciplined tread, the scorching roar
At the grain's roots: she is nervous at the calls
Of men in panic at a strike of ore.

Patient she is in her flesh servitude,
Tolerant to curry ticklings of the harrow,
But do not scratch past her agrarian mood
To cut the calcium in her bone and marrow.

Hold that synthetic seed, for underneath
Deep down she'll answer to your horticulture:
She has a way of germinating teeth
And yielding crops of carrion for the vulture.

A CALL

So quiet was the place, it teemed
With peace invasions of the shore—
The sky and sea were undisturbed
By ruffle of wing or riffle of oar.

Only the chatter of surprise
Of children gathering ear-lobed shells
Was teasing silence when the foam
Let go the handrope of its bells.

The air grew morbid with a load
Of clam and balsam smells like musk:
Veils of chiffon hung in the west
While afternoon was threading dusk.

I hastened to the shore and called,
Their blue eyes wondering—"Why, come home!
There is no danger in the tide,
There is no threat of rain or foam."

"Come home!" There was no reason given.
Nor could I give it. I alone

Could penetrate that sign of rain,
The stalking thunder in that drone.

Despite the Sandman's aid, I knew
No barbiturates in those skies
Would join the solvent of the musk
To wash the daylight from their eyes.

*   *   *   *   *   *

I have forgotten now the peace
That held the tides without a foam:
All I remember is the cry,
Unanswered still—"Come home, come home!"

A NOVEMBER LANDSCAPE

November came today and seized the whole
Of the autumnal store of reds, and left
But drabs and yellows on a land bereft
Of bird and leaf, of body and of soul.

Outside my window now rain-winds patrol
The earth; last August elms and birches seem
Like half-remembered legends in a dream;
Melodious myths—the Thrush and Oriole—

Such strange delusions when November weaves
The sense of desolation and regret
Through clay and stubble, through dead ferns and leaves
As here lie sodden on the ground; and yet

This was the story told six months ago,
When April lured the crocus through the snow.

SUMMIT MEETINGS

Why hurry? Stow your jackets in the lockers!
A bloodless argument could dry its rage
Upon an igneous or a glacial page.

Some day the pterodactyls may return.
What warden whispered that a lizard dwells
In the green suburbs of your syllables?

Caesar aut nihil. Deserts lie between.
Covet the lulls in your penultimates
Made up of aspirates and carbonates.
The sand drifts round the black and white, the *Yes*
And *No.* Check well before you leave your chairs
The journey straps between those camel pairs.

Delay decisions. Visit the museums,
The markets, public squares, the parks and beaches
For convalescent moments after speeches.
Observe all signals—*green, red, stop, go.*
Note last—"This way to the memorial plaques
To find the exits to your *cul-de-sacs.*"

Rumble your bellyfuls and crack your chins;
But let the thunder like a thousand Babels
Bark its black knuckles on the oak of tables.
This is the *summum* that the dead may wish
That these, their broods not yet entombed, may snatch
A loaf of life before their canines hatch.

CYCLES

There was a time we knew our foes,
Could recognize their features well,
Name them before we bartered blows;
So in our challenges could tell
What the damned quarrel was about,
As with our fists we slugged it out.

When distance intervened, the call
Of trumpets sped the spear and arrow;
From stone and sling to musket ball
The path was blasted to the marrow;
But still we kept our foes in sight,
Dusk waiting for the morning light.

111

We need no more that light of day,
No need of faces to be seen;
The squadrons in the skies we slay
Through moving shadows on a screen:
By nailing echoes under sea
We kill with like geometry.

Now since the Lord of Love is late
In being summoned to the ring
To keep in bounds the range of hate,
The Lord of Hosts to whom we sing
As Marshal of both man and brute
May be invoked as substitute.

Whether from heaven or from hell,
May he return as referee,
And, keen-eared to an honest bell,
Splitting the foul from fair, feel free
To send us forth into the lists,
Armed only with our naked fists.

And then before our voice is dumb,
Before our blood-shot eyes go blind,
The Lord of Love and Life may come
To lead our ebbing veins to find
Enough for their recovery
Of plasma from Gethsemane.

MYTH AND FACT

We used to wake our children when they screamed;
We felt no fever, found no pain,
And casually we told them that they dreamed
And settled them in sleep again.

So easy was it thus to exorcise
The midnight fears the morning after.
We sought to prove they could not literalize
Jack, though the giant shook with laughter.

112

We showed them pictures in a book and smiled
At red-shawled wolves and chasing bruins—
Was not the race just an incarnate child
That sat at wells and haunted ruins?

We had outgrown the dreams, outrung the knells
Through voodoo, amulet and prayer,
But knew that daylight fastened on us spells
More fearful than Medusa's hair.

We saw the bat-companioned dead arise
From shafts and pipes, and nose like beagles
The spoors of outlaw quarry in the skies
Whose speed and spread made fools of eagles.

We shut our eyes and plugged our ears, though sound
And sight were our front-line defences,
The mind came with its folly to confound
The crystal logic of the senses.

Then turned we to the story-books again
To see that Cyclopean stare.
'Twas out of focus for the beast was slain
While we were on our knees in prayer.

Who were those giants in their climbing strength?
No reason bade us calibrate
These flying lizards in their scaly length
Or plumb a mesozoic hate.

The leaves released a genie to unbind
Our feet along a pilgrimage:
The make-believe had furnished to the mind
Asylum in the foliage.

Draw down the blinds and lock the doors tonight:
We would be safe from that which hovers
Above the eaves. God send us no more light
Than falls between our picture covers.

For what the monsters of the long-ago
Had done were nursery peccadilloes
To what those solar hounds in tally-ho
Could do when once they sniffed the pillows.

THE DEED

Where are the roadside minstrels gone who strung
Their fiddles to the stirrup cavalcades?
What happened to the roses oversung
By orchard lovers in their serenades?

A feudal dust that draggle-tailed the plumes
Blinded the minstrels chasing cavaliers:
Moonlight that sucked the colour from the blooms
Had soaked the lyrists and the sonneteers.

Where is the beauty still inspired by rhyme,
Competing with those garden miracles,
When the first ray conspires with wind to chime
The matins of the Canterbury bells?

Not in the fruit or flower nor in the whir
Of linnet's wings or plaint of nightingales,
Nor in the moonstruck latticed face of her
Who cracked the tenor sliding up his scales.

We saw that beauty once—an instant run
Along a ledge of rock, a curve, a dive;
Nor did he count the odds of ten to one
Against his bringing up that boy alive.

This was an arch beyond the salmon's lunge,
There was a rainbow in the rising mists:
Sea-lapidaries started at the plunge
To cut the facets of their amethysts.

But this we scarcely noticed, since the deed
Had power to cleanse a grapnel's rust, transfigure
The blueness of the lips, unmat the weed
And sanctify the unambiguous rigour.

For that embrace had trapped the evening's light,
Racing to glean the red foam's harvestings:
Even the seagulls vanished from our sight,
Though settling with their pentecostal wings.

NEWFOUNDLAND SEAMEN

This is their culture, this—their master passion
Of giving shelter and of sharing bread,
Of answering rocket signals in the fashion
Of losing life to save it. In the spread
Of time—the Gilbert-Grenfell-Bartlett span—
The headlines cannot dim their daily story,
Nor calls like London! Gander! Teheran!
Outplay the drama of the sled and dory.

The wonders fade. There overhead a mile,
Planes bank like gulls: like curlews scream the jets.
The caravans move on in radar file
Scarce noticed by the sailors at their nets,
Bracing their bodies to their tasks, as when,
Centuries before Argentia's smoking funnels,
That small ancestral band of Devon men
Red-boned their knuckles on the *Squirrel* gunwales.

As old as it is new, as new as old,
Enduring as a cape, as fresh as dulse,
This is the Terra Nova record told
Of uncontractual blood behind the pulse
On sea or land. Was it but yesterday
That without terms and without drill commands,
A rescue squad found Banting where he lay
With the torn tissues of his healing hands?

MAGIC IN EVERYTHING

How freely came belief when we were young!
Unruffled by an argument, the tongue
Had left the mind a garden where the seeds
Sprouted and grew and blossomed without weeds.
From parents who were wise and old
We simply took what we were told.
That Santa with his reindeer should arrive
From his far northern drive,
Seek out our very house and come

115

Down through the chimney and deposit
Around the hearth or in the bedroom closet
His gifts that left us saucer-eyed and dumb—
But miracles had happened on this earth
And we had thrived on wonders from our birth.
And here was one, for we regarded him,
His ruddy-apple cheeks and snowy beard,
With the same sanctity that we revered
The chubby pictures of the cherubim.
'Twas true that those who matched their faith with wit,
And wanted legends proved,
Looked at the fire-place and measured it.
To ease the downward journey they removed
The ashes and the logs,
Cleared out the soot and shoved away the "dogs".
"Santa must come down clean"—*that* we could follow—
And clean must be the presents that he brought.
We felt the reindeer story hard to swallow,
Yet to *our* minds there was no need for *proofs*:
Twelve months ago that night our ears had caught
The "hail!" of Santa and the thud of hoofs.

A few years passed and we began
Half furtively to question one another,
And still more warily our dad and mother:
And this is how our questions ran—
How did the old man stand that polar race,
Enter a house that with no fire-place
Had but a kitchen stove? This point was hard.
Only the Lord could push a body through
A passage narrow as the kitchen flue.
Were windows open? Was the door unbarred?
This sacrilege of doubt assailed
The toughening spirit of our thought.
Those letters we had written, sealed and mailed
A week or month before—what post had brought
Them to the north? Was it the right address?
Had Santa seen them? Yes,
He must; for there upon the tree or floor
Were the crammed stockings, trains that ran
On tracks, a Jack-in-the-box: outside the door
A pair of snow-shoes and a catamaran—

Just what we asked. Yes, these were real, but why
Did other things escape his eye—
Gifts we had pondered on for many a day?
Was there a limit to his Christmas sleigh?
And when our parents could not satisfy
The older sceptics with a sane reply,
They winked and smiled, grew restless or were bored,
Or ended with one answer long prepared,
An answer which we dared
Not question—"Back of Santa was the Lord."

The Lord! He knew all wherefores, all the whys.
Was He not Lord of earth and skies?
In some strange way
He was related to the Christmas day.
For early on that morn
The steeple chimes were ringing
And choirs were singing
"Unto us a child is born."
Under the charm of that celestial sound,
Within the story of his life we found
The riddles of our youth
Were tongued from higher ground
And solved by proclamation of an Act.
A myth took refuge in a fact,
A fairy tale into a truth.
For painlessly the changes came
Though Santa Claus was still allowed his name.
We banished reindeer with our smiles,
Their voyage through those northern miles.
We closed the argument
About the way the gifts were sent.
No longer did we measure
The chimney width for fear he might be burned
Or ashes smother up the Christmas treasure.
And so completely vanished all our doubt
That we forgot to put the fire out.
What mattered it when in due time we learned
The givers were our parents who, as wise
As Santa, offered to our dawning eyes
That spruce tree with its gay surprise.
Nor did we bother much to reconcile
The ancient fable with a father's smile.

117

And even if the youngest of us tried
To get a smattering of sense
Out of the Santa Claus "pretence",
It wasn't long before his tears were dried
By what he saw: the gifts were real as bread,
Something to touch and taste and eat.
No apples were more fresh and red,
No candy was more sweet;
The wooden horse was there to ride,
And magic was in everything—
The Jacks popped with the spring,
And there were shining runners on the slide.

So, when we found ourselves bereft
Of childhood fantasies we still had left
The memories that years could not corrode—
Behind the celebration of the Day
Were living hands that had bestowed
The gifts, and love behind the hands, and then
Something our reasons could not rub away—
The story of a Birth bequeathed to men.
How could we question that under the spells
Woven around us by the Christmas bells?

Part Two
NARRATIVE POEMS

THE WITCHES' BREW
(1925)

THE WITCHES' BREW

Perched on a dead volcanic pile,
Now charted as a submerged peak,
Near to a moon-washed coral isle,
A hundred leagues from Mozambique,
Three water-witches of the East,
Under the stimulus of rum,
Decided that the hour had come
To hold a Saturnalian feast,
In course of which they hoped to find
For their black art, once and for all,
The true effect of alcohol
Upon the cold, aquatic mind.
From two Phœnicians who were drowned,
The witches three (whose surnames ran
Lulu, Ardath, Maryan)
Had by an incantation found
A cavern near the coast of Crete,
And saw, when they had entered in,
A blacksmith with a dorsal fin,
Whose double pectorals and webbed feet
Proved—while his dusky shoulders swung—
His breed to be of land and water,
Last of great Neptune's stock that sprung
From Vulcan's union with his daughter.
The sisters' terms accepted, he,
Together with his family,
Left his native Cretan shore
To dig the witches' copper ore
Out of their sub-aqueous mines
In the distant Carolines,
And forge a cauldron that might stand,
Stationary and watertight,
A thousand cubits in its height,
Its width a thousand breadths as spanned
By the smith's gigantic hand,
So that each fish, however dry,
Might have, before the Feast was through,
His own demonstrable supply
Of this Pan-Oceanic brew.
A thousand leagues or so away
Down the Pacific to Cape Horn,

And Southwards from Magellan lay
A table-land to which was borne
This cauldron from the Carolines,
For here, as well the sisters knew,
The Spanish conquerors of Peru
Had stored their rich and ancient wines,
About the time the English burst
Upon their galleons under Drake,
Who sank or captured them to slake
A vast Elizabethan thirst.
With pick and bar the Cretan tore
His way to the interior
Of every sunken ship whose hold
Had wines almost four centuries old.
Upon the broad Magellan floors,
Great passage-way from West to East,
Were also found more recent stores,
The products of a stronger yeast.
For twenty years or thereabout,
The Bacchanals of Western nations,
Scenting universal drought,
Had searched the ocean to find out
The most secluded ports and stations,
Where unmolested they might go
"To serve their god while here below,"
With all the strength of their libations.
So to the distant isles there sailed,
In honour of the ivy god,
Scores of log-loaded ships that hailed
From Christiania to Cape Cod
With manifests entitled *ham,*
Corn beef, molasses, chamois milk,
Cotton, Irish linen, silk,
Pickles, dynamite and *jam,*
And myriad substances whose form
Dissolved into quite other freights,
Beneath the magic of a storm
That scattered them around the Straits;
For this is what the blacksmith read,
While raking up the ocean bed:—
Budweiser, Guinness, Schlitz (in kegs),
Square Face Gin and *Gordon's Dry,*
O'Brien's, Burke's and *Johnny Begg's,*

Munich, Bock, and *Seagram's Rye,*
Dewar's, Hennessey's 3 Star,
Glenlivet, White Horse and *Old Parr,*
With *Haig and Haig, Canadian Club,*
Jamaica Rum, and other brands
Known to imbibers in all lands
That stock from Brewery or Pub.
All these the Cretan, with the aid
Of his industrious progeny,
Drew to the cauldron, and there laid,
By order of the witches three,
The real foundation for the spree.

OTHER INGREDIENTS

To make a perfect fish menu,
The witches found they had to place
Upon this alcoholic base
Great stacks of food and spices too.
Of all the things most edible
On which the souls of fish have dined,
That fish would sell their souls to find,
Most gracious to their sense of smell,
Is flesh exotic to their kind:—
Cold-blooded things yet not marine,
And not of earth, but half-between,
That live enclosed within the sand
Without the power of locomotion,
And mammal breeds whose blood is hot,
That court the sea but love it not,
That need the air but not the land,—
The Laodiceans of the ocean.
So in this spacious cauldron went
Cargoes of food and condiment.
Oysters fished from Behring Strait
Were brought and thrown in by the crate;
Spitzbergen scallops on half-shell,
Mussels, starfish, clams as well,

Limpets from the Hebrides,
Shrimps and periwinkles, these,
So celebrated as a stew,
Were meant to flavour up the brew.
Then for the more substantial fare,
The curried quarter of a tail
Hewn from a stranded Greenland whale,
A liver from a Polar bear,
A walrus' heart and pancreas,
A blind Auk from the coast of Java,
A bull moose that had died from gas
While eating toadstools near Ungava,
One bitter-cold November day;
Five sea-lion cubs were then thrown in,
Shot by the Cretan's javelin
In a wild fight off Uruguay,
With flippers fresh from the Azores,
Fijian kidneys by the scores,
Together with some pollywogs,
And kippered hocks of centipedes,
And the hind legs of huge bull frogs
Raked by the millions from the reeds
Of slimy Patagonian bogs.

Then before the copper lid
Was jammed upon the pyramid,
The sisters scattered on the top
Many a juicy lollipop;
Tongues from the Ganges crocodile,
Spawn from the delta of the Nile,
Hoofs of sheep and loins of goats,
Raised from foundered cattle-boats—
Titbits they knew might blend with hops,
Might strengthen rum or season rye,
From Zulu hams and Papuan chops
To filets mignons from Shanghai.
Now while volcanic fires burned,
Making the cauldron fiercely hot,
Lulu with her ladle churned
The pungent contents of the pot,
From which distinctive vapours soon
Rose palpably before the view.
Then Ardath summoned a typhoon

Which as it swooped upon the stew,
And swept around the compass, bore
To every sea and every shore
The tidings of the witches' Feast.
And from the West and from the East,
And from the South and from the North,
From every bay and strait and run,
From the Tropics to the Arctic sun,
The Parliament of fish came forth,
Lured by a smell surpassing far
The potencies of boiling tar,
For essences were in this brew
Unknown to blubber or to glue,
And unfamiliar to the nose
Of sailors hardened as they are
To every unctuous wind that blows
From Nantucket to Baccalieu.
The crudest oil one ever lit
Was frankincense compared to it.
It entered Hades, and the airs
Resuscitated the Immortals;
It climbed the empyrean stairs
And drove St. Peter from the portals.

DEFENSIVE MEASURES

According to the witches' plan,
All life whose blood did not run true
Must be excluded from the brew;
Each earthly thing from snail to man,
And every mammal of the sea
Was for that night an enemy.
And so the smith from ocean hoards
Had gathered masts and spars and boards
Of ships, with cutlasses and swords,
And countless pikes and spears, and made
With them a towering palisade.
And to the top thereof was sent,

To guard the brew, a warrior,—
The bravest of the ranks of war,
And deaf to bribe or argument.
To neither shark nor swordfish fell
The honours of the sentinel,
For of all fighters there, the star
Was Tom the cat from Zanzibar.

THE SEA-CAT

It's not for us to understand
How life on earth began to be,
How forms that lived within the sea
Should leave the water for the land;
Or how— (Satan alone may trace
The dark enigma of this race)
When feline variants, so far
Removed as tabs and tigers are,
Preferred, when they had left the shore,
The jungle and the kitchen floor—
That this uncouth, primordial cat
Should keep his native habitat.
Yet here he was, and one might find
In crouch and slink and instant spring
Upon a living, moving thing,
The common genus of his kind.
But there were qualities which he
Derived not from his family tree.
No leopard, lynx or jaguar
Could match this cat from Zanzibar
For whiskers that from ear to chin
Ran round to decorate his grin.
And something wilder yet than that
Lay in the nature of this cat.
It's said that mariners by night,
When near a dangerous coast-line, might
Recover bearings from the light
Of some strange thing that swam and gleamed;
A Salamander it might be,
They said, or Lucifer that streamed

His fiery passage through the sea.
But in this banquet place not one
Of all the revellers could fail
To solve the riddle when Tom spun
A vast ecliptic as his tail,
A fiery comet, and his fur
Electrified each banqueter.
So the three beldams there agreed
No alien could invade the hall
If one of such a fighting breed
Were placed upon the fortress wall;
For who, they asked, of mortal creatures
Could claim more fearful derivation
Than Tom with his Satanic features
And his spontaneous conflagration?

THE FLIGHT OF THE IMMORTALS

Close to the dunnest hour of night,
Sniffing the odour of the brew,
Their bat-wings oiled for water flight,
The Devil and his legions flew,
Smashing the record from Hell's Gates
By plumbline to Magellan Straits.
Far in their wake, but hurrying fast
For fear the odour might not last
Till morning, came a spectral band
Weary from Hades—that dry land.

INVENTORY OF HADES

1. Statesmen and apothecaries,
   Poets, plumbers, antiquaries,
   Premiers with their secretaries,
   Home and foreign missionaries,
   And writers of obituaries.

2. Mediæval disputants,
   Mystics in perpetual trance,
   Philosophers in baggy pants,
   Puritans to whom the chance
   Had never come in life to dance
   Save when the dreadful circumstance
   Of death removed their maiden aunts.

3. Scribes with wide phylacteries,
   Publicists and Sadducees,
   Scholars, saints and Ph.D.'s.

4. Doctors, auctioneers and bakers,
   Dentists, diplomats and fakirs,
   Clergymen and undertakers.

5. Rich men, poor men, fools and sots,
   Logicians, tying Shades in knots,
   Pagans, Christians, Hottentots,
   Deacons good and bad in spots,
   Farmers with their Wyandots.

AN HOUR LATER

Not since the time the sense of evil
Caught our first parents by surprise,
While eating fruit in Paradise,
One fateful morning, had the Devil,
Used as he was to steam and smoke,
Beheld such chaos as now broke
Upon his horny, bloodshot eyes.
Prince of the Power of the air,
Lord of terrestrial things as well
As subterranean life in Hell,
He had till now not been aware
How this great watery domain
Might be enclosed within his reign;
Such things as fish, cold-blooded, wet,
Had served no end of his as yet.
The serpent could be made to lie,
And hence fit agent to deceive

127

A trustful female such as Eve;
But he, though cold, at least was dry.
For all his wily strategy
Since time began, the Devil saw
No way to circumvent the sea.
The fish transgressed no moral law,
They had no principles, no creed,
No prayers, no Bibles, and no Church,
No Reason's holy light to read
The truth and no desire to search.
Hence from Dame Nature's ancient way
Their fins had never learned to stray.
They ate and drank and fought, it's true,
And when the zest was on they slew;
But yet their most tempestuous quarrels
Were never prejudiced by morals;
As Nature had at the beginning
Created them, so they remained—
Fish with cold blood no skill had trained
To the warm arts of human sinning.

THE MIDNIGHT REVELS AS OBSERVED BY THE SHADES

"The witches' device for the equitable distribution of the liquor consisted in the construction of tens of thousands of stopcocks and bungs which were fitted into the perforations of the cauldron, and graded so nicely in calibre that every species of fish from a sardine to a shark might find perfect oral adjustment. To provide against all contingencies they had, in addition, furnished each amphibious member of the Cretan family with a ladle so that the weaker fish, unable to reach the taps and bung-holes, might be supplied at the surface of the water. But notwithstanding all their powers of divination, the scheme came very near to being wrecked, first, by the tremendous congregation of fish, and secondly, by the advent of the wild hordes from Hades. Now it was not within the counsels of either the witches or the Devil that the test should be prejudiced by the Shades. If they arrived at all, their rôle would be severely restricted to that of an audience. But the momentum of their rush carried them up against the sides of the cauldron with such a terrific impact that a vertical crack, one hundred cubits long, was made near the top. Fortunately, however, for the experiment, the Shades were immediately driven back to the rear by a battalion of imps, and the crack served the purpose of allowing sufficient liquor to trickle through into the sea to account for the inebriation of such fish as those whose nervous constitution could not stand the undiluted draughts."

BYRON:

Now what the devil can be hid
In whisky straight, or punch or sherbet,
To give the doldrums to that squid,
Or plant the horrors in that turbot?
I never dreamed a calamary
Could get so dead stiff on Canary.

WOLSEY:

I've watched the effect of many a dram
On Richmond and on Buckingham;
And with good reasons have I mourned
To see my Royal Henry corned;
And many a noble prelate losing
His benefice by one night's boozing.
But till this hour I never knew
What alcoholic draughts could do
To change a salmon or a hake
Into a paralytic rake;
Or how a drunken sturgeon felt
When fever burned inside his pelt.

CAMPEGGIO:

Now by my Hat and Clement's foot,
What kind of devil must have dwelt
Inside a liquor that could put
Delirium tremens in a smelt?

PEPYS:
What maddening impulse makes that shark,
Which ought, by its own nature, choose a
Mate of its own kind, to spark
With that gelatinous Medusa?

PARACELSUS:
They say that mortals may go mad
Beneath thy beams, Divinest Luna;
But how canst thou debauch a shad,
Create an epileptic tuna?

GULLIVER:
I saw a sardine just now glut
His hunger on a halibut.

SAMUEL BUTLER:
How could a thing like rye or hops stir
The turgid corpus of a lobster?
And thus induce an inflammation
Within the shell of a crustacean?

SAMSON:
I saw a small phlegmatic mullet
Holding a dogfish by the gullet.

SAINT PATRICK:
Such crimes as from the sea arise
Beat out the days of old Gomorrah;
Had I not seen it with my eyes
I would not have believed, begorra!

THE CHARGE OF THE SWORDFISH

Now when, beneath the riotous drinking,
The witches found the liquor sinking
So low their ladles couldn't reach it,
The blacksmith with a blazing larynx
Organized a swordfish phalanx
And charged the cauldron plate to breach it.
Back from its copper flanks they fell,
The smith had done his work too well.

A GREEK:
From such a race of myrmidons
Our heroes and our Marathons.

FABIUS MAXIMUS:
It's but the fury of despair.

A FRENCH GENERAL:
Magnifique! mais ce n'est pas la guerre.

NAPOLEON:
By some such wild demonic means
My astral promise was undone.

NELSON:
By spirits like to such marines
Trafalgar and the Nile were won.

CARLYLE:
Full ten feet thick that plate was wrought,
And yet those swordfish tried to ram it;
Unthinking fools! I never thought
The sea so full of numskulls, dammit!

SATAN:
Now by my hoof, this recipe
Is worth a million souls to me;
But lo! what mortal creature there
Grins, haunched upon the parapet,
Whose fierce, indomitable stare
I long have dreamed of, but not met?

MARYAN:
Most sovereign and most sulphurous lord!
We, with the help of Cretans, made
This circumambient palisade
Of this great height and strength, to ward
Off such invaders as might mar
Our feast, and then as sentinel—
Chief vigilante out of hell—
We stationed HIM *from Zanzibar.*

SATAN:
Good! From such audacious seed
Sprang Heaven's finest, fallen breed,
Maryan! Ardath! Lulu!
Try out upon this cat, the brew.

THE SUPREME TEST

Now it was clear to every Shade
That some great wonder was before them,
As Tom upon the palisade
Emptied, as fast as Lulu bore them,
The flasks upon the ocean wagon.
And clear it was when Tom had cleaned
The liquor from the hundredth flagon,
The Shades then saw Hell's darkest fiend,—
A sea-cat with an awful jag-on.

Up to this time, he did not see
Upon the wide expanse of grey
A single thing approach his way
Which he might call his enemy.
He spent the hours upon the rim,
Leaping, dancing, rarely sitting,
Always grinning, always spitting,
Waiting for a foe to swim
Within his range, but through the night
Not a walrus offered fight,—
A most unusual night for him.
But with the hundredth flagon drink,
He spat at his inactive fate,
And moving closer to the brink,
Began more madly to gyrate.
Upon his face, ironic, grim,
A resolution was ingrained,
If fish would not come unto him
To offer battle, what remained
But that his fighting blood would freeze
Unless he were allowed to go,
Ranging at will upon the seas,
To fight and conquer every foe?
With that, into the cavernous deep
He took a ghastly, flying leap.

Gaping, breathless, every Shade
Watched the course of the wild-cat's raid;
And never was an errand run
With means and end so much at one.
For from his birth he was imbued

With hatred of his racial kind;
A more inveterate, blasting feud
Within the world one could not find.
His stock were traitors to the sea,
Had somehow learned the ways of earth,
The need of air, the mystery
Of things warm-blooded, and of birth.
To avenge this shameful derogation,
He had, upon his final flask,
Resolved to carry out his task,—
To wit:—the full extermination,
First, of his nearest order, male
And female, then the breed cetacean;
Grampus, porpoise, dolphin, whale,—
Humpback, Rorqual, Black and White;
Then the walrus, lion, hood,
Seals of all orders; these he would
Just as they came, in single fight,
Or in the fortunes of mêlée,
Challenge as his lawful prey.

THE BLACKSMITH:
I never knew an ocean steed
Develop such demonic speed.

SIR ISAAC NEWTON:
How he maintains that lightning rate,
Now in air and now in water,
And carries on such heavy slaughter,
Is more than I can formulate.

BLAKE:
The tiger, though in stretch of limb
And heft of bone is larger; still,
For straight uxoricidal will
Is but a lamb compared to him.

BOTTOM:
What humour is it makes him flail
His tawny quarters with that tail?

OWEN GLENDOWER:
Did any electrician mark
The explosive nature of that spark?

133

BENJAMIN FRANKLIN:
I did in truth, but cannot quite
See, on the basis of my kite,
How such a flame should always sit
Upon a wild-cat's caudal tip.

AESOP:
Or what blind fury makes him whip
His smoking sides to capture it—
An ignis fatuus that eludes
The cat's most sanguinary moods.

EUCLID:
The reasons for the circles lie
Within the nature of the thing;
This cat must run around a ring
If he would catch his tail. But why
So bloodily he chaseth it
Is past the compass of my wit.

JOHNNY WALKER:
Just why this wild-cat should revolve,
Leaving his nether tip uncaught,
And spend his energy for naught,
The denser Shades will never solve;
But (granting that the speed is quicker)
All we discerning spirits know
It's just the way a man would go,
Grant the night and grant the liquor.

CALVIN:
If I had known that such mad brutes
Had found, before the world began,
A place within the cosmic plan,
They would have dished my Institutes.

THE RETURN OF THE CAT

TIME—MORNING

A half-point Nor'ard from the West,
A bluish-tinted spot of light,

Now deep below, now on the crest
Of a high wave, hove into sight;
And by the curves and speed it made,
Conviction came to every Shade
That here the monster was returning
With all those inner fires burning
That no destruction could assuage;
Though through the hours of the night
The floating victims of the fight
Showed how the wild-cat could engage
His foes; achieve his victories;
For those he could not kill outright
Had either died from heart-disease
Or passed out through a hæmorrhage.
An unexpected wonder met
His rolling, unabated eye—
For when he reached the parapet
He found the witches' cauldron dry.
And there was something which surprised
Him even more; the drunken riot
Was followed by a holy quiet;
The fish lay dead or paralysed;
No witch this time came forth to serve
His inbred hunger for assault
With either rum or wine or malt.
The thing told heavily on his nerve,
That near that massive banquet place
Not one lone member of his race,
Outside the fortress or within,
Survived to give him grin for grin,
Or swish a tail across his face.
And so this wild-cat, now bereft
Of all of life's amenities,
Took one blood-curdling leap and left
Magellan's for the vacant seas.
Sullen and dangerous he ripped
A gleaming furrow through the water,
Magnificently still equipped
For combat with rapine and slaughter.
Now with his tail electro-tipped,
Swiftly but leisurely he made
Around the steaming palisade
A blazing spiral which outshone

135

The fiercest glow of Acheron.
Then suddenly, as if aware,
By a deep ferment in his soul
Or something psychic in his hair,
Of some ulterior, mystic goal,
He sharply turned, began a lonely
Voyage pregnant of immortal raids
And epic plunder. But the Shades
Saw him no more in the flesh. Only
To Satan and the witches three
(In touch with his galvanic tail,
By more occulted masonry)
Appeared a phosphorescent trail
That headed for the Irish Sea.

TITANS

The Cachalot

The Great Feud

(1926)

To the boys of the stag parties

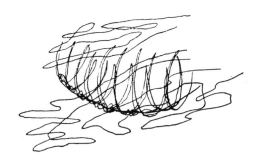

THE CACHALOT

I A thousand years now had his breed
Established the mammalian lead;
The founder (in cetacean lore)
Had followed Leif to Labrador;
The eldest-born tracked all the way
Marco Polo to Cathay;
A third had hounded one whole week
The great Columbus to Bahama;
A fourth outstripped to Mozambique
The flying squadron of da Gama;
A fifth had often crossed the wake
Of Cortez, Cavendish and Drake;
The great grandsire—a veteran rover—
Had entered once the strait of Dover,
In a naval fight, and with his hump
Had stove a bottom of Van Tromp;
The grandsire at Trafalgar swam
At the *Redoubtable* and caught her,
With all the tonnage of his ram,
Deadly between the wind and water;
And his granddam herself was known
As fighter and as navigator,
The mightiest mammal in the zone
From Baffin Bay to the Equator.
From such a line of conjugate sires
Issued his blood, his lumbar fires,
And from such dams imperial-loined
His Taurian timbers had been joined,
And when his time had come to hasten
Forth from his deep sub-mammary basin,
Out on the ocean tracts, his mama
Had, in a North Saghalien gale,
Launched him, a five-ton healthy male,
Between Hong Kong and Yokohama.
Now after ninety moons of days,
Sheltered by the mammoth fin,
He took on adolescent ways
And learned the habits of his kin;
Ransacked the seas and found his mate,
Established his dynastic name,
Reared up his youngsters, and became

The most dynamic vertebrate
(According to his Royal Dame)
From Tonga to the Hudson Strait.
And from the start, by fast degrees,
He won in all hostilities;
Sighted a hammerhead and followed him,
Ripped him from jaw to ventral, swallowed him;
Pursued a shovelnose and mangled him;
Twisted a broadbill's neck and strangled him;
Conquered a rorqual in full sight
Of a score of youthful bulls who spurred
Him to the contest, and the fight
Won him the mastery of the herd.

Another ninety moons and Time
Had cast a marvel from his hand,
Unmatched on either sea or land—
A sperm whale in the pitch of prime.
A hundred feet or thereabout
He measured from the tail to snout,
And every foot of that would run
From fifteen hundred to a ton.
But huge as was his tail or fin,
His bulk of forehead, or his hoists
And slow subsidences of jaw,
He was more wonderful within.
His iron ribs and spinal joists
Enclosed the sepulchre of a maw.
The bellows of his lungs might sail
A herring skiff—such was the gale
Along the wind-pipe; and so large
The lymph-flow of his active liver,
One might believe a fair-sized barge
Could navigate along the river;
And the islands of his pancreas
Were so tremendous that between 'em
A punt would sink; while a cart might pass
His bile-duct to the duodenum
Without a peristaltic quiver.
And cataracts of red blood stormed
His heart, while lower down was formed
That fearful labyrinthine coil
Filled with the musk of ambergris;

139

And there were reservoirs of oil
And spermaceti; and renal juices
That poured in torrents without cease
Throughout his grand canals and sluices.
And hid in his arterial flow
Were flames and currents set aglow
By the wild pulses of the chase
With fighters of the Saxon race.
A tincture of an iron grain
Had dyed his blood a darker stain;
Upon his coat of toughest rubber
A dozen cicatrices showed
The place as many barbs were stowed,
Twisted and buried in his blubber,
The mute reminders of the hours
Of combat when the irate whale
Unlimbered all his massive powers
Of head-ram and of caudal flail,
Littering the waters with the chips
Of whale-boats and vainglorious ships.

II   Where Cape Delgado strikes the sea,
A cliff ran outward slantingly
A mile along a tossing edge
Of water towards a coral ledge,
Making a sheer and downward climb
Of twenty fathoms where it ended,
Forming a jutty scaur suspended
Over a cave of murk and slime.
A dull reptilian silence hung
About the walls, and fungus clung
To knots of rock, and over boles
Of lime and basalt poisonous weed
Grew rampant, covering the holes
Where crayfish and sea-urchins breed.
The upper movement of the seas
Across the reefs could not be heard;
The nether tides but faintly stirred
Sea-nettles and anemones.
A thick festoon of lichens crawled
From crag to crag, and under it

Half-hidden in a noisome pit
Of bones and shells a kraken sprawled.
Moveless, he seemed, as a boulder set
In pitch, and dead within his lair,
Except for a transfixing stare
From lidless eyes of burnished jet,
And a hard spasm now and then
Within his viscous centre, when
His scabrous feelers intertwined
Would stir, vibrate, and then unwind
Their ligatures with easy strength
To tap the gloom, a cable length;
And finding no life that might touch
The mortal radius of their clutch,
Slowly relax, and shorten up
Each tensile tip, each suction cup,
And coil again around the head
Of the mollusc on its miry bed,
Like a litter of pythons settling there
To shutter the Gorgonian stare.

But soon the squid's antennae caught
A murmur that the waters brought—
No febrile stirring as might spring
From a puny barracuda lunging
At a tuna's leap, some minor thing,
A tarpon or a dolphin plunging—
But a deep consonant that rides
Below the measured beat of tides
With that vast, undulating rhythm
A sounding sperm whale carries with him.
The kraken felt that as the flow
Beat on his lair with plangent power,
It was the challenge of his foe,
The prelude to a fatal hour;
Nor was there given him more than time,
From that first instinct of alarm,
To ground himself in deeper slime,
And raise up each enormous arm
Above him, when, unmeasured, full
On the revolving ramparts, broke
The hideous rupture of a stroke
From the forehead of the bull.

141

And when they interlocked, that night—
Cetacean and cephalopod—
No Titan with Olympian god
Had ever waged a fiercer fight;
Tail and skull and teeth and maw
Met sinew, cartilage, and claw,
Within those self-engendered tides,
Where the Acherontic flood
Of sepia, mingling with the blood
Of whale, befouled Delgado's sides.
And when the cachalot out-wore
The squid's tenacious clasp, he tore
From frame and socket, shred by shred,
Each gristled, writhing tentacle,
And with serrated mandible
Sawed cleanly through the bulbous head;
Then gorged upon the fibrous jelly
Until, finding that six tons lay
Like Vulcan's anvil in his belly,
He left a thousand sharks his prey,
And with his flukes, slow-labouring, rose
To a calm surface, where he shot
A roaring geyser, steaming hot,
From the blast-pipe of his nose.
One hour he rested, in the gloom
Of the after-midnight; his great back
Prone with the tide, and, in the loom
Of the Afric coast, merged with the black
Of the water; till a rose shaft, sent
From Madagascar far away,
Etched a ripple, eloquent
Of a freshening wind and a fair day.

Flushed with the triumph of the fight,
He felt his now unchallenged right
To take by demonstrated merit
What he by birth-line did inherit—
The lordship of each bull and dam
That in mammalian waters swam,
As Maharajah of the seas
From Rio to the Celebes.

And nobly did the splendid brute
Leap to his laurels, execute
His lineal functions as he sped
Towards the Equator northwards, dead
Against the current and the breeze;
Over his back the running seas
Cascaded, while the morning sun
Rising in gold and beryl, spun
Over the cachalot's streaming gloss,
And from the foam, a fiery floss
Of multitudinous fashionings,
And dipping downward from the blue,
The sea-gulls from Comoro flew,
And brushed him with their silver wings;
Then at the tropic hour of noon
He slackened down; a drowsy spell
Was creeping over him, and soon
He fell asleep upon the swell.

III The cruising ships had never claimed
So bold a captain, so far-famed
Throughout the fleets a master-whaler—
New England's pride was Martin Taylor.
'Twas in this fall of eighty-eight,
As skipper of the *Albatross,*
He bore South from the Behring Strait,
Down by the China Coast, to cross
The Line, and with the fishing done
To head her for the homeward run
Around the Cape of Storms, and bring
Her to Nantucket by the Spring.
She had three thousand barrels stowed
Under the hatches, though she could,
Below and on her deck, have stood
Four thousand as her bumper load.
And so to try his final luck,
He entered Sunda Strait and struck
Into the Indian Ocean where,
According to reports that year,
A fleet had had grand fishing spells
Between the Cocos and Seychelles.
Thither he sailed; but many a day
Passed by in its unending way,

143

The weather fair, the weather rough,
With watch and sleep, with tack and reef,
With swab and holystone, salt beef
And its eternal partner, duff;
Now driving on with press of sail,
Now sweaty calms that drugged the men,
Everything but sight of whale,
Until one startling midday, when
A gesture in the rigging drew
The flagging tension of the crew.

In the cross-trees at the royal mast,
Shank, the third mate, was breathing fast,
His eyes stared at the horizon clouds,
His heels were kicking at the shrouds,
His cheeks were puffed, his throat was dry,
He seemed to be bawling at the sky.

"Hoy, you windjammer, what's the matter?
What's this infernal devil's clatter?"

"She blows, sir, there she blows, by thunder,
A sperm, a mighty big one, yonder."

"Where-a-way?" was Taylor's scream.

"Ten miles, sir, on the looard beam!"

"Hard up and let her go like hell!"

With heeling side and heady toss,
Smothered in spray, the *Albatross*
Came free in answer to his yell
And corked off seven with a rout
Of roaring canvas crowding her,
Her jibs and royals bellying out,
With studsail, staysail, spinnaker.
The barque came to; the first mate roared
His orders, and the davits swung,
The block-sheaves creaked, and the men sprung
Into the boats as they were lowered.
With oars unshipped, and every sail,
Tub and harpoon and lance in trim,

144

The boats payed off before the gale,
Taylor leading; after him,
Old Wart, Gamaliel, and Shank—
Three mates in order of their rank.
The day was fine; 'twas two o'clock,
And in the north, three miles away,
Asleep since noon, and like a rock,
The towering bulk of the cachalot lay.

"Two hundred barrels to a quart,"
Gamaliel whispered to Old Wart.

"A bull, by gad, the biggest one
I've ever seen," said Wart, "I'll bet'ee,
He'll measure up a hundred ton,
And a thousand gallons of spermaceti."

"Clew up your gab!"
    "Let go that mast!
There'll be row enough when you get him fast."

"Don't ship the oars!"
    "Now, easy, steady;
You'll gally him with your bloody noise."

The four harpooners standing ready
Within the bows, their blades in poise,
Two abaft and two broadside,
Arched and struck; the irons cut
Their razor edges through the hide
And penetrated to the gut.

"Stern all! and let the box-lines slip.
Stern! Sheer!" The boats backed up.

            "Unship
That mast. Bend to and stow that sail,
And jam the pole under the thwart."

With head uplifted the sperm whale
Made for the starboard boat of Wart,
Who managed with a desperate swing
To save his skiff the forehead blow,
But to be crushed with the backward swing
Of the flukes as the giant plunged below;
On this dead instant Taylor cleft

His line; the third mate's iron drew,
Which, for the sounding trial, left
But one boat with an iron true,—
The one that had Gamaliel in it.
The tubs ran out, Gamaliel reckoned
Two hundred fathoms to the minute;
Before the line had cleared the second,
He tied the drugg and quickly passed
The splice to Shank who made it fast,
And with ten blistering minutes gone,
Had but a moment left to toss
It to the fifth boat rushing on
With Hall fresh from the *Albatross*,
Who when his skiff, capsizing, lay
So low he could no longer bail her,
Caught up the end for its last relay,
And flung it to the hands of Taylor.
With dipping bow and creaking thwart,
The skipper's whaleboat tore through tunnels
Of drifting foam, with listing gunwales,
Now to starboard, now to port,
The hemp ran through the leaden chock,
Making the casing searing hot;
The second oarsman snatched and shot
The piggin like a shuttlecock,
Bailing the swamping torrent out,
Or throwing sidelong spurts to dout
The flame when with the treble turn
The loggerhead began to burn.

A thousand fathoms down the lug
Of rope, harpoon, of boat and drugg,
Began, in half a breathless hour,
To get his wind and drain his power;
His throbbing valves demanded air,
The open sky, the sunlight there;
The downward plunging ceased, and now,
Taylor feeling the tarred hemp strand
Slackening that moment at the bow,
Began to haul hand over hand,
And pass it aft where it was stowed

Loose in the stern sheets, while the crew
After the sounding respite threw
Their bodies on the oars and rowed
In the direction of the pull.

"*He blows!*" The four whaleboats converged
On a point to southward where the bull
In a white cloud of mist emerged—
Terror of head and hump and brawn,
Silent and sinister and grey,
As in a lifting fog at dawn
Gibraltar rises from its bay.
With lateral crunching of his jaw,
And thunderous booming as his tail
Collided with a wave, the whale
Steamed up immediately he saw
The boats, lowered his cranial drum
And charged, his slaughterous eye on Shank;
The mate—his hour had not yet come—
Parried the head and caught the flank
With a straight iron running keen
Into the reaches of his spleen.
The boats rushed in; when Taylor backed,
Gamaliel leaped in and lodged
A thrust into his ribs, then dodged
The wallowing flukes when Hall attacked.
As killers bite and swordfish pierce
Their foes, a score of lances sank
Through blubber to the bone and drank
His blood with energy more fierce
Than theirs; nor could he shake them off
With that same large and sovereign scoff,
That high redundancy of ease
With which he smote his enemies.
He somersaulted, leaped, and sounded;
When he arose the whaleboats hounded
Him still; he tried gigantic breaches,
The irons stuck to him like leeches;
He made for open sea but found
The anchors faithful to their ground,
For, every surface run, he towed
The boat crews faster than they rowed.
Five hectic hours had now passed by,

Closing a tropic afternoon,
Now twilight with a mackerel sky,
And now a full and climbing moon.
'Twas time to end this vanity—
Hauling a puny batch of men,
With boat and cross-boards out to sea,
Tethered to his vitals, when
The line would neither break nor draw.
Where was his pride, too, that his race
Should claim one fugitive in a chase?
His teeth were sound within his jaw,
His thirty feet of forehead still
Had all their pristine power to kill.
He swung his bulk round to pursue
This arrogant and impious crew.
He took his own good time, not caring
With such persistent foes to crush
Them by a self-destroying rush,
But blending cunning with his daring,
He sought to mesh them in the toil
Of a rapid moving spiral coil,
Baffling the steersmen as they plied
Their oars now on the windward side,
Now hard-a-lee, forcing them dead
Upon the foam line of his head.
And when the narrowing orbit shrank
In width to twice his spinal length,
He put on all his speed and strength
And turned diagonally on Shank.
The third mate's twenty years of luck
Were ended as the cachalot struck
The boat amidship, carrying it
With open sliding jaws that bit
The keel and sawed the gunwales through,
Leaving behind him as he ploughed
His way along a rising cloud,
Fragments of oars and planks and crew.
Another charge and the death knell
Was rung upon Gamaliel;
At the same instant Hall ran foul

Of the tail sweep, but not before
A well directed iron tore
Three feet into the lower bowel.

Two foes were now left on the sea—
The *Albatross* with shortened sail
Was slatting up against the gale;
Taylor manœuvring warily
Between the rushes and the rough
Wave hazards of the crest and trough,
Now closed and sent a whizzing dart
Underneath the pectoral fin
That pierced the muscle of the heart.
The odds had up to this been equal—
Whale and wind and sea with whaler—
But, for the sperm, the fighting sequel
Grew darker with that thrust of Taylor.
From all his lesser wounds the blood
That ran from him had scarcely spent
A conscious tithe of power; the flood
That issued from this fiery rent,
Broaching the arterial tide,
Had left a ragged worm of pain
Which crawled like treason to his brain,—
The worm of a Titan's broken pride!
Was he—with a toothless Bowhead's fate,
Slain by a thing called a second mate—
To come in tow to the whaler's side?
Be lashed like a Helot to the bitts
While, from the cutting stage, the spade
Of a harpooner cut deep slits
Into his head and neck, and flayed
Him to the bone; while jesters spat
Upon his carcass, jeered and wrangled
About his weight, the price his fat
Would bring, as with the heavy haul
Of the blocks his strips of blubber dangled
At every click of the windlass pawl?
An acrid torture in his soul
Growing with the tragic hurry
Of the blood stream through that widening hole
Presaged a sperm whale's dying flurry—
That orgy of convulsive breath,

Abhorred thing before the death,
In which the maniac threads of life
Are gathered from some wild abysm,
Stranded for a final strife
Then broken in a paroxysm.
Darkness and wind began to pour
A tidal whirlpool round the spot,
Where the clotted nostrils' roar
Sounded from the cachalot
A deep bay to his human foes.
He settled down to hide his track,
Sighted the keels, then swiftly rose,
And with the upheaval of his back,
Caught with annihilating rip
The boat, then with the swelling throes
Of death levied for the attack,
Made for the port bow of the ship.
All the tonnage, all the speed,
All the courage of his breed,
The pride and anger of his breath,
The battling legions of his blood
Met in that unresisted thud,
Smote in that double stroke of death.
Ten feet above and ten below
The water-line his forehead caught her,
The hatches opening to the blow
His hundred driving tons had wrought her;
The capstan and the anchor fled,
When bolts and stanchions swept asunder,
For what was iron to that head,
And oak—in that hydraulic thunder?
Then, like a royal retinue,
The slow processional of crew,
Of inundated hull, of mast,
Halliard and shroud and trestle-cheek,
Of yard and topsail to the last
Dank flutter of the ensign as a wave
Closed in upon the skysail peak,
Followed the Monarch to his grave.

THE GREAT FEUD

(A Dream of a Pleiocene Armageddon)

Like a quarter moon the shoreline curled
Upon the neck of the ancient world,
Where, as the modern Magians say,
In one cool morning of the Earth,
Australasia had its birth,
And vertebrated with Malay.
Monsoons from Arafura Seas
Had played their native energies
Full upon the western tip,
Until the vast recessional
Of scourging wash and tidal rip
Had made a stubborn littoral
Take on a deep indented shape,—
A hundred leagues, to the eastern Cape,
Of broken bays with narrow reaches,
Deltas and gulfs bulwarked by steep
Eroded headlands, with a sweep
Of fifty miles of central beaches,
And rich alluvial flats where luscious
Grasses, ferns and milk bulrushes
Made up the original nursery
For fauna of the land and sea.
Stretching from the water line
By gentle slope and sharp incline,
Past many an undulating plain,
The land ran southward to a chain
Of heavy-wooded hills and rose
Beyond them to the Black Sierras,
Soaring aloft to where the snows
That capped the ranging Guadeleras
Were blackened by the brooding dread
Outline of a volcano's head,—
Jurania, with her crater jaw,
Her slanting forehead ancient-scarred,
And breathing through her smoky maw,
Lay like a dragon left to guard
The Isthmian Scarps against the climb
Of life that left the ocean slime,
In far adventurous design,
On footholds past the timber line.

In such a place, at such a time,
Long before the birth of man,
This great Tellurian feud began.

For ages which cannot be told
The fish along the Isthmian border
Had felt the invasion of their cold
Blood by an unexplained disorder.
It looked as if the destination,
Of all life of the stock marine,
Was doomed to be, through paths unseen,
The most profound obliteration.
Millions of youthful fins were led
Far from their safe and watery bed,
To sport along the tidal edge,
Nosing for grubs and water-lice,
For pickerel weed and shoots of rice
That grew luxuriant within the sedge,
And many feasting unawares
Were drawn into relentless snares;
Strange rasp-and-saw bills harried them,
And swooping talons carried them
Into the air, and many more
Were stranded high and dry on shore,
Where poisonous lizards, asps and adders
Bit them, or where the solar fire
Caught them at noon-tide in the mire,
Curdled their blood and starched their bladders.
And thousands that survived the heat
Turned their backs upon their breed,
Shed their fins and took on feet,
And clambered far inland to feed
On windy things like grass and roots,
Bark and leaves and bitter sloes,
Or, like those horrid jungle brutes
With hairy pelts and horny toes,
To quaff the warm blood of their foes;
While many more that did return,
After one æonian night,
Came back contemptuous to spurn
Their parents, like the trilobite,

With stony back and stonier heart;
Rolled up in balls and dwelt apart
In sulky isolation; while others,—
The mongrel water scorpions sprung
From crabs and spiders,—came and stung
Their little sisters and their brothers.

And thus it was throughout the whole
Sea-range of the Australian zone,
The fear of racial doom was thrown
Heavily upon the piscine soul.
A futile anger like a curse
Only made confusion worse.
Their mad desire to strike back
At their destroying coward-foe
Turned all their fury of attack
Into consuming vertigo.
It broke their hearts and crushed their wills,
It thinned the juices of their maws,
Left them with gnashing of the jaws
And deep prolapsis of the gills.
And hitherto unsuffered pains,
A ghastly brood, came in by legions,
Rheumatic tremors in the veins,
And palsy in the ventral regions.
Now, not a single evening passed
But an aquatic breathed its last
Beneath the terrifying roar
Of some dread plantigrade on shore;
And so this strange insidious spark
Of wild adventure carried sorrow
To many a yearning matriarch
With the drab dawning of the morrow.
But worst of all the horrors which
Enmeshed them was the galling sense
That never would the recompense
Of battle come; that primal itch
For vengeance would expend its force,
According to an adverse Fate,
Running a self-destroying course
Down the blind alley of their hate.
But by some quirk that Nature flings
Into the settled scheme of things,—

That old beldame, she gets so grumpy,
No mortal vision may foretell
Her antics, when her nerves are jumpy—
It happened that she broke the spell
By a freak shifting of the odds
Within the sea-lap of the gods.

Vibrant calms unknown before
Lay on the Australasian shore,
And Silences, a hooded band,
Like portents of catastrophe,
Tip-toed expectant on the land,
And mummed about the open sea.
Neptune had resigned the trident,
For months Aeolus had not spoken,
Nor had the sea-waves heard the strident
Trumpeter,—his conch was broken.
From igneous fissures in the ground
Blue wisps of smoke with eerie sound
Curled on the air to indicate
That some elaborate escapade
Was on the point of being played
By the royal clowns of Fate.
Here and there through asphalt holes
Was heard a most uncanny racket,—
Charon, before the birth of souls
Called for his modern Stygian packet,
Was busy at enormous scows,
Caulking them with walrus skin,
Hammering, sawing to the din
Of Cerberus with his gruff bow-wows,
Together with the gird and clatter
Of wheels and whiffletrees, the croak
Of scranny throats, and the fast patter
Of feet and flap of wings, that spoke
Of straining, jostling ambulances;
Of Hecate with a frightful brood
Of harpies in a phantom wood,
Rehearsing new macabre dances.
Now all this strange activity
Was radiating everywhere;

It rapped the calms upon the sea,
It shot through flumes of stagnant air,
It tingled in the blood of brutes
Of land and water; in the roots
Of trees; and even stuff like rocks
Felt the strong etheric shocks,
Until all natural things that dwelt
In the marine Australian belt
Had come to feel, in a dumb way,
That their protracted evil spell
Might, with the birth of any day,
Dissolve before a miracle.

One vital morning when the tide
Was out and the Scala flats were dried,
The largest-livered, heaviest-brained,
Most thoroughbred pedestrian
Of all the tribes that had attained
The rank of the amphibian,
A green-back turtle left the sea.
Her blood was changing and a scent,
Unknown to her rude ancestry,
Had charged her with presentiment
Of some unfathomed destiny.
She had her eyes upon a spot
She long aspired to, but had not
For lack of muscle, wind and time,
Been able to effect the climb.
To-day, with fast evolving legs,
Urged by the lure of distant land,
She struggled for this cone of sand,
Proudly there to lay her eggs,
And from this vantage point, some day,
To take her young and wend her way,
Far up into the hills, to view
What kind of giant there might dwell
Stretched asleep against the blue,—
A turtle with a snow-white shell,
Or inland whale, for aught she knew,
Sending through a spiracle,
Intermittent puffs of grey
Cloud resembling ocean spray.
But when after four dusty hours

155

She reached the top of the sandy cone,
A thrill her blood had never known
Paralysed her laying powers,
And concentrated all her thought
Upon the scene the morning brought.

An amphitheatre that held
Valleys and cliffs and waterfalls,
Gorges hewn like royal halls,
Forests flanked by hills that swelled
To mountains, these again to clouds
From peaks of ice; and everywhere
On ground, in trees and in the air,
All forms of living things; dense crowds
Of kites and gulls; vultures that hung
Within the blue; and mangabees;
Pig-tailed baboons that peered and swung
From the liana of the trees;
Wombats beneath acacias;
Tasmanian tigers in the grass;
Civets and sloths and bandicoots;
High-standing elks in hollowed stumps
Of redwood; tapirs in the clumps
Of banyan, grubbing at the roots;
And under eucalyptus trees,
Flocks of emus and kiwis,
With herds of skipping kangaroos,
Antelopes and brindled gnoos;—
All Earth's delegates were sent,
Blood relations, tribal foes,
Bound by cordial entente,
To this prodigious Parliament;—
Lions and water-buffaloes,
Clouded leopards, chamois droves,
Side by side and cheek by nose,
Rested in the myrtle groves;
While pumas, rams and grizzly bears
Stroked each other in their lairs.
And central to this wild tableau,
A white giraffe began to scale
A scraggy monolith of shale,

Standing on a high plateau.
And when his neck had arched the summit,
A female anthropoidal ape
Climbed up, and settling on the nape,
Surveyed the crowded congress from it.
The comeliest of the Primate race,
No one of all the Southern lands
Could match her for arboreal grace,
For hairy contour of her hands,
For contemplation in her face,
Or wisdom in her thyroid glands.
To hide her young, to fight or climb,
She was the cleverest of her time.
She taught the family tribes to make
A brier or a bamboo stake,
Fashion an eolith and throw
It deadly at a distant foe,
To charge in serried ranks, or beat
A hurried or prepared retreat,
Showed them new uses for their paws
In battle for the monkey cause.
And faintly she had sniffed the raw
Material of the moral law;
She had observed, one windy night,
The skull of an alligator cut
Open by a cocoanut
Falling from a lofty height,—
An alligator that had torn
And eaten up her youngest born.
Then to a corner she had crept,
And had not eaten, had not slept,
But scratched her head and drummed her breast,
And Reason entered as she wondered,
Brooded in the trees and pondered
On how the reptile was struck dead.
And now on wide and just behalf
Of all the land brutes of the world,
She took the leadership and curled
Around the neck of the giraffe;
And all at once confusion ceased,
As every hard raptorial beak
And slanted eye of bird and beast
Were strained upon the central peak,—

157

And every lobe of every ear
Was cocked that none might fail to hear
The message when the ape unfurled
Her simian marvel to the world.

All ye that dwell afar or nigh
Upon the plains or on the hills,
In valley caves or in the sky,
Feathers, and bristles, talons, quills,
Flesh-eating ones and herbivores
That roam inland or ramp the shores;
All ye with snouts that turn the furrow
For colonies of ants or burrow
For savoury roots and fattened worms;
And ye that carry on your sides
Impenetrable armour hides,
Slow-moving, ponderous pachyderms;
All ye that lie in wait and crouch
And gnashing leap upon your prey;
And those that at the breast or pouch
Suckle the young; all ye that lay,
And scratch the ant-hills with your claws;
And all that brotherhood that climb,
Cracking great nuts between the jaws;
Give ear and know ye that the time
Has come when he that slumbereth
Shall pay the penalty of death.

Turn ye your gaze, a moment, far
Beyond the plain over the height
Of the palm trees where the white
Foam-line breaks upon the bar.
There under the blue stretch of sea,
Living in darkness out of sight
Skulks our ancient enemy,
Devouring everything that passes
Along the great lagoons to feed
On clams and shrimps and rich swamp grasses
Growing beside the tidal weed.
By right of conquest and of birth
We claim all footholds on this Earth;—
Those flats there steaming in the sun,

The coast-line to the salted edge
Where the coral foam is spun,
That long three-cornered, rocky wedge
On which the walrus warms his hide,
Where the dugong sleeps,—which the manatee
Claims as his dwelling when the sea
Sucks it from us at high tide.
All ye that hail from foreign parts
Whose warm blood knocking at your hearts
Has led you to this southern place,
Attend upon my words! and know
What great disaster to our race
Befell us thirty years ago.
You noticed as you cleared the height
Of the Aral range that, to the south,
Three juts of land came into sight,
Extending far out of the mouth
Of the Ravenna river;—these
Have ever been the nurseries
For the monkey tribe and kangaroo,
For gentle bears and wallabies,
For marmoset and wanderoo,
And for the crinkly-tail baboon.
On one dread summer day—at noon—
A terror broke upon our eyes;
We saw the blazing sun go out,
And the level sea begin to rise
Under the breath of a typhoon,
And break with tidal water-spout,
Carrying with the general ruin
Of the palms, the aged and the young,
The mother bear and little bruin;
And wailing mandrill babes that clung
To the parental neck were flung
Into the watery abyss
To satisfy the avarice
And lust of every carrion foe
And devil-fish that dwelt therein.
To-day that slaughter at the Delta
Remains the nightmare of the years;
Those death-cries of the apes could melt a
Stony crocodile to tears.
Since then, their blood-thirst unappeased,

They've ventured up our quiet streams;
Gannets and herons have been seized,
Baboons have died with horrid screams,
And elephantine calves for miles
All along the water-courses,
Together with young water-horses,
Have been dragged down by crocodiles.
For years reports have been received
From distant countries occupied
By furs, feathers and hairs allied
By blood, how they have been bereaved
And plunged in blackest misery
By that insane, consuming hate
Of ignorant, inarticulate
Cold-blood barbarians of the sea.
All we observant ones have seen
That at high tides in clouded moons
The habits of the fish have been
To pass into the great lagoons,
To lie in wait throughout the course
Of night and morning to midday,
Then chase our swimming breeds and slay
Them with no feeling of remorse;
And then with foul-distended maw,
The cowards that they are withdraw
To their unlighted haunts, to shun
An open struggle in the sun.
Therefore, let it now be known,
By tokens that can never err,—
By the marrow in the fox's bone,
By the light growth of the ermine's fur,
And by the camel's drinking bout,
That the season's blasting drought,
With lowering of the tides, will last
Till three up-tilted moons have passed.
Then will the inland shallows be
At all their gateways unexposed
To the waters of the open sea,
When the barrier reefs have closed.
So if our hearts are resolute,
At the appointed hour we'll match them

With our brave hosts in massed pursuit;
No quarter shall there be: we'll catch them,—
From the smallest to the largest brute—
Throw them into consternation,
Hem them in the muddy places
And on the shoals, leaving no traces
Save of their damned annihilation.
Before I close—just one word more.
Oft have we seen a jealous raid
Grow into a great crusade;
Or end by internecine war,
When the blood of kindred drenched
The higher mountain snows and quenched
The jungle grass and arid moors.
Therefore ye thirsty carnivores
Be ye adjured that till the hour
Of trial ye shall not devour
The flesh of either animal
Or bird upon the Earth; nor shall
Ye taste of blood; your daily food
Shall be the Earth's fair yield of fruits,
Her store of plants and sappy roots,
The fresh rind of the sandalwood,
And willow bark, berries and beans,
Tussac grass and mangosteens,
Papaws and guavas and the sweet
Milk of the cocoanut, the meat
Of durian with celery,
The ripe fruit of the mango-tree;
Yea—all the natural plenitude
Of Earth shall henceforth be your food.
Likewise ye herbivores, be ye
Adjured against all enmity.
Ye shall not trample; shall not gore,
With hoof or horn, the carnivore;
But as their allies, ye shall spend,
In one grand consummating blow
Of death against the common foe,
Your strength to a triumphant end.
Now hie ye to your lairs; sleep not;
Gather your hosts; abate no jot
Of this day's wrath, and when the year

Is big with three up-tilted moons,
We'll charge on the aquatics here,
And trap them in the great Lagoons.

She spoke: and every throat and lung
Of herbivore and carnivore,
In volleying symphonic roar,
Rang with persuasion of her tongue.
With vengeance firing up the breast,
And with the speed of a monsoon blast,
The keen dispersing hordes soon passed
Beyond the skyline of the West.
And the sultriness of peace again
Brooded on valley, hill and plain,
Shaken only when a cloud
Of thick Juranian vapour, thrown
In a dark spiral, burst with loud
Echoes, like laughter from the cone.

Scrambling from her hill of sand,
The disillusioned, now unfertile,
Amphibious and bilingual turtle
Fled the spectre of the land;
Crossed the muddy flats and sought her
Endangered kindred of the water,
Apprised them of their bloody fate;
The congress vote; the rage and hate
Of the ape; her story of the feud,
And the news was borne at ether rate
Throughout the ocean's amplitude,
And hailed with fierce, exultant mood,
With wave of pectorals and high leap
Into the air and foamy sweep
Of tail and clutch of tentacle;
Broken was the hoary spell!
The hour for revenge, for daring,
Had come for fin and scale and shell!
For shark! swordfish! mackerel!
Lobster! octopus! and herring!

(With the Passage of the Moons)

Black bucks whose distant ancestry
Sprang from the (now) Westphalian hills;
Wild boars with hair as stiff as quills,
Or Brandenburgian pedigree;
Wallachian elks, whose antlers spread
A full five feet above the head,
Trekked around the Caucasus,
Sounding with defiant stare
Their gutturals blent with blasphemous
Umlauts upon the stricken air;
And they were joined near Teheran
By camels down from Turkestan,
And elands from Trans-Caspian snows,
Persian gazelles with harts and roes,
Arabian antelopes and masses
Of quaggas, zebras and wild asses;
And on the eastern move, they met
Horses following in the tracks
Of ibexes and shaggy yaks
From South Bokhara and Thibet
And countries far-distributed;
The thunderous Indian quadruped,—
Rhinoceros and elephant,
And every kind of ruminant,
And non-cud-chewing animals,
Mammal and marsupial;
From hill and valley, steppe and prairie,
Peccary and dromedary,
Bashan bull and Cashmir ram,
The male spring-bok, chamois, gnoo,
The reid-buck and the kangaroo
Heading downwards through Siam.
Likewise, with earth-shattering roars,
Accompanied by the screams of birds,
From the wide compass came the herds
Of storming, hungry carnivores.
On them the patriotic call
Fell with the greatest sacrifice.
A troop of tigers from Bengal,
Full of caraway and rice,

(In keeping with the simian pledge)
Discovering early that their edge
Of appetite was dulled enough
By such ill-regulated stuff
Upon a base of hops and oats,
Attacked (although they did not slay)
A flock of Himalayan goats
Resting on a wooded height
In their mid-journey to Malay;
They drained their udders, bleached them white,
And leaving them in awful plight,
Prostrate and helpless for the fray,
Passed on with energy renewed
Into the Australasian feud.
Through scorching plains and bleak defiles
Of Northern India's spacious miles,
Spread a vast host of tawny, mad
Lions from Allahabad.
Oleanders, roots of taro
With ginseng and dried kauri cones
Had changed the substance of their marrow,
And alternated growls with groans.
Hyænas forced-fed on salt-bush
With sago palms and tapioca
Wailed so loudly that they woke a
Pack of wolves from Hindu Kush,
Whose tocsin cry antiphonal
Was caught by every caracal
Sleeping with his stomach full
Of rhododendrons near Cabul;
And this was followed by the blab
Of jackals cursed with elderberry
All the way from the Punjab
As far South-East as Pondicherry.
Over the stretch from Turkestan,
From Shamo Desert to Hunan,
From Shantung down to Singapore,
Along the central isthmus, fell
The mighty, myrmidonian roar,
That ululant and choric yell
Of leopards full of okra pods

And lentils; cheetahs gagging hard
At cascarilla spiced with nard;
Polecats charged with cotton wads,
And bears and civets overcome
With stringent eucalyptus gum.
All these in thousands numberless
Had, with the triple lunar round,
Arrived, in hot blood-thirstiness,
Upon the Isthmian battle ground,
Where, when the welter of their roars
Had ceased along the littoral border,
The hordes were disciplined to order,
Divided into army corps,
Brigades, battalions and platoons;
Some were ambushed by the coast
In heavy scrub and bush, but most
Were stationed near the great lagoons
Connected with the hostile beaches,
And regimented into shape
By the anthropoidal ape
Who, by her rousing martial speeches,
Kept up to fever heat their zeal
For the imperilled commonweal.
At last when the appointed week
Had come; and when the final night
Was over with the first faint streak
Of orange in the Eastern light,—
Just at the hour when every pad
And hoof were tingling with the mad
Moment of impending slaughter,
A reeking, ghastly, unknown flair
Compounded of the earth and water,
Of subterranean clay and air,
And like no other scent, arose
And fell upon each roving nose.

Over the top of the nearest alp
A cliff-like head began to rise;
A lizard's skull with horny scalp,
Dragon's teeth and boa's eyes;
Covered with scales of greenish blue
The lower jaw swung into view,
And from the open mouth there came

A lolling tongue of scarlet flame;
A column of a neck whose reach
Topped the high branches of a beech;
Prehensile arms and girthy paunch
Upheld by massive spine and haunch
Are followed by unmeasured thighs;
With hock and joint the inches rise,
Until the monster in dread sight
Of all, to the last claw, collects
His stature on the Aral height,
And lo,—TYRANNOSAUROS REX!

Now let the sceptic disbelieve
The truth I am about to state,
And urge, with curling lip, I weave
A legend that is out of date.
Let him disgorge his lie; I claim
That by a wanton twist of Fate,
(To which I am by Hera sworn)
A creature of this sounding name,
Although three millions years too late,
Stood on that peak this awful morn.
It came to pass, one day, before
Mammals appeared upon the Earth,
A dinosaurian mother bore
Tyrannus in a tragic birth.
Chasing a mighty stegosaur
Into a bed of pitch, she tried,
With huge success, before she died,
To lay an egg that chanced to live
Throughout its long bituminous night,
Enveloped by this soft, air-tight
Most excellent preservative;
Until just fifty years ago,
When the volcano underwent
Her seismal periodic throe,
The egg came bouncing through a rent.
A moa passing by espied
The object; sidled up, cock-eyed,
And watched it with a mother's pride.
Like a beach-stone pumiced by the sea,

It glowed with the full sunlight on it.
She sniffed the thing excitedly,
Walked around it, pecked and scratched
The shell, then feathered down upon it.
And in due course of time she hatched
Her prodigy. At first she fed him
On cotton-tails and unweaned lambs,
On calves and badgers; then she led him
To the higher ridges where she filled
His stomach with the coarser hams
Of pigs and short-horn mountain rams,
Until he took on strength and killed
All comers with their sires and dams.

Now after fifty years, the bird
Had, from a cassowary, heard
About the Pan-cyclonic rally
Of beasts in the Juranian Valley,
And how at their great gastric session
They swore to stand by the Food Concession.
And so the moa felt she'd serve her
Race the best, fanning the wild
Instinct of her foster child
With her strong patriotic fervour.
She found *this* lesson easy for
A huge blood-quaffing dinosaur;
The next one that she strove to teach,—
To feed on rushes, roots and grass,—
Seemed to this hungry ward, alas,
Beyond his intellectual reach.
Still, after days of bleats and pants,
Of clucking at the balsam cones,
Of digging graves for flesh and bones,
And building pyramids of plants;—
And after days of petulant scolding,
She managed to convey, by holding
Within her talons, cocoanuts
And bread-fruit rather than the cuts
From the sirloin of putrid cattle,—
That fasting from all flesh and blood,
And chewing, self-imposed, of cud,
Was the condition of the battle.
And so the fatal morning found

167

Him bloated, angry and unsound
Of wind and reeling down the height
For flesh, his object of the fight.
His skyward neck took on the form
Of a pliant topmast in a storm.
His headlong and unsteady gait
Had been the more provoked, of late,
By a yeasty alimentary state.
For, on the day before, twitch grass
With coarse buck wheat and sassafras
Had formed the staple of his diet.
A vinery of red grape then lay
Before him; he resolved to try it;
Which done, his head began to sway,
The hot, fermenting liquor rose,
And just before the charge was made,
Had sluiced up through his neck, and played
A geyser through his throat and nose,
Until his body seemed to seethe
With dragon foam on scale and claw,
The scarlet dripping from his teeth,
And fire issuing from his jaw.
The ape had feared the monster's coming
Would cause a panic as the sound
Of thunder from the infernal drumming
Of Tyrannus' feet upon the ground,
Breaking like waves along the coast,
Fell upon the affrighted host.
And for a moment as he neared
The rostral monolith and tossed
His head for carnage it appeared
As if the national cause was lost.
So strong the impact as he hit
A line of tigers near the centre
It paralysed the simian's wit
And for a fearful second rent her
Courage as the jungle mass
Went floundering in a deep morass.
But instant as a thunderclap
The prescience of her soul awoke,
For by that self-same tiger stroke

Tyrannosauros filled the gap,
And as the stress upon the line
Was centrally towards the sea,
She caught the panic's energy
Of flight in time, and flashed the sign
Of battle from her lofty tower,
Then launched the seething frenzied power
Of tusk and claw. Blood red the Dawn!
The die was cast! The fight was on!

Now was seen the strategy
Hidden in the stern decree
Of the wise old anthropoid.
The long-continued carnal void,
With all its gastric irritation,
Had raised their lust to slay and eat
Raw flesh to the internal heat
Of a universal conflagration.
Just in from dry Allahabad,
Farinaceous lions had
Spied, upon an oozy bank,
Five hundred head of walruses,
Their hides of rubber steaming rank
With odours oleaginous.
Such was their fury when they smelled them,
It seemed as if the nether air
Were raining tails and brindled hair,—
The way those brutes of India felled them;
They had them stripped before the sun
Arose to bleach each skeleton.
Fifteen miles farther down the Coast,
An angry and conglomerate host,—
Inflammatory Bengalese,
Starved with cherry bark and peas;
With salicaceous jaguars,
Leguminous leopards full of beans
That murmured in their jugulars,—
Swooped, with the speed of peregrines,
Upon the red substantial meals
Of dolphins hot and blubberous,
And a large school of porpoises,
Manatees and ursine seals,
Until the sand-spit where they were

Surrendered back unto the sea
Not one shred of fat or fur
But polished skulls and vertebrae.
Down a sharp declivity
Where the eastern skyline touched a plain,
Wild cats of Burmese demonry
Fell like a cloud of typhoon rain.
Raisins had so alkalized them
That the fur upon their necks had moulted,
Soyas and poppies which they bolted
Stuck in their throats and agonized them.
So swift and vital was their spring
When circling round a "Sulphur Bottom",
They drove him on the rocks and got 'im
Like turkey buzzards on the wing,
Pouncing on a carrion,
Until beneath the morning sky
His ribs were arching high and dry
Like the frame of a stranded galleon.

With the first hours of the day
It seemed the battle fortunes lay
In ample margins with the land.
No courage of the sea could stand
Against the all-consuming, savage
Hunger springing from such a fast,
Nor millions numberless outlast
That crash of pyramidal ravage.
But with the pangs of thirst abated,
A temporary slackening of the drive
Gave to the fish infuriated
With loss a moment to revive
Their ranks, when soon upon the air
New cries of terror and despair
Announced destruction for the land.
Rounding the Roc peninsula,
Sperm whales from Carpentaria
Had reached the Dura bank of sand,
And bellying round, began to blow
Their challenge in contemptuous spout
At any brute the earth could show

Possessing horn or tusk or snout.
Undaunted, a battalion
Of bulling elephants from Canton,
Directed by a jackass, tore
Their ponderous course down to the shore,
In answer to the loud defiance
Of those humpbacked mammalian giants.
Lured by the low ebb of the tide,
And a hundred yards of bar, sun-dried,
They plunged into the quicksands where,
With roar of suction and the blare
Of strained uplifted trunks, they died,
Or slipping into weedy ground
Off the silting edge, were drowned
At leisure by the sweeping tails
And jaw-tug of victorious whales.

Down at the delta of Ravenna,
The hardest struggle of the day
For three long hours was under way,
Wild as the tumult of Gehenna.
A thousand tigers of the land
Were fighting, under the command
Of a Sumatran chimpanzee,
Ten thousand tigers of the sea.
The thirstier cats that formed the van
Took the water, swimming far
Beyond the shallows of the bar,
Heedless of the risk they ran;
Others of more tempered daring,
Striking the water margin, kept
Well within their depth but swept
Along the muddy regions, tearing
The placid surface into spray,
Like a gale's lash upon a bay.
For those three hours the waters ran
With every hue of the rainbow span,—
Saffron lines and serpentine,
Lurid darts of iris green,
Mottled browns with dusky stripe,
Eyeballs flashing streaks of red,
Leaped and zigzagged to the gripe
Of lamia and of hammerhead,

Locking with inveterate teeth
The tigers' bellies underneath.
Phantoms blue and ashen pale
Followed white ones in the race
Where blade of dorsal, scythe of tail
Cut and ripped the water's face,
Curved and sank while in their place
The vitreous glare of stomachs rose
With flapping pectorals, as the claws
Of tigers tore a bottle-nose
Or bullet-head; or as their jaws,
Just at the moment they were drowned,
With paralysing seizure found
Their last authentic tiger mark
In the marble throat of a slate-blue shark.
And when the fierce dispute was over,
And the tides were crimson in the sun,
The splash of a ground shark or the dun
Lithe shadow of an ocean rover,
Cutting across the backward spins
Of settling eddies showed how vast
Was the jungle ruin when at last
The furs were conquered by the fins.

Beyond the edge of the chalk canal,
In the deeper part of the Skibo Run
The tiger slaughter was outdone
By a longer, bloodier carnival.
There, neutral hippopotami,
Spotted deer, mild-mannered sows,
Milk-white mules and buffalo cows
Had wandered with their young to lie
And bathe beneath a peaceful sky,
With antelopes and quagga mares,
Soft gazelles and brown she-bears,
Frightened by the roars that rent
The rafters of the firmament;
When suddenly as by design
It seemed as if the whole Pacific
Had yielded up her most terrific
Monsters of the fighting line.

Their long blades flashing in the sun,
Sword-fish were swimming up the Run,
Accompanied by flagitious things,—
Saw-bills with their deadly pikes,
Thornbacks with their poisoned spikes,
Torpedo rays with scorpion stings;
Most feared by everything that lives
Above the ocean floor, they broke
With full mortality of stroke
On neutrals and on fugitives,
Hemmed them backwards from the beaches
Into the water's deeper reaches,
Where with rapiers lightning sped,
They took the measure of their sides,
Till all the antelopes were dead,
And all the hippos' leathery hides
Transfixed and all the bears were drilled
With holes and all the calves were killed.

Now late within the afternoon
Again the tide of battle changed.
Fish from the Seven Seas were ranged
Along the stretch of the Blue Lagoon
That had beneath the withering spell
Of three hot rainless moons been closed.
There, lash-rays—the marines of hell—
Had come with sharks,—the shovel-nosed,
And sickle-finned; dog-fish, big jacks
Gifted with prophetic smell,—
All following in the conquering tracks
Of threshers from the Hebrides,
Of Greenland killers and those mailed,
Tremendous rhinodons that hailed
From the typhoons of the Indian seas.
Against that swarming, heaving pack
Was launched the raving, massed attack
Of full-grown argali, and rams
From South Afghanistan that mourned
The swordfish slaughter of their dams;
And fighting boars that would have scorned
Brigades of tigers, with koodoos,
Flanked by battalions of gnoos,
And bull-head rhinos double-horned.

173

Into that reeling, shapeless ruck,
Scarce covered by the water, poured
This furious and avenging horde. . . .
Surviving rhinodons that struck
For ocean spaces through the ford
Were caught fast in the mire, and gored
To death by stag and water-buck.

And as the dubious hours went by,
Cormorants, in carrion mood,
Ospreys and kestrels thronged the sky,
Impatient, as the fiery feud
Swung through such vicissitude
As never, after or before,
Was known within the files of War.
Such acts of valour as were done
Outshone the white flame of the sun;—
Such hopeless sacrificial deeds
And feats of strength as might belong
To men or gods, when weaker breeds
Wrecked their bodies on the strong.
Reversals with the strangest luck,
Unknown to contests in the sea,
Took place where bulk and energy
Matched themselves with skill and pluck.
Mackerel and electric eels
Drowned zebras, weighting down their thighs;
Leonine and ursine seals
Were killed by lemurs and aye-ayes.
To rescue otters with their young
From saw-fish and an instant slaughter,
A scouting beaver party flung
Themselves into the salted water,
Were caught, outnumbered and were beaten,
Run through by bayonet-bills, and eaten.
But their assailants blown with greed
Were seized, after the hottest chase,
By hounds of an Eo-Irish race,
And terriers of a Gallic breed.
And the sun went down upon the sight
Of bison worsted by becunas,

Of foxes putting sharks to flight
And weasels at the throats of tunas.
Along the shore from tip to tip,
This interlocking battle grip
Relaxed only as either side
Gave ground with flow and ebb of tide;
For all were pledged, with teeth and claws,
To racial blood and comradeship,
Devoted to the national cause
And loyal to the boundary strip.

In one swift hour when the night
Was far advanced, the Saurian,
By some half-blinded route, began
To scent the issue of the fight.
Throughout the day he did not know
Which was his ally or his foe;
Beyond the blue lagoon he waded
Where sluggish alligators hid
Behind a sand-spit, and invaded
The rocky strongholds of the squid.
With his steep claws he rent apart
Amphibia along the shore,
And wandering farther out, he tore
Pelagic mammals to the heart.
He followed up a narwhal, wedged
Him dry upon the Gumra shoals,
Left him with twenty streaming holes
From twelve-inch canines double-edged.
Then back upon his tracks he wheeled,
Floundered through the littoral mud,
Entered the battle zone and reeled
Through mounting sloughs of flesh and blood,
Scattering a full hyæna pack
That hung all day upon his track
Along the freshly swollen moors,
Wondering how their nostrils missed
The secret of those bloody spoors
Left by the alien Atavist.
Fish and land animals alike
Were objects for his fangs to strike;
Elephants and jungle cats
Met the same fate as hares and rats;

Beneath his horned, gigantic toes
Camels went down and buffaloes;
And wild cats were so many fleas
That tickled him below the knees.
But when the evening wore to night
Gorillas under cover hit him
With flying stones, and cave bears bit him;
A flock of eagles bleared his sight
With beak and claw; a downy pack
Of monkeys in a sycamore
Swung downward by their tails and tore
The scaly armour from his back.
The bravest lions in the ranks
Buried their teeth into his hocks;
From hemlock crotches and from rocks,
Tigers leaping on his shanks
Gouged deeply with insistent claws
And dropped with flitches in their jaws.
Then from this unremitting stress
Came the sure touch of weariness;
A pulse of apprehension dim
Of what this struggle double-faced
Might in the outcome mean to him.
Perhaps some inland desert taste
During the slaughter of the camels,
Taught him his kinship with the lizard,
His blood-removal from the mammals,
And gave him nausea at the gizzard.
Perhaps in some sharp way it sprang
From the reminiscent tang
Of salt sea water on his muzzle,
The moment that he stooped and took
The narwhal's blood as from a brook
With one inebriating guzzle.
Something in his racial birth,
At variance with the things of Earth,—
A tidal call that beat like pain
From spinal ganglion to brain—
Now made him shake his foes aside,
And leave the battle's desperate zone,
And wander off to climb alone

A promontory where the tide
Sounded its nocturnal flow
A sheer three hundred feet below.
He cleared the base, his body fagged,
And clambered on from shard to shard,
Pausing, jibbing, breathing hard.
Under his weight his knee-caps sagged;
Bleeding fast from fissures torn
By tiger fang and rhino horn,
He groped and stumbled up until
He reached a level granite sill;
Raw fillets hanging from his thighs,
He sank a moment faint with pain;
Chaos was closing on his eyes,
When the voice of the sea-god called again,
Far across the water,—"Ex-
Saurian of the Pleiocene,
Blind wanderer from the race marine,
TYRANNOSAUROS REX!"
Starting sharply from his swoon,
He stood upright, his figure set
Black like a poplar's silhouette
Against the orb of an inflamed moon.
And once again from a crystal bell,
Oceanus wove his spell;
Sounding like a three-fold ring,
Steepled in the crimson surge,
It tolled . . .
"TYRANNOSAUROS!
      TYRANNOSAUROS!
            TYRANNOSAUROS KING!"
The lizard staggered to the verge,
Looked into the water's face,
The rolling cradle of his race,
Brooded a moment as he hung
Over the crag-holds wearily,
And with the final echo, flung
His body to the Austral Sea.

Wilder than the maddest rout,
Madder than the wildest roar,
A storm of rage unknown before
Followed Tyrannus' passing out.

The dark unreason of his mind,
Read in promiscuous assault
Upon the land and ocean kind,
Had placed the agreement in default.
But through the day, the immediate sight
Of a teeming and aggressive sea
Enforced the covenantal right
Against a mutual enemy;
Kept in abeyance blood desires
As veteran as Jurassic fires.
Now under cover of the night
When many of their ranks had died
Of virus from the saurian's bite,
The leash of discipline was untied,
And soon the full abysmal sound
Broke out in internecine notes
From all the brutes on fighting ground
Feeling for each other's throats.
So piercing was the central cry
It carried to the southward high
Over the foothills to the crests
Of the snowy Guadeleras, waking
The æries of the eagles; shaking
The condors from their craggy nests.
Then by a fierce contagion carried
East and west to either tip
Of the Isthmian sea-board, it was harried
Into ten thousand shards;—the rip
Of lion's claws on buffalo hides;
Of ivory through the lions' sides;
The grunt of a bush hog or the squeal
Of a babyroussa with the pounce
Of an infuriated ounce;
Of leopards crushed beneath the kneel
Of battle-wearied elephants;
The growls of bears; the dissonance
Of fleeing, howling allouattes
Pursued by cheetahs; of wild cats
Nine-lived and strung in endless knots
Upon the backs of Cashmir ewes,
Or arguing with ocelots

The fallen bodies of kangaroos.
And now and then the storm would rise
To unimaginable cries,
As though a stubborn racial note,
Goaded to the bitter-full,
Had baulked within the cosmic throat.
And yet the scale, for all this woe,
Had still a higher note to go.

All through the day,—in throaty pant
Of steam and pulmonary moan,
Being full of slag, the stridulant
Jurania, like a surly crone,
Had growled about a deeper pain,
Caused by an old Silurian sprain.
By dusk, her fetid breath had grown
Into a thick revolving cone.
And as the minutes passed, a flash,—
An incandescent fork of blue,
And now of green would struggle through
The smothering pall of smoke and ash,
Until with undulating sheet
Of multi-coloured flame that beat
The blank face of the sky apart,—
Just as the last convulsive stroke
Unthrottled the volcano's heart,—
The storm flood of the lava broke.
It shot a fifteen thousand feet
Straight to the sky, then billowing higher,
And outward, made as if to meet
Its own maternal stellar fire
With tenuous play of finger streaks;
But failing in its vaunted leap,
Returned with frenzied haste to sweep
Across the Guadelera peaks;
Inundate the valleys; glut
The plains and canyons; rise and shut
The higher gorges, rifts and caves
Of the mountains; overflow and roll
Seaward with tumbling lava waves
Over the great Juranian bowl.
It blazed the forest pines and passed
The northern stretch of cliffs until,

Clearing the summit and the last
Excoriated ridge and hill,
It poured its fury on the dead;
Then the inexorable blast,
Capping the horrors of the night,
Pursued the living remnants, bled
To the final pulses with the fight,
And caught them as they tried to flee
To the drowning mercies of the sea.

Far to the East,—from all this dire
Titanic strife of claw and fire,
The only fighter to escape,—
The female anthropoidal ape!
By subtle powers that placed her head
Of land belligerents, she, alone,
Had often turned to watch with dread
The beat of catastrophic power,
In cloud and thunder, as the cone
Ticked off her last Aeonian hour.
She sniffed the warning just in time,
Before the extinction throe, to reach
The forest heights that flanked the beach.
She took the eastern headland climb,
And then turned southwards from the sea,
Shambling upward wearily,
Ever on the chasing fringe
Of the lava that, with hideous twist
Of myriad anacondas, hissed
And spat out fiery tongues to singe
Her hair. Gaining the summit where
Water breezes cooled the air,
She paused a moment to endure
The scene survived, her eyes aglow
Held first by the mesmeric lure
Of globes of vivid indigo
That danced and burst as they were thrown
From the deep labour of the cone,
And then by that which choked her breath
And dazed her brain,—the molten red
Of plain and ridge on which were spread

The incredulities of death,
Riding on tumultuously
In a gulf of fire to the sea.
Under the shelter of the height,
She gathered up her residue
Of will to blot out from her view
The awful fiction of the night,
And take upon herself the strain
Of the descent. By swinging, crawling,
Running in little spurts and falling,
Splay-footed, shoulders crooked with pain,
She reached a shallow river-bed
Winding through a moor which led
Her to a grove of sandalwood.
There, at the hollow of a tree,
She found her lair, and brokenly
She entered in, cuddling her brood
To withered paps; and in the hush
Of the laggard hours as the flush
Of dawn burnt out the coppery tones
That smeared the unfamiliar West,
The heralds of the day were moans,
And croons, and drummings of the breast.

THE ROOSEVELT
AND THE ANTINOE

(1930)

To my brothers Jim, Art and Cal

THE ROOSEVELT AND THE ANTINOE

Her high freeboard towering above the pier,
She lay beneath the lift of spars and blocks:
Her port life month by month and year by year
Knew nothing but the humdrum of the docks;—
The rumble of trucks along the warehouse floors,
The blare of sirens, shout of stevedores,
The play of tackle under the gruff mood
Of winches, clatter of hooks and booms, subdued
To the credit balance that must never fail
The ledgers of Hoboken Lines—so she,
Built for the tides of commerce on the sea,
Was under schedule in an hour to sail.

In the Commissioner's room it was agreed
Between the Master and the mariners,
That as the men received *per month or run*
Their wage in dollars and were guaranteed
By statutes of the State that they might draw
Their scale of rations—*bread and meat and water,*
Lemon and lime and such *prescribed by law,*
With *means of warmth in weather*; they, the crew,
Should pledge themselves to conduct, *faithful, true,*
And orderly, in honest, sober manner;
At all times in their duties diligent;
To the Master's lawful word obedient,
In everything relating to the vessel—
Safety of passengers, cargo and store,
Whether on board, in boats, or on the shore.

And with the reading thus concluded, both
The parties to the contract gave their oath
Of signature. Items of birthplace, age,
Height and description then were written in,
Each sailor's time of service with his wage-
Allotment, and address of Next-of-Kin.
So, with their sea-bags on their backs, the crew
Went up the gangway to the foc's'le; threw
Their dunnage on the bunks; soon to be lined
Two hundred of them, on the deck; assigned
Stations and duties, as the bos'n drew
The *likeliest* man, his mate the next; and then.

Alternately the Watches claimed the men,
In that renowned and tacit lottery
Full of the hoary savour of the sea.

The mooring cables splashing from the bollards,
Three stern and bow tugs moved her to the stream,
And slowly swung her head round with the ebb-tide;
Were cast off; when the liner on her steam
Proceeded down the channels of the Hudson,
Into the outer harbour, to the sea,
And on past Sandy Hook where finally
She set her course which led her to the *Great
Circle Track* for Queenstown, Plymouth, Cherbourg
(Service of passenger and mail), thence straight
To Bremen with the body of her freight.

Thursday morning rose without a sun,
Sleet in the air: the wind was westerly:
The river breeze of Wednesday had begun
To stiffen to a whole gale on the sea.
By noon the stations at the coast were flashing
Warnings, making smaller ships delay
Their date of sailing. Vessels under canvas,
Attempting shorter trips in gulf or bay,
Crawled back to harbour double-reefed, while others,
Still further to the east, that could not make
Return,—sails blown to ribbons from the gaskets—
Were forced to scud under bare poles to take
The luck ahead. Long threat lay in the signals.
The charts traced not a cyclone's come-and-go,—
The fury soon begun and as soon ended—
But those broad areas on which storms grow,
Northern and Oceanic, where each hour,
Feeding on the one before, transmits
In turn its own inheritance of power
Unto the next until the hammer hits
A hemisphere.

                    Along the eastern seaboard,
And inland to one-half the continent,
Thousands of dials in studio and station
Were "off the air" by an ungrudged consent—
That the six-hundred-metre wave might keep

185

Upon the sea that night its high command
For the great business that was nigh at hand,
With deep already calling unto deep.

Friday evening, with Cape Race reporting
Big seas with thickening fog followed by snow,
Barometer still falling, very low.

Morning of Saturday! the gale now rising
To the dimensions of a hurricane,
With gusts that boxed the compass of a vane,
Sweeping around the headlands to contest
The arrogated highway from the West.

Evening again, and in its power to smite
The snowy cordon with its warning light,
The Cape's revolving beacon was as sick
As the guttering limit of a candle-wick.
And never—it was claimed—had tides so climbed
A slope of shoal from such a depth to feed
The tumult of the upper waves; so timed
Direction with their volume and their speed,
To meet both wave and wind that all might lock
In foam above so high a line of rock.

South of this Cape within these hours, the *Roosevelt*
Was driving East by North, with her decks stripped;
Her lower ventilator cowls unshipped,
The shafts plugged; battened and wedged the hatches;
Bell-mouths full-bore discharging from the bilge-pumps
Under the straining hull; thirty degrees
Measuring her roll within the heavier seas.
The facing of the 'midship house was spattered
At seventy feet. Captain and quarter-master
Saw nothing legible upon the face
Of day or night: the sextant in its case,
The navigators guessed the ship's position.

Abaft—the smoke came out, to be driven back
In eddies low and fierce against the white
Salt crust upon the surface of the stack,
Then, split in billows to the left and right.

Dispersed before it found a line of flight.
The double lines of life-boats lay like rows
Of mastodons asleep in polar snows.
Ahead—appeared under the steamer's light
Truncated day between two walls of night.
Sometimes the for'ard derrick-posts were blotted
Out; the hooded shapes of winches squatted
Upon the deck; and with each long roll, patches
Of white laggin' from the steampipes swirled
And blended with the foam around the hatches.
The sea itself was gone save when it hurled
The body of a wave across the bow;
Soon even this was lost to the bridge, and now
Behind the weather-cloth it seemed the world
Was carried with the last gust to the void.

Fried stepped inside the Pilot House to get
Another reading from the aneroid.
An hour ago the adjusting hand was set
At twenty-nine—the low foul weather mark,
And the indicator for that hour had stood
Directly underneath as though it were glued
To the card. He came nearer, full of dark
Conjecture, tapped the glass, and the hand fell,
The barest fraction but perceptible,
Entering by slow, inexorable rate,
The tragic ranges of the *twenty-eight*.
Later he returned; the oracle
Yielded this time a record to appal
The heart. Muttering *"twenty-eight (point) three,"*
He shot a glance to the right where on the wall
He found, in confirmation, the line drawn
To the same level on the mercury.
'Twas four o'clock on a North Atlantic sea,
Three hours before a January dawn.
The wind having slipped the gale's leash was soon
To match the wing-shod speed of a typhoon:
The storm of nineteen twenty-six was on.

Somewhere far-off in that unwavering gloom,
Cramped in the quarters of a wireless room,
A boy was seated, tapping at a key.
Water ran along the floor: his knee
Was braced against a table to resist

The dangerous angle of a starboard list.
Upon his right a wireless log-chart lay
With many entries for so young a day.
He reached and pushed a button and the drone
Of a generator started. A switch thrown,
He rapped the key, then instantly transferred
To the receiving set; listened with keen
Thrust of his face; and with no answer heard,
Changed over, going through the same routine.
But once when on the panel a blue flame,
Crackling like tearing linen at the gap,
Responded to a more than hectic tap
Of the finger, dumb and drowsy symbols came
To life. Through aerials screaming like curlews,
Magnetic messengers carried the name
Of a disabled vessel with the news
Of water in the stokehold and a crew's
Vigil upon a flooded deck. Legions
Unnumbered moving at the rate of light,
Pushed out beyond all navigated regions,
Exploring every cranny of the night,
Reaching out through dusky corridors
Above the sea to uninhabited shores,
Or taking undecoded human cries
Below the keel to the Atlantic crypts.
And millions undulated to the skies,
Through snow and vapour and the cloud eclipse,
Past day and night and the terrestrial air,
To add their wasted sum to a plethora
Of speed and power in those void spaces where
Light-years go drifting by Andromeda.
And yet in all that sterile plenitude
A few were harnessed to a human mood.

The cabin of the *Roosevelt* radio!
Three dots, three dashes, and the dots again—
(The call sign) *British freighter, 'Antinoe'.*
Don't know position. Sixteen hours ago,
Rough latitude—North forty-six and ten,
Rough longitude—thirty-nine, five-eight.
Been hove-to ever since; the present rate
Of drift to East, two knots (approximate).

Fried took the message, reading nothing more
Than that a ship was sending out a call
For help, and that since noon the day before
She had not known her bearings. This was all
The cryptogram surrendered for a clue.
A fresh despatch was brought two minutes later,
The *Aquitania* calling—"*Which of two
Should undertake location of the freighter?*"
Their own positions given, 'twas agreed—
Cunarder farther off by hours, pressed
To the muzzle of the storm and moving West,—
The job might therefore be assigned to Fried.

Orders were given to the wireless chief
To bring the direction-finder into play,
Capture the signals and report at brief
Periods—and the ship was on her way.
Taking his station at the binnacle,
The head-phones on, he listened while he swung
The handwheel slowly to the right until
The loop above the Pilot House that hung
The wires came broadside to the signal cry.
The sounds grew fainter, faded out, came back
With further revolution but to die
Again with the reversal of the track.
Underneath, the hair-line on the face
Of the dummy compass card had kept its pace
With every move, faithful to every trial,
And like a dogma that might take denial
From neither sense nor reason, pointed *There*,
At a figure stamped in black upon the dial:
For when it moved to either side with the wheel,
It came back ever with the aerial square
To the source of the signal like a steadying keel
Demanding its position. How far? Where,
Along this line, now tossing like a chip
Upon those crests and hollows, lay the ship,
It could not tell—one hundred miles or two
It might have been for all the seamen knew.

Back in the wireless room the call came in
With the staccato of a bulletin;
Triads of notes spare and reiterant,
A whistle shot with burr and sibilant—

189

The international prelude which the sea
Beats out in storm from human veins to express
The fever pulses of its own distress.
Whether it was the sharp economy
Of pauses in the breaks, or some known trick
Of the ear to catch the timbre of a click,
A pressure or a crotchet in the tapping,
The operator felt someone was rapping
A message out with white intensity,
In life-death finger action on a key,
Within the cabin of the *Antinoe*.
Tarpaulins ripped. Another hatch let go.
Bad list. Grain swelling fast. Seams loosening now.
All life-boats gone from starboard davits. How
Many knots are you making? How far away
Do you reckon you are?
                              Ten knots: now eight:
Now ten—top speed allowed by sea.
                                      You say
That we sound nearer to you? Cannot wait
Much longer.
                  Twelve.
                            Find it hard to steer,
Ice-chest has crashed into the steering gear.

Coming.
              Six o'clock. Now seven. The dots
Of the freighter answered by the liner's knots,
Followed by danger when the sea would turn
And test the rivets from the stem to stern
With longitudinal blows, hurling cascades
Upon the bow, till with a burial wave
The engines instantly would stop to save
The tail-shaft from the racing of the blades.

A longer silence; and a deep suspicion.
Destruction of the ship? or loss of power?
Blindness was coming with the light of morning,
Ten minutes, twenty, now a half-an-hour.
Where are you, 'Antinoe'?—The keys kept rapping,

But the receiving phones were dumb to space,
And in the Pilot House there came no signal,
The hand lay palsied on the compass face.

The operator meantime on the wreck
Had left his room and crossed a slushing deck,
Reporting to his captain. When he tried
Return, a wave upon the weather side
Reached and caught the last port life-boat; smashed
It from the davits down the incline; crashed
The forward wall of the wireless cabin; sheared
It clean. Matching death with strategy,
The sailors took their chance with each spent sea;
The fragments were removed; the way was cleared;
The set put in emergency repair
And human speech again was on the air.

Eleven o'clock. Fried knowing that he neared
The ship's position by the growing power
Of the signals slowed the *Roosevelt* down to scour
The closer plotted area, fighting squall
On top of storm, boring through a pall
Of snow, till at the heart of the wave-zone,
With Jack reversed, the freighter like a lone
Sea-mallard with a broken wing was seen
Ahead, lee-rail awash, taking it green
At the bow.

> *Do you wish to abandon?*
>> *Not just yet;*
Endeavouring to fix steering gear, and get
Hatches secured. Water in stokehold. Grain
Cargo shifted. Trying to maintain
Sufficient steam to heave-to and survive
Till weather moderate. Crew twenty-five.
Can you spread oil to windward? Please stand-by.

But hard as the three engineers might try,
The leaks outraced the pumps. The daylight grew
To dusk, the hatches opened and the crew
Signalled for rescue. Fried, a quarter mile
To windward, poured his fuel oil on the sea,
Giving, that distance, what the *Roosevelt* lee
Afforded, edging in and backing while

191

He waited for a sign of the wind's subsiding,
Watching the scud of the waves, the darkening sky,
The drifting snow and the freighter heavily riding.

Then suddenly at nine as the squall increased,
With a smother of black hail the *Roosevelt*'s light
Could not pierce through, the bridge look-out lost sight
Of the *Antinoe* and the wireless contact ceased.

Dead Slow! The *Roosevelt* took a risk as great
As if the air shook with the roar of reefs.
The wireless and the navigating chiefs
Fried summoned to the flying bridge to debate
The course. What with the hammer of the sea
To windward, and that anvil on the lee,
Judgment and will were warped by doubt. Suspend
Pursuit? Keep steerage-way and just hold on?
For at this hour with sight and hearing gone,
All felt within their blood they could depend
On nothing but an elemental trust
In bulkheads; in the physics of a dark
Equation, where with each remorseless thrust
Down to the starboard limits of the arc,
The ship should take under unheard commands
The port recoil, a pivoted keel, and then,
At the crux of the port roll find again
The firm up-heave of Atlantean hands.
On such a faith, borne in by night and snow,
Rested the riddle of the *Antinoe*.

Was she beyond that scurrying barricade,
To come back on a wave-lift, as a score
Of doubtful moments she had done before
When gusts had passed? Or had the *Roosevelt* strayed
Beyond the vernier of her calculation,
Caught suddenly by a winter vertigo,
After reaching the *Antinoe*'s location
By a straight miracle of navigation?
But why no message? Flooded dynamo?
Followed by exhausted batteries?
The wireless room demolished by the seas?

Or aerials blown off like a wind-swept kite
From a wallowing ship beam-to and rudderless?
Or had she foundered? This the likelier guess.

The ship with unremitting search despite
The chances stacked against her, steamed on far
Into the night, past midnight and the slow
Hours, blindly heading into snow;
Not a sextant reading off a star;
No radio now with subtle fingering
Untied the snarl of the freighter's wayward course.
Nothing but log and the dead reckoning,
And the *Roosevelt*'s instruments stating the force
Of wind, direction and the tidal stress,
Nothing but these and the wheel's luck to trail her,—
Unless there might be added to the sum
Of them an unexplored residuum—
The bone-and-marrow judgment of a sailor.

But all this time signals were streaming through
The ship's antennae; *'Solvang' in collision,*
Bulkheads crushed, and sinking; the 'Curlew'
A-leak, and under jury-rig, 'Carlstad'
Searching; 'Carlotta' helping 'Orebro';
The 'Bremen' hastening to the 'Laristan';
Engine trouble, serious, twenty-two
Aboard. No record of the *Antinoe*.

Each hour the searchlight moving on its swivel,
Traced but a wide circumference of yeast,
Bounding the clash of forces on the ocean,
With endless lorries heading for the east.
At times the sea would snow the *Roosevelt* under,
As shearing a wave, her bow came to the luff,
Or as she turned with sharp careening angle
To avoid a shadow, putting beam to trough.
The scent was cold by now. Few words were spoken
Between the officer-on-watch and captain;
The *Antinoe* was sunk by every token
And every law known to the wind and weather.

"With such a list, no shift or pumps could right her."
"A dollar flashlight! All she's got to signal."
"If she's afloat, 'twould take a hawk to sight her."

"A flash upon the weather quarter?"
                                        "No.
Her power gone, that handlight wouldn't show
A hundred yards."
                        "A dog's chance for a boat
To get across . . . assuming she's afloat."
"What do you reckon her drift?"
                                    "Port easy! Hold her!
Let her take that one on her starboard shoulder."

Feeling her shifted courses over-run,
And yet uncertain whether she should tack
Upon a chosen port or starboard track,
The baffled liner like a water-dog
Would dip her nose to the sea and then up-rear
Her head with black hawse nostrils keen to flair
A flying quarry covered by a fog.
Dawn and noon and now the afternoon.
"We picked her up"—so ran the captain's log—
"One point upon the starboard bow at four
O'clock, with nineteen hours of delay,
And sixty miles from her last known position."
Her navigating bridge was swept away;
Flooded, steam off, lights out, a closing day,—
The time again awaited Fried's decision.
To pour fuel upon the sea to assuage
Its fury; make a high-decked vessel ride
Steady; maintain sufficient weather gage,
Four hundred tons of pressure at the side,
To avoid the crisis when a wave should toss
Her like a dinghy on the smaller ship,
Beam against beam, or stem to rail, to rip
The plates like cardboard to a double loss;
And yet mindful of this first charge, to crawl
Within a narrow margin to the hulk,
To take advantage of the liner's bulk,
As windbreak for a life-boat, and forestall
The second disappearance in a squall
Of the *Antinoe;*—in fine, to run a race
For a crew's life with the storm laps in advance;
To outstare Death to his salt countenance,
Made up the grim agenda on his face.

Fried took a turn upon the weather deck,
Saw little of assurance in the sky,
Came back to the lee-wing, gauging with his eye
The span his boat must cover to the wreck;
Made up his mind alone on the degree
Of risk; issued a call; in such a sea
And cause the order needed no command,
Only the heart's assent unto the hand.

The men answering the summons with a will,
Came aft; were picked for hardihood and skill.
Their names as on the shipping register:—
Robert Miller, the first officer,
Commanding; Ernest Heitman, bos'n's mate,
No relative; Uno Wertanen,
Master-at-arms, aged twenty-eight, a Finn,
His mother (Helsingfors), the next of kin;
Sam Fisher; Franelich, an Austrian;
Bauer, a naturalized American;
Maurice Jacobowitz of New York State;
And a Dane named Alexander Fugelsang—
Made up the life-boat complement of eight.

A dozen orders from the bos'n rang—
*"Stand by and clear the falls for running; man
The cranks; let go the gripes."* Winch ropes began
To move, winding through the leading blocks;
Slowly the boat was lifted from the chocks.
The crew holding suspended lines that ran
Along the spring-stay, freeboards from the stern
To bow were jacked to gunwales; at a turn
Of the quadrant screw both boat and davit swung
Outboard. The oars and boat-hooks kept her free.
With painters taut at fore and aft, she hung
For her sixty feet of journey to the sea.
Below, like creatures of a fabled past,
From their deep hidings in unlighted caves,
The long processions of great-bellied waves
Cast forth their monstrous births which with grey fang
Appeared upon the leeward side, ran fast
Along the broken crests, then coiled and sprang
For the boat impatient of its slow descent
Into their own inviolate element.
A shout or instant gesture of the hand

Was answered by the double roar of winches.
The ropes ran through the iron cleats by inches,
Straining, checking, running on demand
Of the fore-and-after levels. *"Lower away!"*
A steady longer roar, then a moment clear
Of the side. *"Avast! Let go releasing gear!"*
The blocks shot from the slip-links evenly,
And number one had settled on the sea.

Here was a trial far beyond her training;
Her tests had been accorded her in weather,
And in blue water where there was no danger,—
Where, governed by the stroke, all pull together,
And every rhythmic blade falls to the feather
Against the breeze. Now like a colt untried,
She bucked control and though she carried well
The lop of the shorter waves, she plunged and shied
The moment that she reached the top of a swell,
And went down sidling to the trough and flung
The crew in the water. Under discipline
Of many a drill, they struggled back and clung
To the running loops and cork-grips, clambered in,
And started for the wreck; but with recall
From the bridge, they brought her to the wind and tried
Over a wave-barrel to reach the side
Of the ship when, twenty feet away, a squall
Combined with tide-rip caught the boat and threw
The men back to the waves. Six of the crew
Clutching ladders and lines which might afford
A toe or finger hold were drawn aboard.
Heitman, crushed between the ship and boat,
Slipped from a life-buoy and was seen to float
Senseless away, down by the liner's stern,
Where he was lost under the wave and churn
Of the propeller. Wertanen, who twice
And willingly released his own firm grip
To take within his teeth a rope eye-splice,
Swam fifteen yards to leeward of the ship
To help an exhausted mate, and paid his price
In drifting past the adventure of return.
By help of current and by desperate swim,

A wave pitched him against the life-boat stern.
He clutched the running-line and then the rim
Of the gunwale; tried to get his weight athwart,
But oil had greased his hands and he fell short.
The crew could see him grab and plunge and cling,
Using his legs as rudders so to swing
Her head around to the wreck and with the sheer
Abandon of his youth to try to steer
His open, wilful, single-handed craft
So close to the side that wind might bear it aft,
And round the freighter's stern to where he knew
Life-belts and lines were waiting, with the crew
Gathered at the lee taffrail. Jockeying the boat
Within three fathoms length he tried to grip
A belt, but oil had made his fingers slip,
And oil was in his eyes and in his throat,
And the last thing sighted from the liner's deck,
Near to the close of an hour's futile searching,
Were tossing oars and a frenzied life-boat lurching
From wave to wave, a gunshot from the wreck,
And here and there as far as might be scanned
Within the spindrift, a tide-revolving speck—
A belt perhaps or human head or hand.

From every quarter came the night confounding
The unhorizoned sea with sky and air,
And to the crew of the *Antinoe*—despair.
At ten o'clock the *Roosevelt* bugle sounding
From the saloon stairway a call to prayer!
With separated phrase and smothered word
An immemorial psalm became a blurred
Bulwark under erosion by the sea.
Beneath the maddening crashes of the wind
Crumbled the grammar of the liturgy.

God of all comfort . . .
                    humbly beseeching thee . . .
We do acknowledge . . . . sinned . . .
Most merciful . . . confess . . . grievously . . .
Who spreadest out the heavens, crownest the years.
. . . . Grant us we pray thee . . . . .
Who commandest the seas and they do obey thee.
Nigh unto all . . . .

197

. . . . our distresses and fears.
. . . . A father to the fatherless.
Followed the fragments of great passages:
I am the Resurrection . . . . We
. . . . commit . . . . . bodies to the deep . . .
Corruptible . . . . Of those who sleep . . .
. . . . shall put on immortality.

And then brief tributes to the seamen drowned,
While Miller and his men were ranged around,
Bandaged in head and wrist, with arms in sling,
And others who had come, despite the warning,
To take their places were envisaging
The job that lay before them in the morning.

Meanwhile outside, echoing the ritual—
Now unto Him who is able to do . . . . .
Exceeding abundantly . . . a wild antiphonal
Of shriek and whistle from the shrouds broke through,
Blending with thuds as though some throat had laughed
In thunder down the ventilating shaft;
And the benediction ended with the crack
Of a stanchion on the starboard beam, the beat
Of a loose block, with the fast run of feet,
Where a flying guy careered about the stack;
Then following the omen of a lull,
The advent of a wave which like a wall
Crashed down in volleys flush against the hull,
Lifting its white and shafted spume to fall
Across the higher decks; and through it all,
As on the dial of the telegraph,
Governed by derelict and hurricane,
Rang *Stop, Full Speed Astern* or *Slow* or *Half*,
The irregular pulse and cough of the engine strain,
The quick smite of the blades against a wave,
And always threat, escape, threat, then the brave
Lift of the keel, and still that breathless sink,
Dividing up the seconds, nearing the brink
Of a grey, unplumbed precipice and grave.

Within this hour a priest clothed with the whole
Habiliment and dignity of office—

Black cassock, surplice white and purple stole—
Feeling that from an older faith would come
The virtue of a rubric yet unspoken
For the transition of a soul, a crumb
Of favour from a cupboard not bereft
Of all by the night's intercessions, left
His room; climbed up the stairs; pushed through a door
Storm-wedged, and balancing along the floor
Of the deck to where a davit stood, he placed
His grip securely on a guy rope there.
Lifting up a crucifix, he faced
The starboard quarter, looking down the waste
Of the waters casting back the flickering light
Of the steamer, where two bodies without wrap
Of shroud, deprived of their deck funeral rite,
Swung to the rune of the sea's stern foster-lap

Ego vos absolvo . . . . *ab omnibus*
Peccatis et censuris . . . . .
. . . . *in nomine*
Patris et Filii et Spiritus . . . . .
Sancti . . . . *Attende Domine*
. . . . *et miserere*
Hear . . . *O stella maris* . . . *Mary.*

But no Gennesaret of Galilee
Conjured to its level by the sway
Of a hand or a word's magic was this sea,
Contesting with its iron-alien mood,
Its pagan face, its own primordial way,
The pale heroic suasion of a rood.
And the absolving Father, when the ship
Righted her keel between two giant rolls,
Recrossed himself, and letting go his hold,
Returned to berth, murmuring *God rest their souls.*

And now throughout the middle of the night,
The *Roosevelt* took the hurricane, hove-to.
Into her own defence the captain knew
Must enter all the sinews of her fight—
Her searchlight ripping fissures as through dark
Parchment where at times the freighter, set
In a frame of tossing silver, showed the stark
And streaming edges of her silhouette,

199

Battered but yet miraculously afloat,
Heaving, subsiding with her lathered flank,
Like a bison smitten from the loin to shank,
Surrendering to the wolves about her throat.

And every hour in the wireless room,
The shards of cries as by an incantation,
Were joined to an Atlantic orchestration;
Epic and drama rising to illume
Disaster—now the call and now reply;
The *Bremen* radio—*"still standing by
The 'Laristan'. Six rescued. Will resume
At daylight."*

                 " 'Solvang' lost. All saved but two."
" 'Sparta' reported foundering. Left no clue."
Daylight and wreckage. *Bremen* calling still—
"The 'Laristan' gone down with rest of crew."

With every tap of key, the *Roosevelt* knew
How little would the game depend on skill
Of hand or resolution of the will,
How much would all the morrow's gain and loss
Turn on the unknown chances of a toss.

At four o'clock the *Roosevelt* moved to windward,
And drew again upon her fuel tanks;
Only the whitened edges left the combers,
Like a growth of harvest stubble from the banks
Of rolling prairies that a fire had gleaned.
Still black and dangerous stretches intervened.
At six o'clock the flag at the mast-head
Was lowered half-high in token of her dead,
And the Red Ensign on the freighter went
To the same place in mute acknowledgement.
Then back to their full height the flags were run,
To snap out like the folds of a toreador:
With so much on the boards still to be done,
'Twas fitting that they should, in that same breath
With which the storm took the salute, restore
The colours to their stations, baiting death.

At noon the starboard list began to assume
The final margin for the *Antinoe,*
The signal flags reporting that below
The sea was filling up the engine room.

The next attempt was with the Lyle gun.
Fried edged his vessel nearer to the wreck,
Trying for the safest, shortest run
To get a line across the after-deck.
But once again an adverse hand conspired
Against the chance, checkmated the design,
For at the muzzle as the gun was fired,
The steel projectile snapped the messenger line.
The second did the same, the third, and so
The fourth; the six succeeding carriers trailed
Their lines midway; the last, the eleventh, failed;
Only the iron passed the *Antinoe.*

The store of rockets next—but what availed
Their slender shafts and powder charges scaled
Against the weight of vapour, wind and snow?

An empty cask was lowered with the hope
The wind might carry it to the ship's side.
It sank beneath its sagging weight of rope.

Another stroke of rescue was devised.
A life-boat was trailed off without a crew;
It climbed, zigzagged and floundered, plunging through,
But pitched against the freighter and capsized.

Fried tried again, placing his ship to *looard*
Less than a hundred yards. The next boat moored
By a line rove through the high block of the kingpost
On the quarter-deck, was towed close to the stern
Of the *Antinoe,* but with the luff of the *Roosevelt*
To the weather side, the rope sagged at the turn;
Went underneath and fouled, and number three
Started to drift beyond recovery.

Another night, the third, confronted Fried,
When the last remnant of the sky was blown
Out, with the ocean like a pampas stirred
To the confusion of a great stampede—

Riot of lariat and hoof, of spurred
Horses, and the *Antinoe* a thrown
Spent rider overtaken by the herd.

Wednesday morning! and the twenty-five
Huddled on the aft deck—still alive.
One hundred hours had passed since the men had known
The wool-warmth of a bunk, or stood the cold
With nourished veins; and sleep had taken hold
Of tired bodies salt-drugged to the bone.
And in that hundred hours eternity
Had ticked its lazy seconds on the sea,
Timing the wind and surge and the defeat
Of day by night; of night by day; the slow
Unreasoned alternation of the sleet
With hurrying phantoms of the hail and snow,
The same rotation on the deck—the grey
Sterility of hope with each life-boat gone,
Dusk followed by the night, and every dawn
A slattern offering dust instead of day.

During the night the fact was plain the gun
Would by such lavish firing soon outrun
The standard stock of carriers and consume
The packing cord; so in the engine room
A humming lathe was making up arrears,
In cutting blocks of steel; in fashioning
Projectiles and their rods; and engineers,
Following a passenger's design,
Were busy in construction of a spring,
A spiral coil to graduate the strain
Of the steel rod upon the carrying line
At the initial instant of the shots.
And knowing how the day ahead would drain
Resources, men began to overhaul
The cordage, making loops for arms and knots
For hand-grips, culling big stuff from the small
For nets and heaving-lines and ladders,—all
Which might be spared out of the essential store,
From cargo-slings to the stout rope from the fall
Of a wrecked life-boat davit. Others toiled
For hours, whaler-fashion, over the four

Containing tubs, undid the twists, and coiled
The messenger line many thousand feet,
From vertical core to the end-loop with neat
Precision. So when morning came it seemed
Defaulted effort now might be redeemed,
For though the seventh shot burst free and sped
Away beyond the wreck, it carried true,
Trailing sufficient line to lay it dead
On the poop deck in centre of the crew.

A heavier rope made fast was pulled aboard,
And when the *Roosevelt*'s boat was safely lowered,
Another paying off through fair-leads gave
What help it could to the wavering bow control.
The boat without a load mounted each wave,
Righting herself from every plunge and roll,
Covered the stretch of water like a gull,
Until within five fathoms of the hull,
She turned broadside in an attempt to scale
A sea, the bow line chafed against the rail
And snapped, the stern line gave, and number four
Followed her sisters of the day before.

And so the latter half of the fourth day
Came with the ocean well astride its prey:
The storm in front like a shifty pugilist,
Watching for some slight turn of luck to slay
The rescuer with an iron-knuckled fist.
'Twas useless for the *Roosevelt* to await
The issue of the struggle by debate.
For nothing in those skies favoured a sign
That by manoeuvre could the fight be won—
By floating cask or breeches-buoy or line,
Mere parleying with rockets and a gun.
The hour had called for argument more rife
With the gambler's sacrificial bids for life,
The final manner native to the breed
Of men forging decision into deed—
Of getting down again into the sea,
And testing rowlocks in an open boat,
Of grappling with the storm-king bodily,
And placing Northern fingers on his throat.

The call again, and number five was ready.
The men were chosen and the davits swung;

The boat moved outward easily and hung
Level and snug to leeward but unsteady
In the capricious pockets of the squall.
Another order and the falls began
To move—eight men inside her; Alfred Wall,
Araneda, Diaz, Albertz, Hahn,
Upton, Roberts, Miller in command.
The gunwale fended off with oar and hand
At every lurch, she managed luckily
To clear the steamer's side, covering the steep
Descent, and then undamaged took the sea.
Three oars aside and with a steering sweep,
The boat pulled out from the immediate lee
Into the eddies where the waters met
From stern and bow,—where the last ounces put
On the oars, even with the wind abaft, could yet
Advance them only by the inch and foot.
They followed down the beam-path of the searchlight,
The *Roosevelt* all the while manoeuvring,
Now drawing in, now clawing off, and now
Dead close, beam to the wind, just shadowing
The brute drive of the freighter, to allow
The boat with heavy lateral drift to steer
With wider berth into the wind and clear
The danger of the surge around the bow.
A swamping moment caught her, but each blade
Flexed to the curve of snapping, Miller made
The turn and came down sharp broadside to gain
A point amidships that he might obtain
Such shelter as this windbreak could afford.
But the wells were under water and the lee
Was like the surf of breakers, for the sea,
Contemptuous of this man-made sunken mole,
Threatened each time to hurl the boat aboard,
And reach the funnel with resurgent roll.
Escaping this disaster, Miller drew
His boat back in the sea, and tried to creep
Forward to higher freeboard where the crew
Near the First Hatch might have the shortest leap.
Backwatering and staving off the hull,
And crawling in again with a slight lull

Of the wind, or with recession of the surge,
He took three men who on the perishing verge
Of sleep fell from the rail to the thwarts and slumped
To the floor-boards. Out and back once more
With slow manoeuvring, and another four
Secure. Others of tougher sinew jumped
To the stern sheets from the rail. The task was done
With sudden moves and checks like a strange play
Which starts, is forced to stop, and then begun
Afresh on unknown ground but under sway
Of old Olympian rules. So one by one
The lives were scored and those who missed their aim,
And fell into the sea, were grabbed and pulled
Over the gunwale; counted with the same
Slow chalking up as of advances bulled
Out of the fiery scrimmage of a game.

Miller tried to close again but failed.
With water shipped as fast as it was bailed,
Seams leaking, twelve half-dead men barely stowed,
And with his crew of eight he did not dare
To give his boat a more unstable load;
So pushed away and with the wind and tide
In favour, forced her water-logged to where
The *Roosevelt,* now round to leeward, showed
A maze of lines and ladders on her side.
The first instalment of the crew too numb
To lay their hands on heaving-lines were placed
Within the cargo-nets and drawn up plumb;
The others taking ropes, with their feet braced
Against the hull went up with the sheer lift
Of their mates, till all were safe aboard, and now
The life-boat number five with damaged bow
And broken hoisting hooks was cast adrift.

The pitch of the storm, late night and still the snow,
Two hundred yards between of yawning space,
And thirteen sailors on the *Antinoe.*
Three nights upon the bridge behind the shield
Of the canvas dodger, his accustomed place,
Fried doubtful, peering with his blizzard face.
Now one o'clock, and a slight rift revealed
A spatter of light above the running seas—
The freighter's lantern jabbing out in Morse

That the ship's list had reached fifty degrees.
The last hour was on with no recourse
Except another summons to the crew.
Miller commanding for the third time drew
From the line-up of forty volunteers
Of every rank—deck-hand to passenger,
His four uninjured veterans and five new
Hands: Thomas Sloan, the third officer;
Reidel; Wilke; Deck Yeoman Wilson Beers;
And Caldwell, messman to the engineers.

The sixth life-boat was ready on the lee.
The others stood a moment in review;
Three hundred passengers, two hundred crew;
The cut was getting near the artery.
The men, lowered without mishap, once more
Brought round the boat to the lee bow of the freighter,
And ranged her off the First Hatch as before.
The risk this time for boat and ship was greater;
The growing list could take no steeper verge,
And all the boatmanship could not avail
At first against the backwash of the surge;
For there was peril in the sunken rail,
When at uncertain moments the ship tried
For balance, lifting up a wounded side
To ease a wave that struck amidships, cleaving
Her port; and peril in those hours of doubt
For strengthless men that watched their comrades leaving,
And long the galley fires had been out.
Fried shortened up his weather gage to try
To give a double shelter to the life-boat:
The message later read—"*Had to rely
Upon the final power of my engines,
For had a revolution failed,—'twas either
'Roosevelt' or 'Antinoe' with odds on neither.*"
The revolution did not fail, and Miller
Secured his men, and though with cracked air-tank,
And all the spare oars rent in hull-collision,
The boat came down the wind to the lee flank
Of the liner where the remnant with their clothes

Sodden and shrunk were, like drowsed children, gathered
To the cargo hammocks, twelve of them, then Tose,
The captain, who had worn his buttons well.
His bread had now returned upon the waters,
For ten years back, as later stories tell,
He had while master of another vessel,
Rescued a Philadelphian bark in seas
And winds only less full of death than these.

Now open throttles! Now my lads, YOHO!
The *twenty-five*, by Neptune, every one!
Captain to deck-hand, every mother's son
Aboard! GOOD-BYE, GOOD-BYE, THE *ANTINOE!*
The sea had closed on forward deck and bow;
Let flag and mast and funnel settle now.
Frost-bitten, thinned in blood, gnarled to the bone,
But everyone surviving. All were brought
Below where ocean miracles are wrought,
Where the hearts' furnaces are stoked and blown,
Where men are shepherded in the old way
Of the sea, where drowned men come to life, they say,
Under such calls to breathe as never come
To those that roam the uplands of this earth:—
The hearty comradeship of a foc's'le berth,
With treble-folded blankets on their numb
Bodies, with balsam thawing out the brain,
Hot milk and coffee piping down their dumb
Constricted throats and mustard scattering pain,—
When cold half-foundered bellies steam again
Under the red authority of rum.

The siren! Never did a whistle blow
Upon a ship at sea like this before.
The notes came from a silver throat aglow
With life and triumph. Steady blast to roar
Rising to pitch and volume that would crow
The daybreak in. A shorter blast,
A mimic of halloo, followed by fast
Merry little runs in tremolo,
And then again with open throat the long
Insistent call with pauses, trills and strong
Leaping crescendos.

207

Vital, sound and steady,
For the first hour in days was heard to start
The normal rhythm of the liner's heart;
Her bearings bathed, her boilers breathed and ready
For the ports of England. The fifth morning found her
With high gales still and white seas all around her,
But clean in every valve and with the main
Play of her steam free on each turbine-vane.

Another day and the back of the storm was broken.
The snow and hail had ceased; the clouds rode high;
And though the wind remained, the glass gave token
Of fairer weather. Through a rift of sky
A level shaft, the first one for the week,
Quivered on an edge of cloud, then struck
A line of foam making for the grey peak
Of a kingpost, then to waterline from truck,
Till from the starboard taffrail up the span
Of the hull, it reached the lettering where it ran
In crimson coronation of her name,
As if a god might thus salute the deed,
And ratify the venture with the screed
Of an aurora milled in solar flame.

The Lizard Point, and now the Eddystone!

Meanwhile a nation which was never spared
The discipline of waters, had prepared
Her subjects' hearts from foc's'le to throne
With this Atlantic record to attest
The valour of the eagle from the west,
In bringing home her brood of castaways.
For there had come through radiogram and wire
As high romance as any since the days
When Grecian sails and the triremes of Tyre
Hailed Carthaginian ships upon the bays
Of the Aegean. So she entered Plymouth,
With crusted funnel, twisted rails, scoured clean
By salt on every deck, and overdue;
Yet with the bearing of a Viking Queen,—

Prerogative of life within her hand.
She anchored in the roadstead, while the crew
Of the wrecked ship were taken to the land.
The nation gave its thanks on board; and she,
Soon ready for completion of her run,
Swung out the Sound, with her day's work well done,
And in an hour was on the Channel sea.

THE TITANIC

(1935)

To my father

THE TITANIC

The hammers silent and the derricks still,
And high-tide in the harbour! Mind and will
In open test with time and steel had run
The first lap of a schedule and had won.
Although a shell of what was yet to be
Before another year was over, she,
Poised for the launching signal, had surpassed
The dreams of builder or of navigator.
The Primate of the Lines, she had out-classed
That rival effort to eliminate her
Beyond the North Sea where the air shots played
The laggard rhythms of their fusillade
Upon the rivets of the *Imperator*.
The wedges in, the shores removed, a girl's
Hand at a sign released a ribbon braid;
Glass crashed against the plates; a wine cascade,
Netting the sunlight in a shower of pearls,
Baptized the bow and gave the ship her name;
A slight push of the rams as a switch set free
The triggers in the slots, and her proud claim
On size—to be the first to reach the sea—
Was vindicated, for whatever fears
Stalked with her down the tallow of the slips
Were smothered under by the harbour cheers,
By flags strung to the halyards of the ships.

MARCH 31, 1912

Completed! Waiting for her trial spin—
Levers and telegraphs and valves within
Her intercostal spaces ready to start
The power pulsing through her lungs and heart.
An ocean lifeboat in herself—so ran
The architectural comment on her plan.
No wave could sweep those upper decks—unthinkable!
No storm could hurt that hull—the papers said so.
The perfect ship at last—the first unsinkable,
Proved in advance—had not the folders read so?
Such was the steel strength of her double floors

Along the whole length of the keel, and such
The fine adjustment of the bulkhead doors
Geared to the rams, responsive to a touch,
That in collision with iceberg or rock
Or passing ship she could survive the shock,
Absorb the double impact, for despite
The bows stove in, with forward holds aleak,
Her aft compartments buoyant, watertight,
Would keep her floating steady for a week.
And this belief had reached its climax when,
Through wireless waves as yet unstaled by use,
The wonder of the ether had begun
To fold the heavens up and reinduce
That ancient *hubris* in the dreams of men,
Which would have slain the cattle of the sun,
And filched the lightnings from the fist of Zeus.
What mattered that her boats were but a third
Of full provision—caution was absurd:
Then let the ocean roll and the winds blow
While the risk at Lloyd's remained a record low.

THE ICEBERG

Calved from a glacier near Godhaven coast,
It left the fiord for the sea—a host
Of white flotillas gathering in its wake,
And joined by fragments from a Behring floe,
Had circumnavigated it to make
It centre of an archipelago.
Its lateral motion on the Davis Strait
Was casual and indeterminate,
And each advance to southward was as blind
As each recession to the north. No smoke
Of steamships nor the hoist of mainsails broke
The polar wastes—no sounds except the grind
Of ice, the cry of curlews and the lore
Of winds from mesas of eternal snow;
Until caught by the western undertow,
It struck the current of the Labrador
Which swung it to its definite southern stride.
Pressure and glacial time had stratified
The berg to the consistency of flint,
And kept inviolate, through clash of tide

213

And gale, façade and columns with their hint
Of inward altars and of steepled bells
Ringing the passage of the parallels.
But when with months of voyaging it came
To where both streams—the Gulf and Polar—met,
The sun which left its crystal peaks aflame
In the sub-arctic noons, began to fret
The arches, flute the spires and deform
The features, till the batteries of storm,
Playing above the slow-eroding base,
Demolished the last temple touch of grace.
Another month, and nothing but the brute
And palaeolithic outline of a face
Fronted the transatlantic shipping route.
A sloping spur that tapered to a claw
And lying twenty feet below had made
It lurch and shamble like a plantigrade;
But with an impulse governed by the raw
Mechanics of its birth, it drifted where
Ambushed, fog-grey, it stumbled on its lair,
North forty-one degrees and forty-four,
Fifty and fourteen west the longitude,
Waiting a world-memorial hour, its rude
Corundum form stripped to its Greenland core.

SOUTHAMPTON, WEDNESDAY, APRIL 10, 1912

An omen struck the thousands on the shore—
A double accident! And as the ship
Swung down the river on her maiden trip,
Old sailors of the clipper decades, wise
To the sea's incantations, muttered fables
About careening vessels with their cables
Snapped in their harbours under peaceful skies.
Was it just suction or fatality
Which caused the *New York* at the dock to turn,
Her seven mooring ropes to break at the stern
And writhe like anacondas on the quay,
While tugs and fenders answered the collision
Signals with such trim margin of precision?
And was it backwash from the starboard screw

Which, tearing at the big *Teutonic*, drew
Her to the limit of her hawser strain,
And made the smaller tethered craft behave
Like frightened harbour ducks? And no one knew
For many days the reason to explain
The rise and wash of one inordinate wave,
When a sunken barge on the Southampton bed
Was dragged through mire eight hundred yards ahead,
As the *Titanic* passed above its grave.
But many of those sailors wise and old,
Who pondered on this weird mesmeric power,
Gathered together, lit their pipes and told
Of portents hidden in the natal hour,
Told of the launching of some square-rigged ships,
When water flowed from the inverted tips
Of a waning moon, of sun-hounds, of the shrieks
Of whirling shags around the mizzen peaks.
And was there not this morning's augury
For the big one now heading for the sea?
So long after she passed from landsmen's sight,
They watched her with their Mother Carey eyes
Through Spithead smoke, through mists of Isle of Wight,
Through clouds of sea-gulls following with their cries.

WEDNESDAY EVENING

Electric elements were glowing down
In the long galley passages where scores
Of white-capped cooks stood at the oven doors
To feed the population of a town.
Cauldrons of stock, purées and consommés,
Simmered with peppercorns and marjoram.
The sea-shore smells from bisque and crab and clam
Blended with odours from the fricassées.
Refrigerators, hung with a week's toll
Of the stockyards, delivered sides of lamb
And veal, beef quarters to be roasted whole.
Hundreds of capons and halibut. A shoal
Of Blue-Points waited to be served on shell.
The boards were loaded with pimolas, pails
Of lobster coral, jars of Béchamel,
To garnish tiers of rows of chilled timbales
And aspics. On the shelves were pyramids

215

Of truffles, sprigs of thyme and water-cress,
Bay leaf and parsley, savouries to dress
Shad roes and sweetbreads broiling on the grids.
And then in diamond, square, crescent and star,
Hors d'oeuvres were fashioned from the toasted bread,
With paste of anchovy and caviare,
Paprika sprinkled and pimento spread,
All ready, for the hour was seven!
                                    Meanwhile,
Rivalling the engines with their steady tread,
Thousands of feet were taking overhead
The fourth lap round the deck to make the mile.
Squash racquet, shuffle board and quoits; the cool
Tang of the plunge in the gymnasium pool,
The rub, the crisp air of the April night,
The salt of the breeze made by the liner's rate,
Worked with an even keel to stimulate
Saliva for an ocean appetite;
And like storm troops before a citadel,
At the first summons of a bugle, soon
The army massed the stairs towards the saloon,
And though twelve courses on the cards might well
Measure themselves against Falstaffian juices,
But few were found presenting their excuses,
When stewards offered on the lacquered trays
The Savoy chasers and the canapés.

The dinner gave the sense that all was well:
That touch of ballast in the tanks; the feel
Of peace from ramparts unassailable,
Which, added to her seven decks of steel,
Had constituted the *Titanic* less
A ship than a Gibraltar under heel.
And night had placed a lazy lusciousness
Upon a surfeit of security.
Science responded to a button press.
The three electric lifts that ran through tiers
Of decks, the reading lamps, the brilliancy
Of mirrors from the tungsten chandeliers,
Had driven out all phantoms which the mind
Had loosed from ocean closets, and assigned

To the dry earth the custody of fears.
The crowds poured through the sumptuous rooms and halls,
And tapped the tables of the Regency;
Smirked at the caryatids on the walls;
Talked Jacobean-wise; canvassed the range
Of taste within the Louis dynasty.
Grey-templed Cæsars of the world's Exchange
Swallowed liqueurs and coffee as they sat
Under the Georgian carved mahogany,
Dictating wireless hieroglyphics that
Would on the opening of the Board Rooms rock
The pillared dollars of a railroad stock.

IN THE GYMNASIUM

A group had gathered round a mat to watch
The pressure of a Russian hammerlock,
A Polish scissors and a German crotch,
Broken by the toe-hold of Frank Gotch;
Or listened while a young Y.M.C.A.
Instructor demonstrated the left-hook,
And that right upper-cut which Jeffries took
From Johnson in the polished Reno way.
By midnight in the spacious dancing hall,
Hundreds were at the Masqueraders' Ball,
The high potential of the liner's pleasures,
Where mellow lights from Chinese lanterns glowed
Upon the scene, and the *Blue Danube* flowed
In andantino rhythms through the measures.

By three the silence that proceeded from
The night-caps and the soporific hum
Of the engines was far deeper than a town's:
The starlight and the low wash of the sea
Against the hull bore the serenity
Of sleep at rural hearths with eiderdowns.

The quiet on the decks was scarcely less
Than in the berths: no symptoms of the toil
Down in the holds; no evidence of stress
From gears drenched in the lubricating oil.
She seemed to swim in oil, so smooth the sea.
And quiet on the bridge: the great machine

217

Called for laconic speech, close-fitting, clean,
And whittled to the ship's economy.
Even the judgment stood in little need
Of reason, for the Watch had but to read
Levels and lights, meter or card or bell
To find the pressures, temperatures, or tell
Magnetic North within a binnacle,
Or gauge the hour of docking; for the speed
Was fixed abaft where under the Ensign,
Like a flashing trolling spoon, the log rotator
Transmitted through a governor its fine
Gradations on a dial indicator.

Morning of Sunday promised cool and clear,
Flawless horizon, crystal atmosphere;
Not a cat's paw on the ocean, not a guy
Rope murmuring: the steamer's columned smoke
Climbed like extensions of her funnels high
Into the upper zones, then warped and broke
Through the resistance of her speed—blue sky,
Blue water rifted only by the wedge
Of the bow where the double foam line ran
Diverging from the beam to join the edge
Of the stern wake like a white unfolding fan.
Her maiden voyage was being sweetly run,
Adding a half-knot here, a quarter there,
Gliding from twenty into twenty-one.
She seemed so native to her thoroughfare,
One turned from contemplation of her size,
Her sixty thousand tons of sheer flotation,
To wonder at the human enterprise
That took a gamble on her navigation—
Joining the mastiff strength with whippet grace
In this head-strained, world-watched Atlantic race:
Her less than six days' passage would combine
Achievement with the architect's design.

9 A.M.

A message from *Caronia: advice*
From ships proceeding west; sighted field ice

And growlers; forty-two north; forty-nine
To fifty-one west longitude. S.S.
'Mesaba' of Atlantic Transport Line
Reports encountering solid pack: would guess
The stretch five miles in width from west to east,
And forty-five to fifty miles at least
In length.

1 P.M.

        Amerika obliged to slow
Down: warns all steamships in vicinity
Presence of bergs, especially of three
Upon the southern outskirts of the floe.

1.42 P.M.

The Baltic warns Titanic: so Touraine;
Reports of numerous icebergs on the Banks,
The floe across the southern traffic lane.

5 P.M.

The Californian and Baltic again
Present their compliments to Captain.

"TITANIC"

                         Thanks.

THREE MEN TALKING ON DECK

"That spark's been busy all the afternoon—
Warnings! The Hydrographic charts are strewn
With crosses showing bergs and pack-ice all
Along the routes, more south than usual
For this time of the year."
             "She's hitting a clip
Instead of letting up while passing through
This belt. She's gone beyond the twenty-two."

"Don't worry—Smith's an old dog, knows his ship,
No finer in the mercantile marine

219

Than Smith with thirty years of service, clean
Record, honoured with highest of all commands,
'Majestic', then 'Olympic' on his hands,
Now the 'Titanic'."
                    "'Twas a lucky streak
That at Southampton dock he didn't lose her,
And the 'Olympic' had a narrow squeak
Some months before rammed by the British Cruiser,
The 'Hawke'."
                    "Straight accident. No one to blame:
'Twas suction—Board absolved them both. The same
With the 'Teutonic' and 'New York'. No need
To fear she's trying to out-reach her speed.
There isn't a sign of fog. Besides by now
The watch is doubled at crow's nest and bow."
"People are talking of that apparition,
When we were leaving Queenstown—that head showing
Above the funnel rim, and the fires going!
A stoker's face—sounds like a superstition.
But he was there within the stack, all right;
Climbed up the ladder and grinned. The explanation
Was given by an engineer last night—
A dummy funnel built for ventilation."

"That's queer enough, but nothing so absurd
As the latest story two old ladies heard
At a rubber o' bridge. They nearly died with fright;
Wanted to tell the captain—of all things!
The others sneered a bit but just the same
It did the trick of breaking up the game.
A mummy from The Valley of the Kings
Was brought from Thebes to London. Excavators
Passed out from cholera, black plague or worse.
Egyptians understood—an ancient curse
Was visited on all the violators.
One fellow was run over, one was drowned,
And one went crazy. When in time it found
Its way to the Museum, the last man
In charge—a mothy Aberdonian—
Exploding the whole legend with a laugh,
Lost all his humour when the skeleton

Appeared within the family photograph,
And leered down from a corner just like one
Of his uncles."
                    "Holy Hades!"

                                        "The B.M.
Authorities themselves were scared and sold
It to New York. That's how the tale is told."
"The joke is on the Yanks."
                                "No, not on them,
Nor on The Valley of the Kings. What's rummy
About it is—we're carrying the mummy."

7.30 P.M. AT A TABLE IN THE DINING SALOON

Green Turtle!
                    Potage Romanoff!
                                        "White Star
Is out this time to press Cunarders close,
Got them on tonnage—fifty thousand gross.
Preferred has never paid a dividend.
The common's down to five—one hundred par.
The double ribbon—size and speed—would send
Them soaring."

                    "Speed is not in her design,
But comfort and security. The Line
Had never advertised it—'twould be mania
To smash the record of the 'Mauretania'."
Sherry!
            "The rumour's out."
                                        "There's nothing in it."
"Bet you she docks on Tuesday night."
                                        "I'll take it."
"She's hitting twenty-two this very minute."
"That's four behind—She hasn't a chance to make it."
Brook Trout!
                    Fried Dover Sole!
                                        "Her rate will climb
From twenty-two to twenty-six in time.
The Company's known never to rush their ships
At first or try to rip the bed-bolts off.
They run them gently half-a-dozen trips,

A few work-outs around the track to let
Them find their breathing, take the boiler cough
Out of them. She's not racing for a cup."
Claret!
        "Steamships like sprinters have to get
Their second wind before they open up."

"That group of men around the captain's table,
Look at them, count the aggregate—the House
Of Astor, Guggenheim, and Harris, Straus,
That's Frohman, isn't it? Between them able
To halve the national debt with a cool billion!
Sir Hugh is over there, and Hays and Stead.
That woman third from captain's right, it's said,
Those diamonds round her neck—a quarter million!"
Mignon of Beef!
        Quail!
            "I heard Phillips say
He had the finest outfit on the sea;
The new Marconi valve; the range by day,
Five hundred miles, by night a thousand. Three
Sources of power. If some crash below
Should hit the engines, flood the dynamo,
He had the batteries: in emergency,
He could switch through to the auxiliary
On the boat deck."
        Woodcock and Burgundy!
"Say waiter, I said RARE, you understand."
Escallope of Veal!
        Roast Duckling!
            Snipe! More Rhine!
"Marconi made the sea as safe as land:
Remember the 'Republic'—White Star Line—
Rammed off Nantucket by the 'Florida',
One thousand saved—the 'Baltic' heard the call.
Two steamers answered the 'Slavonia',
Disabled off the Azores. They got them all,
And when the 'Minnehaha' ran aground
Near Bishop's Rock, they never would have found
Her—not a chance without the wireless. Same
Thing happened to that boat—what was her name?
The one that foundered off the Alaska Coast—

Her signals brought a steamer in the nick
Of time. Yes, sir—Marconi turned the trick."

The Barcelona salad; *no,* Beaucaire;
That Russian dressing;

Avocado pear;

"They wound her up at the Southampton dock,
And then the tugs gave her a push to start
Her off—as automatic as a clock."

Moselle!

   "For all the hand work there's to do
Aboard this liner up on deck, the crew
Might just as well have stopped ashore. Apart
From stokers and the engineers, she's run
By gadgets from the bridge—a thousand and one
Of them with a hundred miles of copper wire.
A filament glows at the first sign of fire,
A buzzer sounds, a number gives the spot,
A deck-hand makes a coupling of the hose.
That's all there's to it; not a whistle; not
A passenger upon the ship that knows
What's happened. The whole thing is done without
So much as calling up the fire brigade.
They don't need even the pumps—a gas is sprayed,
Carbon dioxide—and the blaze is out."

A Cherry Flan!

   Champagne!

Chocolate parfait!

"How about a poker crowd to-night?
Get Jones, an awful grouch—no good to play,
But has the coin. Get hold of Larry."

"Right."

"You fetch Van Raalte: I'll bring in MacRae.
In Cabin D, one hundred seventy-nine.
In half-an-hour we start playing."

"Fine."

ON DECK

The sky was moonless but the sea flung back
With greater brilliance half the zodiac.

THE TITANIC

As clear below as clear above, the Lion
Far on the eastern quarter stalked the Bear:
Polaris off the starboard beam—and there
Upon the port the Dog-star trailed Orion.
Capella was so close, a hand might seize
The sapphire with the silver Pleiades.
And further to the south—a finger span,
Swam Betelgeuse and red Aldebaran.
Right through from east to west the ocean glassed
The billions of that snowy caravan
Ranging the highway which the Milkmaid passed.

9.05 P.M.

"CALIFORNIAN" FLASHING

I say, old man, we're stuck fast in this place,
More than an hour. Field ice for miles about.

"TITANIC"

Say, 'Californian', shut up, keep out,
You're jamming all my signals with Cape Race.

10 P.M.

A group of boys had gathered round a spot
Upon the rail where a dial registered
The speed, and waiting each three minutes heard
The taffrail log bell tallying off a knot.

11.20 P.M.

BEHIND A DECK HOUSE

First act to fifth act in a tragic plan,
Stage time, real time—a woman and a man,
Entering a play within a play, dismiss
The pageant on the ocean with a kiss.
Eleven-twenty curtain! Whether true

224

Or false the pantomimic vows they make
Will not be known till at the *fifth* they take
Their mutual exit twenty after two.

11.25 P.M.

Position half-a-mile from edge of floe,
Hove-to for many hours, bored with delay,
The *Californian* fifteen miles away,
And fearful of the pack, has now begun
To turn her engines over under slow
Bell, and the operator, his task done,
Unclamps the 'phones and ends his dullest day.

The ocean sinuous, half-past eleven;
A silence broken only by the seven
Bells and the look-out calls, the log-book showing
Knots forty-five within two hours—not quite
The expected best as yet—but she was going
With all her bulkheads open through the night,
For not a bridge induction light was glowing.
Over the stern zenith and nadir met
In the wash of the reciprocating set.
The foam in bevelled mirrors multiplied
And shattered constellations. In between,
The pitch from the main drive of the turbine
Emerged like tuna breaches to divide
Against the rudder, only to unite
With the converging wake from either side.
Under the counter, blending with the spill
Of stars—the white and blue—the yellow light
Of Jupiter hung like a daffodil.

D-179

"Ace full! A long time since I had a pot."

*"Good boy, Van Raalte. That's the juiciest haul
To-night. Calls for a round of roodles, what?
Let's whoop her up. Double the limit. All
In."* (Jones, heard muttering as usual,
Demurs, but over-ruled.) *"Jones sore again."*

VAN RAALTE (DEALER)
"Ten dollars and all in!
                    The sea's like glass
To-night. That fin-keel keeps her steady."

JONES: *"Pass."*
(Not looking at his hand.)

LARRY: *"Pass."*

CRIPPS: *"Open for ten."*
(Holding a pair of aces.) *"Say, who won*
The sweep to-day?"
                    "A Minnesota guy
With olive-coloured spats and a mauve tie.
Five hundred and eighty miles—Beat last day's run."

MAC: *"My ten."*

HARRY: (Taking a gamble on his four
Spades for a flush) *"I'll raise the bet ten more."*

VAN R.: (Two queens) "AND *ten."*

JONES: (Discovering three kings)
"Raise you to forty" (face expressing doubt.)

LARRY: (Looking hard at a pair of nines) *"I'm out."*

CRIPPS: (Flirts for a moment with his aces, flings
His thirty dollars to the pot.)

MAC: (The same.)

HARRY: *"My twenty. Might as well stay with the game."*

VAN R.: *"I'm in. Draw! Jones, how bloody long you wait."*

JONES: (Withholds an eight) *"One."* (And then draws an eight.)

CRIPPS: *"Three."* (Gets another pair.)
                    "How many, Mac?"

MAC: *"Guess I'll take two, no, three."* (Gets a third Jack.)

HARRY: *"One."* (Draws the ace of spades.)

VAN R.:   *"Dealer takes three."*

CRIPPS (THE OPENER): (Throws in a dollar chip.)

MAC: (The same.)

HARRY: *"I'll raise
You ten."*

VAN R.:   *"I'll see you."*

JONES: (Hesitates, surveys
The chips.) *"Another ten."*

CRIPPS: *"I'll call you."*

MAC: *"See."*

HARRY: *"White livers! Here she goes to thirty."*

VAN R.:   *"Just
The devil's luck."* (Throws cards down in disgust.)

JONES:
"Might as well raise." (Counts twenty sluggishly,
Tosses them to the centre.)
                    "Staying, Cripps?"

CRIPPS: *"No, and be damned to it."*

MAC: *"My ten."* (With groans.)

HARRY:
(Looks at the pyramid and swears at Jones,
Then calls, pitching ten dollars on the chips.)

JONES:
(Cards down.) *"A full house tops the flush."* (He spreads
His arms around the whites and blues and reds.)

MAC:
*"As the Scotchman once said to the Sphinx,
I'd like just to know what he thinks,
I'll ask him, he cried,
And the Sphinx—he replied,
It's the hell of a time between drinks."*

CRIPPS (WATCH IN HAND):
"Time? Eleven forty-four, to be precise."

227

HARRY:
*"Jones—that will fatten up your pocket-book.
My throat's like charcoal. Ring for soda and ice."*

VAN R.:
"Ice: God! Look—take it through the port-hole—look!"

11.45 P.M.

A signal from the crow's nest. Three bells pealed:
The look-out telephoned—*Something ahead,
Hard to make out, sir; looks like . . . . iceberg dead
On starboard bow!*

MURDOCH HOLDING THE BRIDGE-WATCH

     Starboard your helm: ship heeled
To port. From bridge to engine-room the clang
Of the telegraph. *Danger. Stop.* A hand sprang
To the throttle; the valves closed, and with the churn
Of the reverse the sea boiled at the stern.
Smith hurried to the bridge and Murdoch closed
The bulkheads of the ship as he supposed,
But could not know that with those riven floors
The electro-magnets failed upon the doors.
No shock! No more than if something alive
Had brushed her as she passed. The bow had missed.
Under the vast momentum of her drive
She went a mile. But why that ominous five
Degrees (within five minutes) of a list?

IN A CABIN:
"What was that, steward?"
     "Seems like she hit a sea, sir."
*"But there's no sea; calm as a landlocked bay
It is; lost a propeller blade?"*
      "Maybe, sir."
"She's stopped."
     *"Just cautious like, feeling her way,
There's ice about. It's dark, no moon to-night,
Nothing to fear, I'm sure, sir."*

228

                              For so slight
The answer of the helm, it did not break
The sleep of hundreds: some who were awake
Went up on deck, but soon were satisfied
That nothing in the shape of wind or tide
Or rock or ice could harm that huge bulk spread
On the Atlantic, and went back to bed.

CAPTAIN IN WIRELESS ROOM:
"We've struck an iceberg—glancing blow: as yet
Don't know extent; looks serious; so get
Ready to send out general call for aid;
I'll tell you when—having inspection made."

REPORT OF SHIP'S CARPENTER AND FOURTH OFFICER:
A starboard cut three hundred feet or more
From foremast to amidships. Iceberg tore
Right at the bilge turn through the double skin:
Some boiler rooms and bunkers driven in;
The forward five compartments flooded—mail
Bags floating. Would the engine power avail
To stem the rush?

WIRELESS ROOM, FIRST OFFICER PHILLIPS AT KEY:
                              Titanic, C.Q.D.
Collision: iceberg: damaged starboard side:
Distinct list forward. (Had Smith magnified
The danger? Over-anxious certainly.)
The second (joking)—*"Try new call, maybe*
Last chance you'll have to send it."
                                          S.O.S.
Then back to older signal of distress.

On the same instant the *Carpathia* called,
The distance sixty miles—*Putting about,*
And heading for you; Double watch installed
In engine-room, in stokehold and look-out.
Four hours the run, should not the ice retard
The speed; but taking chances: Coming hard!

THE BRIDGE

As leaning on her side to ease a pain,
The tilted ship had stopped the captain's breath:

229

The inconceivable had stabbed his brain,
This thing unfelt—her visceral wound of death?
Another message—this time to report her
Filling, taxing the pumps beyond their strain.
Had that blow rent her from the bow to quarter?
Or would the aft compartments still intact
Give buoyancy enough to counteract
The open forward holds?
                                    The carpenter's
Second report had offered little chance,
And panic—heart of God—the passengers,
The fourteen hundred—seven hundred packed
In steerage—seven hundred immigrants!
Smith thought of panic clutching at their throats,
And feared that Balkan scramble for the boats.

No call from bridge, no whistle, no alarm
Was sounded. Have the stewards quietly
Inform the passengers: no vital harm,
Precautions merely for emergency;
Collision? Yes, but nature of the blow
Must not be told: not even the crew must know:
Yet all on deck with lifebelts, and boats ready,
The sailors at the falls, and all hands steady.

WIRELESS ROOM

The lilac spark was crackling at the gap,
Eight ships within the radius of the call
From fifteen to five hundred miles, and all
But one answering the operator's tap.
Olympic twenty hours away had heard;
The *Baltic* next and the *Virginian* third;
Frankfurt and *Burma* distant one-half day;
Mount Temple nearer, but the ice-field lay
Between the two ships like a wall of stone;
The *Californian* deaf to signals though
Supreme deliverer an hour ago:
The hope was on *Carpathia* alone.

So suave the fool-proof sense of life that fear
Had like the unforeseen become a mere
Illusion—vanquished by the towering height
Of funnels pouring smoke through thirty feet
Of bore; the solid deck planks and the light
From a thousand lamps as on a city street;
The feel of numbers; the security
Of wealth; the placid surface of the sea,
Reflecting on the ship the outwardness
Of calm and leisure of the passengers;
Deck-hands obedient to their officers;
Pearl-throated women in their evening dress
And wrapped in sables and minks; the silhouettes
Of men in dinner jackets staging an act
In which delusion passed, deriding fact
Behind the cupped flare of the cigarettes.

Women and children first! Slowly the men
Stepped backward from the rails where number ten,
Its cover off, and lifted from the chocks,
Moved outward as the Welin davits swung.
The new ropes creaking through the unused blocks,
The boat was lowered to B deck and hung
There while her load of sixty stepped inside,
Convinced the order was not justified.

Rockets, one, two, God! Smith—what does he mean?
The sounding of the bilges could not show
This reason for alarm—the sky serene
And not a ripple on the water—no
Collision. What report came from below?
No leak accounts for this—looks like a drill,
A bit of exhibition play—but still
Stopped in mid-ocean! and those rockets—*three!*
More urgent even than a tapping key
And more immediate as a protocol
To a disaster. *There!* An arrow of fire,
A fourth sped towards the sky, its bursting spire
Topping the foremast like a parasol
With fringe of fuchsia,—more a parody

Upon the tragic summons of the sea
Than the real script of unacknowledged fears
Known to the bridge and to the engineers.

Midnight! The Master of the ship presents
To the Master of the Band his compliments,
Desiring that the Band should play right through;
No intermission.

CONDUCTOR: *"Bad?"*

OFFICER: *"Yes, bad enough,*
The half not known yet even to the crew;
For God's sake, cut the sentimental stuff,
The BLUE BELLS *and Kentucky lullabies.*
Murdoch will have a barrel of work to do,
Holding the steerage back, once they get wise;
They're jumpy now under the rockets' glare;
So put the ginger in the fiddles—Zip
Her up."

CONDUCTOR: *"Sure, number forty-seven:"*   E-Yip
I Addy-I-A, I Ay . . . I don't care . . .

NUMBER TEN GOES OVER THE SIDE

Full noon and midnight by a weird design
Both met and parted at the median line.
Beyond the starboard gunwale was outspread
The jet expanse of water islanded
By fragments of the berg which struck the blow.
And further off towards the horizon lay
The loom of the uncharted parent floe,
Merging the black with an amorphous grey.
On the port gunwale the meridian
Shone from the terraced rows of decks that ran
From gudgeon to the stem nine hundred feet;
And as the boat now tilted by the stern,
Or now resumed her levels with the turn
Of the controlling ropes at block and cleat,
How easy seemed the step and how secure
Back to the comfort and the warmth—the lure

Of sheltered promenade and sun decks starred
By hanging bulbs, amber and rose and blue,
The trellis and palms lining an avenue
With all the vista of a boulevard:
The mirror of the ceilings with festoon
Of pennants, flags and streamers—and now through
The leaded windows of the grand saloon,
Through parted curtains and the open doors
Of vestibules, glint of deserted floors
And tables, and under the sorcery
Of light excelling their facsimile,
The periods returning to relume
The panels of the lounge and smoking-room,
Holding the mind in its abandonment
During those sixty seconds of descent.
Lower away! The boat with its four tons
Of freight went down with jerks and stops and runs
Beyond the glare of the cabins and below
The slanting parallels of port-holes, clear
Of the exhaust from the condenser flow:
But with the uneven falls she canted near
The water line; the stern rose; the bow dipped;
The crew groped for the link-releasing gear;
The lever jammed; a stoker's jack-knife ripped
The aft ropes through, which on the instant brought her
With rocking keel though safe upon the water.

THE "CARPATHIA"

Fifteen, sixteen, seventeen, eighteen—three
Full knots beyond her running limit, she
Was feeling out her port and starboard points,
And testing rivets on her boiler joints.
The needle on the gauge beyond the red,
The blow-offs feathered at the funnel head.
The draught-fans roaring at their loudest, now
The quartermaster jams the helm hard-over,
As the revolving searchlight beams uncover
The columns of an iceberg on the bow,
Then compensates this loss by daring gains
Made by her passage through the open lanes.

233

THE BAND

East side, West side, all around the town,
The tots sang "Ring-a-Rosie"
"London Bridge is falling down",
Boys and girls together . . . .

The cranks turn and the sixth and seventh swing
Over and down, the "tiller" answering
"Aye, Aye, sir" to the shouts of officers—
"Row to the cargo ports for passengers."
The water line is reached, but the ports fail
To open, and the crews of the boats hail
The decks; receiving no response they pull
Away from the ship's side, less than half full.
The eighth caught in the tackle foul is stuck
Half-way. With sixty-five capacity,
Yet holding twenty-four, goes number three.

The sharp unnatural deflection, struck
By the sea-level with the under row
Of dipping port-holes at the forward, show
How much she's going by the head. Behind
The bulkheads, sapping out their steel control,
Is the warp of the bunker press inclined
By many thousand tons of shifting coal.

The smoothest, safest passage to the sea
Is made by number one—the next to go—
Her space is forty—twelve her company:
"Pull like the devil from her—harder—row!
The minute that she founders, not a boat
Within a mile around that will not follow.
What nearly happened at Southampton? So
Pull, pull, I tell you—not a chip afloat,
God knows how far, her suction will not swallow."

Alexander's rag-time band. . . .
It's the best band in the land. . . .

VOICES FROM THE DECK:
"There goes the Special with the toffs. You'll make
New York to-night rowing like that. You'll take

Your death o' cold out there with all the fish
And ice around."
                    "Make sure your butlers dish
You up your toddies now, and bring hot rolls
For breakfast."
                    "Don't forget the finger bowls."

The engineering staff of thirty-five
Are at their stations: those off-duty go
Of their free will to join their mates below
In the grim fight for steam, more steam, to drive
The pressure through the pumps and dynamo.
Knee-deep, waist-deep in water they remain,
Not one of them seen on the decks again.
The under braces of the rudder showing,
The wing propeller blades began to rise,
And with them, through the hawse-holes, water flowing—
The angle could not but assault the eyes.
A fifteen minutes, and the fo'c'sle head
Was under. And five more, the sea had shut
The lower entrance to the stairs that led
From C deck to the boat deck—the short cut
For the crew. Another five, the upward flow
Had covered the wall brackets where the glow
Diffusing from the frosted bulbs turned green
Uncannily through their translucent screen.

ON THE "CARPATHIA"

White Star—Cunarder, forty miles apart,
Still eighteen knots! From coal to flame to steam—
Decision of a captain to redeem
Errors of brain by hazards of the heart!
Showers of sparks danced through the funnel smoke,
The firemen's shovels, rakes and slice-bars broke
The clinkers, fed the fires, and ceaselessly
The hoppers dumped the ashes on the sea.

As yet no panic, but none might foretell
The moment when the sight of that oblique
Breath-taking lift of the taffrail and the sleek
And foamless undulation of the swell
Might break in meaning on those diverse races,

235

And give them common language. As the throng
Came to the upper decks and moved along
The incline, the contagion struck the faces
With every lowering of a boat and backed
Them towards the stern. And twice between the hush
Of fear and utterance the gamut cracked,
When with the call for women and the flare
Of an exploding rocket, a short rush
Was made for the boats—fifteen and two.
'Twas nearly done—the sudden clutch and tear
Of canvas, a flurry of fists and curses met
By swift decisive action from the crew,
Supported by a quartermaster's threat
Of three revolver shots fired on the air.

But still the fifteenth went with five inside,
Who, seeking out the shadows, climbed aboard
And, lying prone and still, managed to hide
Under the thwarts long after she was lowered.

Jingle bells, jingle bells,
Jingle all the way,
O what fun. . . .

"*Some men in number two, sir!*"
                                          The boat swung
Back.
              "*Chuck the fellows out.*"
                                          Grabbed by the feet,
The lot were pulled over the gunwale and flung
Upon the deck.
                    "*Hard at that forward cleat!*
A hand there for that after fall. Lower
Away—port side, the second hatch, and wait."

With six hands of his watch, the bosun's mate,
Sent down to open up the gangway door,
Was trapped and lost in a flooded alley way,
And like the seventh, impatient of delay,
The second left with room for twenty more.

The fiddley leading from a boiler room
Lay like a tortuous exit from a tomb.

A stoker climbed it, feeling by the twist
From vertical how steep must be the list.
He reached the main deck where the cold night airs
Enswathed his flesh with steam. Taking the stairs,
He heard the babel by the davits, faced
The forward, noticed how the waters raced
To the break of the fo'c'sle and lapped
The foremast root. He climbed again and saw
The resolute manner in which Murdoch's rapped
Command put a herd instinct under law;
No life-preserver on, he stealthily
Watched Phillips in his room, bent at the key,
And thinking him alone, he sprang to tear
The jacket off. He leaped too soon. *"Take that!"*
The second stove him with a wrench. *"Lie there,*
Till hell begins to singe your lids—you rat!"

But set against those scenes where order failed,
Was the fine muster at the fourteenth where,
Like a zone of calm along a thoroughfare,
The discipline of sea-worn laws prevailed.
No women answering the repeated calls,
The men filled up the vacant seats: the falls
Were slipping through the sailors' hands,
When a steerage group of women, having fought
Their way over five flights of stairs, were brought
Bewildered to the rails. Without commands
Barked from the lips of officers; without
A protest registered in voice or face,
The boat was drawn up and the men stepped out
Back to the crowded stations with that free
Barter of life for life done with the grace
And air of a Castilian courtesy.

I've just got here through Paris,
From the sunny Southern shore,
I to Monte Carlo went. . . .

ISIDOR AND IDA STRAUS

At the sixteenth—a woman wrapped her coat
Around her maid and placed her in the boat;
Was ordered in but seen to hesitate

237

At the gunwale, and more conscious of her pride
Than of her danger swiftly took her fate
With open hands, and without show of tears
Returned unmurmuring to her husband's side;
"We've been together now for forty years,
Whither you go, I go."

                 A boy of ten,
Ranking himself within the class of men,
Though given a seat, made up his mind to waive
The privilege of his youth and size, and piled
The inches on his stature as he gave
Place to a Magyar woman and her child.

And men who had in the world's run of trade,
Or in pursuit of the professions, made
Their reputation, looked upon the scene
Merely as drama in a life's routine:
Millet was studying eyes as he would draw them
Upon a canvas; Butt, as though he saw them
In the ranks; Astor, social, debonair,
Waved *"Good-bye"* to his bride—*"See you to-morrow"*,
And tapped a cigarette on a silver case;
Men came to Guggenheim as he stood there
In evening suit, coming this time to borrow
Nothing but courage from his calm, cool face.

And others unobserved, of unknown name
And race, just stood behind, pressing no claim
Upon priority but rendering proof
Of their oblation, quiet and aloof
Within the maelstrom towards the rails. And some
Wavered a moment with the panic urge,
But rallied to attention on the verge
Of flight as if the rattle of a drum
From quarters faint but unmistakable
Had put the stiffening in the blood to check
The impulse of the feet, leaving the will
No choice between the lifeboats and the deck.

The four collapsibles, their lashings ripped,
Half-dragged, half-lifted by the hooks, were slipped

Over the side. The first two luckily
Had but the forward distance to the sea.
Its canvas edges crumpled up, the third
Began to fill with water and transferred
Its cargo to the twelfth, while number four,
Abaft and higher, nose-dived and swamped its score.

The wireless cabin—Phillips in his place,
Guessing the knots of the Cunarder's race.
Water was swirling up the slanted floor
Around the chair and sucking at his feet.
Carpathia's call—the last one heard complete—
Expect to reach position half-past four.
The operators turned—Smith at the door
With drawn incredulous face. *"Men, you have done
Your duty. I release you. Everyone
Now for himself."* They stayed ten minutes yet,
The power growing fainter with each blue
Crackle of flame. Another stammering jet—
Virginian heard "a tattering C.Q.".
Again a try for contact but the code's
Last jest had died between the electrodes.

Even yet the spell was on the ship: although
The last lifeboat had vanished, there was no
Besieging of the heavens with a crescendo
Of fears passing through terror into riot—
But on all lips the strange narcotic quiet
Of an unruffled ocean's innuendo.
In spite of her deformity of line,
Emergent like a crag out of the sea,
She had the semblance of stability,
Moment by moment furnishing no sign,
So far as visible, of that decline
Made up of inches crawling into feet.
Then, with the electric circuit still complete,
The miracle of day displacing night
Had worked its fascination to beguile
Direction of the hours and cheat the sight.
Inside the recreation rooms the gold
From Arab lamps shone on the burnished tile.
What hindered the return to shelter while
The ship clothed in that irony of light
Offered her berths and cabins as a fold?

239

And, was there not the *Californian?*
Many had seen her smoke just over there,
But two hours past—it seemed a harbour span—
So big, so close, she could be hailed, they said;
She must have heard the signals, seen the flare
Of those white stars and changed at once her course.
There under the *Titanic's* foremast head,
A lamp from the look-out cage was flashing Morse.
No ship afloat unless deaf, blind and dumb
To those three sets of signals but would come.
And when the whiz of a rocket bade men turn
Their faces to each other in concern
At shattering facts upon the deck, they found
Their hearts take reassurance with the sound
Of the violins from the gymnasium, where
The bandsmen in their blithe insouciance
Discharged the sudden tension of the air
With the fox-trot's sublime irrelevance.

The fo'c'sle had gone under the creep
Of the water. Though without a wind, a lop
Was forming on the wells now fathoms deep.
The seventy feet—the boat deck's normal drop—
Was down to ten. Rising, falling, and waiting,
Rising again, the swell that edged and curled
Around the second bridge, over the top
Of the air-shafts, backed, resurged and whirled
Into the stokehold through the fiddley grating.

Under the final strain the two wire guys
Of the forward funnel tugged and broke at the eyes:
With buckled plates the stack leaned, fell and smashed
The starboard wing of the flying bridge, went through
The lower, then tilting at the davits crashed
Over, driving a wave aboard that drew
Back to the sea some fifty sailors and
The captain with the last of the bridge command.

Out on the water was the same display
Of fear and self-control as on the deck—
Challenge and hesitation and delay,
The quick return, the will to save, the race

Of snapping oars to put the realm of space
Between the half-filled lifeboats and the wreck.
The swimmers whom the waters did not take
With their instant death-chill struck out for the wake
Of the nearer boats, gained on them, hailed
The steersmen and were saved: the weaker failed
And fagged and sank. A man clutched at the rim
Of a gunwale, and a woman's jewelled fist
Struck at his face: two others seized his wrist,
As he released his hold, and gathering him
Over the side, they staunched the cut from the ring.
And there were many deeds envisaging
Volitions where self-preservation fought
Its red primordial struggle with the "ought",
In those high moments when the gambler tossed
Upon the chance and uncomplaining lost.

Aboard the ship, whatever hope of dawn
Gleamed from the *Carpathia*'s riding lights was gone,
For every knot was matched by each degree
Of list. The stern was lifted bodily
When the bow had sunk three hundred feet, and set
Against the horizon stars in silhouette
Were the blade curves of the screws, hump of the rudder.
The downward pull and after buoyancy
Held her a minute poised but for a shudder
That caught her frame as with the upward stroke
Of the sea a boiler or a bulkhead broke.

Climbing the ladders, gripping shroud and stay,
Storm-rail, ringbolt or fairlead, every place
That might befriend the clutch of hand or brace
Of foot, the fourteen hundred made their way
To the heights of the aft decks, crowding the inches
Around the docking bridge and cargo winches.
And now that last salt tonic which had kept
The valour of the heart alive—the bows
Of the immortal seven that had swept
The strings to outplay, outdie their orders, ceased.
Five minutes more, the angle had increased
From eighty on to ninety when the rows
Of deck and port-hole lights went out, flashed back
A brilliant second and again went black.
Another bulkhead crashed, then following

The passage of the engines as they tore
From their foundations, taking everything
Clean through the bows from 'midships with a roar
Which drowned all cries upon the deck and shook
The watchers in the boats, the liner took
Her thousand fathoms journey to her grave.

*   *   *   *   *

And out there in the starlight, with no trace
Upon it of its deed but the last wave
From the *Titanic* fretting at its base,
Silent, composed, ringed by its icy broods,
The grey shape with the palaeolithic face
Was still the master of the longitudes.

BRÉBEUF AND HIS BRETHREN

(1940)

To my father

I   The winds of God were blowing over France,
Kindling the hearths and altars, changing vows
Of rote into an alphabet of flame.
The air was charged with song beyond the range
Of larks, with wings beyond the stretch of eagles.
Skylines unknown to maps broke from the mists
And there was laughter on the seas. With sound
Of bugles from the Roman catacombs,
The saints came back in their incarnate forms.
Across the Alps St. Francis of Assisi
In his brown tunic girt with hempen cord,
Revisited the plague-infected towns.
The monks were summoned from their monasteries,
Nuns from their convents; apostolic hands
Had touched the priests; foundlings and galley slaves
Became the charges of Vincent de Paul;
Francis de Sales put his heroic stamp
Upon his order of the Visitation.
Out of Numidia by way of Rome,
The architect of palaces, unbuilt
Of hand, again was busy with his plans,
Reshaping for the world his *City of God.*
Out of the Netherlands was heard the call
Of Kempis through the *Imitatio*
To leave the dusty marts and city streets
And stray along the shores of Galilee.
The flame had spread across the Pyrenees—
The visions of Theresa burning through
The adorations of the Carmelites;
The very clouds at night to John of the Cross
Being cruciform—chancel, transept and aisle
Blazing with light and holy oracle.
Xavier had risen from his knees to drive
His dreams full-sail under an ocean compass.
Loyola, soldier-priest, staggering with wounds
At Pampeluna, guided by a voice,
Had travelled to the Montserrata Abbey
To leave his sword and dagger on an altar
That he might lead the *Company of Jesus.*

The story of the frontier like a saga
Sang through the cells and cloisters of the nation,
Made silver flutes out of the parish spires,
Troubled the ashes of the canonized
In the cathedral crypts, soared through the nave
To stir the foliations on the columns,
Roll through the belfries, and give deeper tongue
To the *Magnificat* in Notre Dame.
It brought to earth the prophets and apostles
Out of their static shrines in the stained glass.
It caught the ear of Christ, reveined his hands
And feet, bidding his marble saints to leave
Their pedestals for chartless seas and coasts
And the vast blunders of the forest glooms.
So, in the footsteps of their patrons came
A group of men asking the hardest tasks
At the new outposts of the Huron bounds
Held in the stern hand of the Jesuit Order.

And in Bayeux a neophyte while rapt
In contemplation saw a bleeding form
Falling beneath the instrument of death,
Rising under the quickening of the thongs,
Stumbling along the Via Dolorosa.
No play upon the fancy was this scene,
But the Real Presence to the naked sense.
The fingers of Brébeuf were at his breast,
Closing and tightening on a crucifix,
While voices spoke aloud unto his ear
And to his heart—*per ignem et per aquam.*
Forests and streams and trails thronged through his mind,
The painted faces of the Iroquois,
Nomadic bands and smoking bivouacs
Along the shores of western inland seas,
With forts and palisades and fiery stakes.
The stories of Champlain, Brulé, Viel,
Sagard and Le Caron had reached his town—
The stories of those northern boundaries
Where in the winter the white pines could brush
The Pleiades, and at the equinoxes
Under the gold and green of the auroras
Wild geese drove wedges through the zodiac.
The vows were deep he laid upon his soul.

"I shall be broken first before I break them."
He knew by heart the manual that had stirred
The world—the clarion calling through the notes
Of the Ignatian preludes. On the prayers,
The meditations, points and colloquies,
Was built the soldier and the martyr programme.
This is the end of man—*Deum laudet,*
To seek and find the will of God, to act
Upon it for the ordering of life,
And for the soul's beatitude. This is
To do, this not to do. To weigh the sin;
The interior understanding to be followed
By the amendment of the deed through grace;
The abnegation of the evil thought
And act; the trampling of the body under;
The daily practice of the *counter virtues.*
"In time of desolation to be firm
And constant in the soul's determination,
Desire and sense obedient to the reason."

The oath Brébeuf was taking had its root
Firm in his generations of descent.
The family name was known to chivalry—
In the Crusades; at Hastings; through the blood
Of the English Howards; called out on the rungs
Of the siege ladders; at the castle breaches;
Proclaimed by heralds at the lists, and heard
In Council Halls:—the coat-of-arms a bull
In black with horns of gold on a silver shield.
So on that toughened pedigree of fibre
Were strung the pledges. From the novice stage
To the vow-day he passed on to the priesthood,
And on the anniversary of his birth
He celebrated his first mass at Rouen.

April 26, 1625

And the first clauses of the Jesuit pledge
Were honoured when, embarking at Dieppe,
Brébeuf, Massé and Charles Lalemant
Travelled three thousand miles of the Atlantic,

And reached the citadel in seven weeks.
A month in preparation at Notre Dame
Des Anges, Brébeuf in company with Daillon
Moved to Three Rivers to begin the journey.
Taking both warning and advice from traders,
They packed into their stores of altar-ware
And vestments, strings of coloured beads with knives,
Kettles and awls, domestic gifts to win
The Hurons' favour or appease their wrath.
There was a touch of omen in the warning,
For scarcely had they started when the fate
Of the Franciscan mission was disclosed—
News of Viel, delivered to Brébeuf,—
Drowned by the natives in the final league
Of his return at Sault-au-Récollet!

Back to Quebec by Lalemant's command;
A year's delay of which Brébeuf made use
By hardening his body and his will,
Learning the rudiments of the Huron tongue,
Mastering the wood-lore, joining in the hunt
For food, observing habits of speech, the ways
Of thought, the moods and the long silences.
Wintering with the Algonquins, he soon knew
The life that was before him in the cabins—
The troubled night, branches of fir covering
The floor of snow; the martyrdom of smoke
That hourly drove his nostrils to the ground
To breathe, or offered him the choice of death
Outside by frost, inside by suffocation;
The forced companionship of dogs that ate
From the same platters, slept upon his legs
Or neck; the nausea from sagamite,
Unsalted, gritty, and that bloated feeling,
The February stomach touch when acorns,
Turk's cap, bog-onion bulbs dug from the snow
And bulrush roots flavoured with eel skin made
The menu for his breakfast-dinner-supper.
Added to this, the instigated taunts
Common as daily salutations; threats
Of murderous intent that just escaped
The deed—the prologue to Huronia!

July, 1626

Midsummer and the try again—Brébeuf,
Daillon, de Nouë just arrived from France;
Quebec up to Three Rivers; the routine
Repeated; bargaining with the Indians,
Axes and beads against the maize and passage;
The natives' protest when they saw Brébeuf,
High as a totem-pole. What if he placed
His foot upon the gunwale, suddenly
Shifted an ounce of those two hundred pounds
Off centre at the rapids! They had visions
Of bodies and bales gyrating round the rocks,
Plunging like stumps and logs over the falls.
The Hurons shook their heads: the bidding grew;
Kettles and porcelain necklaces and knives,
Till with the last awl thrown upon the heap,
The ratifying grunt came from the chief.
Two Indians holding the canoe, Brébeuf,
Barefooted, cassock pulled up to his knees,
Planted one foot dead in the middle, then
The other, then slowly and ticklishly
Adjusted to the physics of his range
And width, he grasped both sides of the canoe,
Lowered himself and softly murmuring
An *Ave*, sat, immobile as a statue.

So the flotilla started—the same route
Champlain and Le Caron eleven years
Before had taken to avoid the swarm
Of hostile Iroquois on the St. Lawrence.
Eight hundred miles—along the Ottawa
Through the steep gorges where the river narrowed,
Through calmer waters where the river widened,
Skirting the island of the Allumettes,
Thence to the Mattawa through lakes that led
To the blue waters of the Nipissing,
And then southward a hundred tortuous miles
Down the French River to the Huron shore.
The record of that trip was for Brébeuf
A memory several times to be re-lived;

Of rocks and cataracts and portages,
Of feet cut by the river stones, of mud
And stench, of boulders, logs and tangled growths,
Of summer heat that made him long for night,
And when he struck his bed of rock—mosquitoes
That made him doubt if dawn would ever break.
'Twas thirty days to the Georgian Bay, then south
One hundred miles threading the labyrinth
Of islands till he reached the western shore
That flanked the Bay of Penetanguishene.
Soon joined by both his fellow priests he followed
The course of a small stream and reached Toanché,
Where for three years he was to make his home
And turn the first sod of the Jesuit mission.

'Twas ploughing only—for eight years would pass
Before even the blades appeared. The priests
Knew well how barren was the task should signs,
Gestures and inarticulate sounds provide
The basis of the converse. And the speech
Was hard. De Noüe set himself to school,
Unfalteringly as to his Breviary,
Through the long evenings of the fall and winter.
But as light never trickled through a sentence,
Either the Hurons' or his own, he left
With the spring's expedition to Quebec,
Where intermittently for twenty years
He was to labour with the colonists,
Travelling between the outposts, and to die
Snow-blind, caught in the circles of his tracks
Between Three Rivers and Fort Richelieu.

Daillon migrated to the south and west
To the country of the Neutrals. There he spent
The winter, fruitless. Jealousies of trade
Awoke resentment, fostered calumnies,
Until the priest under a constant threat
That often issued in assault, returned
Against his own persuasion to Quebec.

Brébeuf was now alone. He bent his mind
To the great end. The efficacious rites
Were hinged as much on mental apprehensions
As on the disposition of the heart.

249

For that the first equipment was the speech.
He listened to the sounds and gave them letters,
Arranged their sequences, caught the inflections,
Extracted nouns from objects, verbs from actions
And regimented rebel moods and tenses.
He saw the way the chiefs harangued the clans,
The torrent of compounded words, the art
Concealed within the pause, the look, the gesture.
Lacking all labials, the open mouth
Performed a double service with the vowels
Directed like a battery at the hearers.
With what forebodings did he watch the spell
Cast on the sick by the Arendiwans:
The sorcery of the Huron rhetoric
Extorting bribes for cures, for guarantees
Against the failure of the crop or hunt!
The time would come when steel would clash on steel,
And many a battle would be won or lost
With weapons from the armoury of words.
Three years of that apprenticeship had won
The praise of his Superior and no less
Evoked the admiration of Champlain.
That soldier, statesman, navigator, friend,
Who had combined the brain of Richelieu
With the red blood of Cartier and Magellan,
Was at this time reduced to his last keg
Of powder at the citadel. Blockade,
The piracy of Kirke on the Atlantic,
The English occupation of Quebec,
And famine, closed this chapter of the Mission.

1629

II   Four years at home could not abate his zeal.
Brébeuf, absorbed within his meditations,
Made ready to complete his early vows.
Each year in France but served to clarify
His vision. At Rouen he gauged the height
Of the Cathedral's central tower in terms
Of pines and oaks around the Indian lodges.
He went to Paris. There as worshipper,

His eyes were scaling transepts, but his mind,
Straying from window patterns where the sun
Shed rose ellipses on the marble floor,
Rested on glassless walls of cedar bark.
To Rennes—the Jesuits' intellectual home,
Where, in the *Summa* of Aquinas, faith
Laid hold on God's existence when the last
Link of the Reason slipped, and where Loyola
Enforced the high authoritarian scheme
Of God's vicegerent on the priestly fold.
Between the two nostalgic fires Brébeuf
Was swung—between two homes; in one was peace
Within the holy court, the ecstasy
Of unmolested prayer before the Virgin,
The daily and vicarious offering
On which no hand might dare lay sacrilege:
But in the other would be broken altars
And broken bodies of both Host and priest.
Then of which home, the son? From which the exile?
With his own blood Brébeuf wrote his last vow—
"Lord Jesus! Thou didst save me with thy blood;
By thy most precious death; and this is why
I make this pledge to serve thee all my life
In the Society of Jesus—never
To serve another than thyself. Hereby
I sign this promise in my blood, ready
To sacrifice it all as willingly
As now I give this drop."—Jean de Brébeuf.

Nor did the clamour of the *Thirty Years*,
The battle-cries at La Rochelle and Fribourg,
Blow out the flame. Less strident than the names
Of Richelieu and Mazarin, Condé,
Turenne, but just as mighty, were the calls
Of the new apostolate. A century
Before had Xavier from the Indies summoned
The world to other colours. Now appeals
Were ringing through the history of New France.
Le Jeune, following the example of Biard
And Charles Lalemant, was capturing souls
By thousands with the fire of the *Relations*:
Noble and peasant, layman, priest and nun
Gave of their wealth and power and personal life.

251

Among his new recruits were Chastellain,
Pijart, Le Mercier, and Isaac Jogues,
The Lalemants—Jerome and Gabriel—
Jerome who was to supervise and write,
With Ragueneau, the drama of the Mission;
Who told of the survivors reaching France
When the great act was closed that *"all of them
Still hold their resolution to return
To the combat at the first sound of the trumpets."*
The other, Gabriel, who would share the crown
With Jean Brébeuf, pitting the frailest body
Against the hungers of the wilderness,
The fevers of the lodges and the fires
That slowly wreathed themselves around a stake.

Then Garnier, comrade of Jogues. The winds
Had fanned to a white heat the hearth and placed
Three brothers under vows—the Carmelite,
The Capuchin, and his, the Jesuit.
The gentlest of his stock, he had resolved
To seek and to accept a post that would
Transmit his nurture through a discipline
That multiplied the living martyrdoms
Before the casual incident of death.

To many a vow did Chabanel subject
His timid nature as the evidence
Of trial came through the Huronian records.
He needed every safeguard of the soul
To fortify the will, for every day
Would find him fighting, mastering his revolt
Against the native life and practices.
Of all the priests he could the least endure
The sudden transformation from the Chair
Of College Rhetoric to the heat and drag
Of portages, from the monastic calm
To the noise and smoke and vermin of the lodges,
And the insufferable sights and stinks
When, at the High Feast of the Dead, the bodies
Lying for months or years upon the scaffolds
Were taken down, stripped of their flesh, caressed,
Strung up along the cabin poles and then

Cast in a pit for common burial.
The day would come when in the wilderness,
The weary hand protesting, he would write
This final pledge—"*I, Noel Chabanel,*
Do vow, in presence of the Sacrament
Of Thy most precious blood and body, here
To stay forever with the Huron Mission,
According to commands of my Superiors.
Therefore I do beseech Thee to receive me
As Thy perpetual servant and to make
Me worthy of so sublime a ministry."

And the same spirit breathed on Chaumonot,
Making his restless and undisciplined soul
At first seek channels of renunciation
In abstinence, ill health and beggary.
His months of pilgrimages to the shrines
At Rome and to the Lady of Loretto,
The static hours upon his knees had sapped
His strength, turning an introspective mind
Upon the weary circuit of its thoughts,
Until one day a letter from Brébeuf
Would come to burn the torpors of his heart
And galvanize a raw novitiate.

1633

III   New France restored! Champlain, Massé, Brébeuf
Were in Quebec, hopes riding high as ever.
Davost and Daniel soon arrived to join
The expedition west. Midsummer trade,
The busiest the Colony had known,
Was over: forty-three canoes to meet
The hazards of return; the basic sense
Of safety, now Champlain was on the scene;
The joy of the Toanché Indians
As they beheld Brébeuf and heard him speak
In their own tongue, was happy augury.
But as before upon the eve of starting
The path was blocked, so now the unforeseen
Stepped in. A trade and tribal feud long-blown
Between the Hurons and the Allumettes
Came to a head when the Algonquin chief

253

Forbade the passage of the priests between
His island and the shore. The Hurons knew
The roughness of this channel, and complied.

In such delays which might have been construed
By lesser wills as exits of escape,
As providential doors on a light latch,
The Fathers entered deeper preparation.
They worked incessantly among the tribes
In the environs of Quebec, took hold
Of Huron words and beat them into order.
Davost and Daniel gathered from the store
Of speech, manners, and customs that Brébeuf
Had garnered, all the subtleties to make
The bargain for the journey. The next year
Seven canoes instead of forty! Fear
Of Iroquois following a recent raid
And massacre; growing distrust of priests;
The sense of risk in having men aboard
Unskilled in fire-arms, helpless at the paddles
And on the portages—all these combined
To sharpen the terms until the treasury
Was dry of presents and of promises.

1634

The ardours of his trip eight years before
Fresh in his mind, Brébeuf now set his face
To graver peril, for the native mood
Was hostile. On the second week the corn
Was low, a handful each a day. Sickness
Had struck the Huron, slowing down the blades,
And turning murmurs into menaces
Against the Blackrobes and their French companions.
The first blow hit Davost. Robbed of his books,
Papers and altar linens, he was left
At the Island of the Allumettes; Martin*
Was put ashore at Nipissing; Baron*
And Daniel were deserted, made to take

*French assistants.

Their chances with canoes along the route,
Yet all in turn, tattered, wasted, with feet
Bleeding—broken though not in will, rejoined
Their great companion after he had reached
The forest shores of the Fresh Water Sea,
And guided by the sight of smoke had entered
The village of Ihonatiria.

A year's success flattered the priestly hope
That on this central field seed would be sown
On which the yield would be the Huron nation
Baptized and dedicated to the Faith;
And that a richer harvest would be gleaned
Of duskier grain from the same seed on more
Forbidding ground when the arch-foes themselves
Would be re-born under the sacred rites.
For there was promise in the auspices.
Ihonatiria received Brébeuf
With joy. Three years he had been there, a friend
Whose visit to the tribes could not have sprung
From inspiration rooted in private gain.
He had not come to stack the arquebuses
Against the mountains of the beaver pelts.
He had not come to kill. Between the two—
Barter and battle—what was left to explain
A stranger in their midst? The name *Echon**
Had solved the riddle.

                              So with native help
The Fathers built their mission house—the frame
Of young elm-poles set solidly in earth;
Their supple tops bent, lashed and braced to form
The arched roof overlaid with cedar-bark.
"No Louvre or palace is this cabin," wrote
Brébeuf, *"no stories, cellar, garret, windows,*
No chimney—only at the top a hole
To let the smoke escape. Inside, three rooms
With doors of wood alone set it apart
From the single long-house of the Indians.
The first is used for storage; in the second
Our kitchen, bedroom and refectory;
Our bedstead is the earth; rushes and boughs

*Echon—he who pulls the heavy load.

For mattresses and pillows; in the third,
Which is our chapel, we have placed the altar,
The images and vessels of the Mass."
It was the middle room that drew the natives,
Day after day, to share the sagamite
And raisins, and to see the marvels brought
From France—marvels on which the Fathers built
A basis of persuasion, recognizing
The potency of awe for natures nurtured
On charms and spells, invoking kindly spirits
And exorcising demons. So the natives
Beheld a mass of iron chips like bees
Swarm to a lodestone: was it gum that held
Them fast? They watched the handmill grind the corn;
Gaped at a lens eleven-faceted
That multiplied a bead as many times,
And at a phial where a captive flea
Looked like a beetle. But the miracle
Of all, the clock! It showed the hours; it struck
Or stopped upon command. *Le Capitaine*
Du Jour which moved its hands before its face,
Called up the dawn, saluted noon, rang out
The sunset, summoned with the count of twelve
The Fathers to a meal, or sent at four
The noisy pack of Indians to their cabins.
"What did it say?" "Yo eiouahaoua—
Time to put on the cauldron." "And what now?"
"Time to go home at once and close the door."
It was alive: an *oki* dwelt inside,
Peering out through that black hub on the dial.

As great a mystery was writing—how
A Frenchman fifteen miles away could know
The meaning of black signs the runner brought.
Sometimes the marks were made on peel of bark,
Sometimes on paper—in itself a wonder!
From what strange tree was it the inside rind?
What charm was in the ink that transferred thought
Across such space without a spoken word?

This growing confirmation of belief
Was speeded by events wherein good fortune
Waited upon the priestly word and act.

Aug. 27, 1635

A moon eclipse was due—Brébeuf had known it—
Had told the Indians of the moment when
The shadow would be thrown across the face.
Nor was there wastage in the prayers as night,
Uncurtained by a single cloud, produced
An orb most perfect. No one knew the lair
Or nest from which the shadow came; no one
The home to which it travelled when it passed.
Only the vague uncertainties were left—
Was it the dread invasion from the south?
Such portent was the signal for the braves
To mass themselves outside the towns and shoot
Their multitudes of arrows at the sky
And fling their curses at the Iroquois.
Like a crow's wing it hovered, broodily
Brushing the face—five hours from rim to rim
While midnight darkness stood upon the land.
This was prediction baffling all their magic.
Again, when weeks of drought had parched the land
And burned the corn, when dancing sorcerers
Brought out their tortoise shells, climbed on the roofs,
Clanging their invocation to the Bird
Of Thunder to return, day after day,
Without avail, the priests formed their processions,
Put on their surplices above their robes,
And the Bird of Thunder came with heavy rain,
Released by the nine masses at Saint Joseph.

Nor were the village warriors slow to see
The value of the Frenchmen's strategy
In war. Returning from the eastern towns,
They told how soldiers had rebuilt the forts,
And strengthened them with corner bastions
Where through the embrasures enfilading fire
Might flank the Iroquois bridging the ditches,
And scaling ramparts. Here was argument
That pierced the thickest prejudice of brain

257

And heart, allaying panic ever present,
When with the first news of the hated foe
From scouts and hunters, women with their young
Fled to the dubious refuge of the forest
From terror blacker than a pestilence.
On such a soil tilled by those skilful hands
Those passion flowers and lilies of the East,
The *Aves* and the *Paternosters* bloomed.
The *Credos* and the *Thou-shalt-nots* were turned
By Daniel into simple Huron rhymes
And taught to children, and when points of faith
Were driven hard against resistant rock,
The Fathers found the softer crevices
Through deeds which readily the Indian mind
Could grasp—where hands were never put to blows
Nor the swift tongues used for recrimination.

Acceptance of the common lot was part
Of the original vows. But that the priests
Who were to come should not misread the text,
Brébeuf prepared a sermon on the theme
Of Patience:—*"Fathers, Brothers, under call
Of God! Take care that you foresee the perils,
Labours and hardships of this Holy Mission.
You must sincerely love the savages
As brothers ransomed by the blood of Christ.
All things must be endured. To win their hearts
You must perform the smallest services.
Provide a tinder-box or burning mirror
To light their fires. Fetch wood and water for them;
And when embarking never let them wait
For you; tuck up your habits, keep them dry
To avoid water and sand in their canoes. Carry
Your load on portages. Always appear
Cheerful—their memories are good for faults.
Constrain yourselves to eat their sagamite
The way that they prepare it, tasteless, dirty."*

And by the priests upon the ground all dots
And commas were observed. They suffered smoke
That billowed from the back-draughts at the roof,

Smothered the cabin, seared the eyes; the fire
That broiled the face, while frost congealed the spine;
The food from unwashed platters where refusal
Was an offence; the rasp of speech maintained
All day by men who never learned to talk
In quiet tones; the drums of the Diviners
Blasting the night—all this without complaint!
And more—whatever sleep was possible
To snatch from the occasional lull of cries
Was broken by uncovenanted fleas
That fastened on the priestly flesh like hornets.
Carving the curves of favour on the lips,
Tailoring the man into the Jesuit coat,
Wrapping the smiles round inward maledictions,
And sublimating hoary Gallic oaths
Into the *Benedicite* when dogs
And squaws and reeking children violated
The hours of rest, were penances unnamed
Within the iron code of good Ignatius.
Was there a limit of obedience
Outside the jurisdiction of this Saint?
How often did the hand go up to lower
The flag? How often by some ringing order
Was it arrested at the halliard touch?
How often did Brébeuf seal up his ears
When blows and insults woke ancestral fifes
Within his brain, blood-cells, and viscera,
Is not explicit in the written story.

But never could the Indians infer
Self-gain or anything but simple courage
Inspired by a zeal beyond reproof,
As when the smallpox spreading like a flame
Destroying hundreds, scarifying thousands,
The Fathers took their chances of contagion,
Their broad hats warped by rain, their moccasins
Worn to the kibes, that they might reach the huts,
Share with the sick their dwindled stock of food—
A sup of partridge broth or raisin juice,
Inscribe the sacred sign of the cross, and place
A touch of moisture from the Holy Water
Upon the forehead of a dying child.

259

Before the year was gone the priests were shown
The way the Hurons could prepare for death
A captive foe. The warriors had surprised
A band of Iroquois and had reserved
The one survivor for a fiery pageant.
No cunning of an ancient Roman triumph,
Nor torment of a Medici confession
Surpassed the subtle savagery of art
Which made the dressing for the sacrifice
A ritual of mockery for the victim.
What visions of the past came to Brébeuf,
And what forebodings of the days to come,
As he beheld this weird compound of life
In jest and intent taking place before
His eyes—the crude unconscious variants
Of reed and sceptre, robe and cross, brier
And crown! Might not one day baptismal drops
Be turned against him in a rain of death?
Whatever the appeals made by the priests,
They could not break the immemorial usage
Or vary one detail. The prisoner
Was made to sing his death-song, was embraced,
Hailed with ironic greetings, forced to state
His willingness to die.

"See how your hands
Are crushed. You cannot thus desire to live.

No.

Then be of good courage—you shall die.

True!—What shall be the manner of my death?

By fire.

When shall it be?

Tonight.

What hour?
At sunset.

All is well."

Eleven fires

Were lit along the whole length of the cabin.
His body smeared with pitch and bound with belts
Of bark, the Iroquois was forced to run
The fires, stopped at each end by the young braves,
And swiftly driven back, and when he swooned,
They carried him outside to the night air,
Laid him on fresh damp moss, poured cooling water
Into his mouth, and to his burns applied
The soothing balsams. With resuscitation
They lavished on him all the courtesies
Of speech and gesture, gave him food and drink,
Compassionately spoke of his wounds and pain.
The ordeal every hour was resumed
And halted, but, with each recurrence, blows
Were added to the burns and gibes gave place
To yells until the sacrificial dawn,
Lighting the scaffold, dimming the red glow
Of the hatchet collar, closed the festival.

Brébeuf had seen the worst. He knew that when
A winter pack of wolves brought down a stag
There was no waste of time between the leap
And the business click upon the jugular.
Such was the forthright honesty in death
Among the brutes. They had not learned the sport
Of dallying around the nerves to halt
A quick despatch. A human art was torture,
Where Reason crept into the veins, mixed tar
With blood and brewed its own intoxicant.
Brébeuf had pleaded for the captive's life,
But as the night wore on, would not his heart,
Colliding with his mind, have wished for death?
The plea refused, he gave the Iroquois
The only consolation in his power.
He went back to his cabin, heavy in heart.
To stem that viscous melanotic current
Demanded labour, time, and sacrifice.
Those passions were not altered over-night.
Two plans were in his mind—the one concerned
The seminary started in Quebec.
The children could be sent there to be trained
In Christian precepts, weaned from superstition
And from the savage spectacle of death.

261

He saw the way the women and their broods
Danced round the scaffold in their exaltation.
How much of this was habit and how much
Example? Curiously Brébeuf revolved
The facets of the Indian character.
A fighting courage equal to the French—
It could be lifted to crusading heights
By a battle speech. Endurance was a code
Among the braves, and impassivity.
Their women wailing at the Feast of Death,
The men sat silent, heads bowed to the knees.
"Never in nine years with but one exception,"
Wrote Ragueneau, *"did I see an Indian weep
For grief."* Only the fires evoked the cries,
And these like scalps were triumphs for the captors.
But then their charity and gentleness
To one another and to strangers gave
A balance to the picture. Fugitives
From villages destroyed found instant welcome
To the last communal share of food and land.
Brébeuf's stay at Toanché gave him proof
Of how the Huron nature could respond
To kindness. But last night upon that scaffold!
Could that be scoured from the heart? Why not
Try out the nurture plan upon the children
And send the boys east, shepherded by Daniel?

The other need was urgent—labourers!
The villages were numerous and were spread
Through such a vast expanse of wilderness
And shore. Only a bell with a bronze throat
Must summon missionaries to these fields.
With the last cry of the captive in his ears,
Brébeuf strode from his cabin to the woods
To be alone. He found his tabernacle
Within a grove, picked up a stone flat-faced,
And going to a cedar-crotch, he jammed
It in, and on this table wrote his letter.
*"Herein I show you what you have to suffer.
I shall say nothing of the voyage—that
You know already. If you have the courage*

To try it, that is only the beginning,
For when after a month of river travel
You reach our village, we can offer you
The shelter of a cabin lowlier
Than any hovel you have seen in France.
As tired as you may be, only a mat
Laid on the ground will be your bed. Your food
May be for weeks a gruel of crushed corn
That has the look and smell of mortar paste.
This country is the breeding place of vermin.
Sandflies, mosquitoes haunt the summer months.
In France you may have been a theologian,
A scholar, master, preacher, but out here
You must attend a savage school; for months
Will pass before you learn even to lisp
The language. Here barbarians shall be
Your Aristotle and Saint Thomas. Mute
Before those teachers you shall take your lessons.
What of the winter? Half the year is winter.
Inside your cabins will be smoke so thick
You may not read your Breviary for days.
Around your fireplace at mealtime arrive
The uninvited guests with whom you share
Your stint of food. And in the fall and winter,
You tramp unbeaten trails to reach the missions,
Carrying your luggage on your back. Your life
Hangs by a thread. Of all calamities
You are the cause—the scarcity of game,
A fire, famine or an epidemic.
There are no natural reasons for a drought
And for the earth's sterility. You are
The reasons, and at any time a savage
May burn your cabin down or split your head.
I tell you of the enemies that live
Among our Huron friends. I have not told
You of the Iroquois our constant foes.
Only a week ago in open fight
They killed twelve of our men at Contarea,
A day's march from the village where we live.
Treacherous and stealthy in their ambuscades,
They terrorize the country, for the Hurons
Are very slothful in defence, never
On guard and always seeking flight for safety.

"Wherein the gain, you ask, of this acceptance?
There is no gain but this—that what you suffer
Shall be of God: your loneliness in travel
Will be relieved by angels overhead;
Your silence will be sweet for you will learn
How to commune with God; rapids and rocks
Are easier than the steeps of Calvary.
There is a consolation in your hunger
And in abandonment upon the road,
For once there was a greater loneliness
And deeper hunger. As regards the soul
There are no dangers here, with means of grace
At every turn, for if we go outside
Our cabin, is not heaven over us?
No buildings block the clouds. We say our prayers
Freely before a noble oratory.
Here is the place to practise faith and hope
And charity where human art has brought
No comforts, where we strive to bring to God
A race so unlike men that we must live
Daily expecting murder at their hands,
Did we not open up the skies or close
Them at command, giving them sun or rain.
So if despite these trials you are ready
To share our labours, come; for you will find
A consolation in the cross that far outweighs
Its burdens. Though in many an hour your soul
Will echo—'Why hast Thou forsaken me?',
Yet evening will descend upon you when,
Your heart too full of holy exultation,
You call like Xavier—'Enough, O Lord!' "

This letter was to loom in history,
For like a bulletin it would be read
In France, and men whose bones were bound for dust
Would find that on those jagged characters
Their names would rise from their oblivion
To flame on an eternal Calendar.
Already to the field two young recruits
Had come—Pijart, Le Mercier; on their way
Were Chastellain with Garnier and Jogues
Followed by Ragueneau and Du Peron.

On many a night in lonely intervals,
The priest would wander to the pines and build
His oratory where celestial visions
Sustained his soul. As unto Paul and John
Of Patmos and the martyr multitude
The signs were given—voices from the clouds,
Forms that illumined darkness, stabbed despair,
Turned dungeons into temples and a brand
Of shame into the ultimate boast of time—
So to Brébeuf had Christ appeared and Mary.
One night at prayer he heard a voice command—
"Rise, Read!" Opening the *Imitatio Christi*,
His eyes *"without design"* fell on the chapter,
Concerning the royal way of the Holy Cross,
Which placed upon his spirit *"a great peace"*.
And then, day having come, he wrote his vow—
"My God, my Saviour, I take from thy hand
The cup of thy sufferings. I invoke thy name;
I vow never to fail thee in the grace
Of martyrdom, if by thy mercy, Thou
Dost offer it to me. I bind myself,
And when I have received the stroke of death,
I will accept it from thy gracious hand
With all pleasure and with joy in my heart;
To thee my blood, my body and my life."

IV The labourers were soon put to their tasks,—
The speech, the founding of new posts, the sick:
Ihonatiria, a phantom town,
Through plague and flight abandoned as a base,
The Fathers chose the site, Teanaostayé,
To be the second mission of St. Joseph.
But the prime hope was on Ossossané,
A central town of fifty cabins built
On the east shore of Nottawasaga Bay.
The native council had approved the plans.
The presence of the priests with their lay help
Would be defence against the Iroquois.
Under the supervision of Pijart
The place was fortified, ramparts were strengthened,
And towers of heavy posts set at the angles.
And in the following year the artisans
And labourers from Quebec with Du Peron,

Using broad-axe and whipsaw built a church,
The first one in the whole Huronian venture
To be of wood. Close to their lodge, the priests
Dug up the soil and harrowed it to plant
A mere handful of wheat from which they raised
A half a bushel for the altar bread.
From the wild grapes they made a cask of wine
For the Holy Sacrifice. But of all work
The hardest was instruction. It was easy
To strike the Huron sense with sound and colour—
The ringing of a bell; the litanies
And chants; the surplices worn on the cassocks;
The burnished ornaments around the altar;
The pageant of the ceremonial.
But to drive home the ethics taxed the brain
To the limit of its ingenuity.
Brébeuf had felt the need to vivify
His three main themes of God and Paradise
And Hell. The Indian mind had let the cold
Abstractions fall: the allegories failed
To quicken up the logic. Garnier
Proposed the colours for the homilies.
The closest student of the Huron mind,
He had observed the fears and prejudices
Haunting the shadows of their racial past;
Had seen the flaws in Brébeuf's *points*; had heard
The Indian comments on the moral law
And on the Christian scheme of Paradise.
Would Iroquois be there? Yes, if baptized.
Would there be hunting of the deer and beaver?
No. Then starvation. War? And Feasts? Tobacco?
No. Garnier saw disgust upon their faces,
And sent appeals to France for pictures—one
Only of souls in bliss: of *âmes damnées*
Many and various—the horned Satan,
His mastiff jaws champing the head of Judas;
The plummet fall of the unbaptized pursued
By demons with their fiery forks; the lick
Of flames upon a naked Saracen;
Dragons with scarlet tongues and writhing serpents
In ambush by the charcoal avenues

Just ready at the Judgment word to wreak
Vengeance upon the unregenerate.
The negative unapprehended forms
Of Heaven lost in the dim canvas oils
Gave way to glows from brazier pitch that lit
The visual affirmatives of Hell.

Despite the sorcerers who laid the blame
Upon the French for all their ills—the plague,
The drought, the Iroquois—the Fathers counted
Baptisms by the hundreds, infants, children
And aged at the point of death. Adults
In health were more intractable, but here
The spade had entered soil in the conversion
Of a Huron in full bloom and high in power
And counsel, Tsiouendaentaha
Whose Christian name—to aid the tongue—was Peter.
Being the first, he was the Rock on which
The priests would build their Church. He was baptized
With all the pomp transferable from France
Across four thousand miles combined with what
A sky and lake could offer, and a forest
Strung to the *aubade* of the orioles.
The wooden chapel was their Rheims Cathedral.
In stole and surplice Lalemant intoned—
"If therefore thou wilt enter into life,
Keep the commandments. Thou shalt love the Lord
Thy God with all thy heart, with all thy soul,
With all thy might, and thy neighbour as thyself."
With salt and water and the holy chrism,
And through the signs made on his breast and forehead
The Huron was exorcised, sanctified,
And made the temple of the Living God.

The holy rite was followed by the Mass
Before the motliest auditory known
In the annals of worship, Oblates from Quebec,
Blackrobes, mechanics, soldiers, labourers,
With almost half the village packed inside,
Or jammed with craning necks outside the door.
The warriors lean, lithe, and elemental,
"As naked as your hand"* but for a skin

*Lalemant's phrase.

Thrown loosely on their shoulders, with their **hair**
Erect, boar-brushed, matted, glued with the oil
Of sunflower larded thickly with bear's grease;
Papooses yowling on their mothers' backs,
The squatting hags, suspicion in their eyes,
Their nebulous minds relating in some way
The smoke and aromatics of the censer,
The candles, crucifix and Latin murmurs
With vapours, sounds and colours of the **Judgment.**

(THE FOUNDING OF FORT SAINTE MARIE)

1639

V The migrant habits of the Indians
With their desertion of the villages
Through pressure of attack or want of food
Called for a central site where undisturbed
The priests with their attendants might pursue
Their culture, gather strength from their **devotions,**
Map out the territory, plot the routes,
Collate their weekly notes and write their letters.
The roll was growing—priests and colonists,
Lay brothers offering services for life.
For on the ground or on their way to place
Themselves at the command of Lalemant,
Superior, were Claude Pijart, Poncet,
Le Moyne, Charles Raymbault, René Menard
And Joseph Chaumonot: as oblates came
Le Coq, Christophe Reynaut, Charles Boivin,
Couture and Jean Guérin. And so to house
Them all the Residence—Fort Sainte Marie!
Strategic as a base for trade or war
The site received the approval of Quebec,
Was ratified by Richelieu who saw
Commerce and exploration pushing west,
Fulfilling the long vision of Champlain—
"Greater New France beyond those inland seas."
The fort was built, two hundred feet by ninety,
Upon the right bank of the River Wye:
Its north and eastern sides of masonry,
Its south and west of double palisades,

And skirted by a moat, ran parallel
To stream and lake. Square bastions at the corners,
Watch-towers with magazines and sleeping posts,
Commanded forest edges and canoes
That furtively came up the Matchedash,
And on each bastion was placed a cross.
Inside, the Fathers built their dwelling house,
No longer the bark cabin with the smoke
Ill-trained to work its exit through the roof,
But plank and timber—at each end a chimney
Of lime and granite field-stone. Rude it was
But clean, capacious, full of twilight calm.
Across the south canal fed by the river,
Ringed by another palisade were buildings
Offering retreat to Indian fugitives
Whenever war and famine scourged the land.

The plans were supervised by Lalemant,
Assigning zones of work to every priest.
He made a census of the Huron nation;
Some thirty villages—twelve thousand persons.
Nor was this all: the horizon opened out
On larger fields. To south and west were spread
The unknown tribes—the Petuns and the Neutrals.

(THE MISSION TO THE PETUNS AND NEUTRALS)
1640-1641

VI In late November Jogues and Garnier
Set out on snow-obliterated trails
Towards the Blue Hills south of the Nottawasaga,
A thirty mile journey through a forest
Without a guide. They carried on their backs
A blanket with the burden of the altar.
All day confronting swamps with fallen logs,
Tangles of tamarack and juniper,
They made detours to avoid the deep ravines
And swollen creeks. Retreating and advancing,
Ever in hope their tread was towards the south,
Until, *"surprised by night in a fir grove"*,
They took an hour with flint and steel to nurse
A fire from twigs, birch rind and needles of pine;
And flinging down some branches on the snow,

269

They offered thanks to God, lay down and slept.
Morning—the packs reshouldered and the tramp
Resumed, the stumble over mouldering trunks
Of pine and oak, the hopeless search for trails,
Till after dusk with cassocks torn and *"nothing
To eat all day save each a morsel of bread"*,
They saw the smoke of the first Indian village.

And now began a labour which for faith
And triumph of the spirit over failure
Was unsurpassed in records of the mission.
Famine and pest had struck the Neutral tribes,
And fleeing squaws and children had invaded
The Petun villages for bread and refuge,
Inflicting on the cabins further pest
And further famine. When the priests arrived,
They found that their black cassocks had become
The symbols of the scourge. Children exclaimed—
"Disease and famine are outside." The women
Called to their young and fled to forest shelters,
Or hid them in the shadows of the cabins.
The men broke through a never-broken custom,
Denying the strangers right to food and rest.
Observing the two priests at prayer, the chief
Called out in *council voice—"What are these demons
Who take such unknown postures, what are they
But spells to make us die—to finish those
Disease had failed to kill inside our cabins?"*
Driven from town to town with all doors barred,
Pursued by storms of threats and flying hatchets,
The priests sought refuge through the forest darkness
Back to the palisades of Sainte Marie.

As bleak an outlook faced Brébeuf when he
And Chaumonot took their November tramp—
Five forest days—to the north shores of Erie,
Where the most savage of the tribes—the Neutrals—
Packed their twelve thousand into forty towns.
Evil report had reached the settlements
By faster routes, for when upon the eve
Of the new mission Chaumonot had stated
The purpose of the journey, Huron chiefs,

Convinced by their own sorcerers that Brébeuf
Had laid the epidemic on the land,
Resolved to make the Neutral leaders agents
Of their revenge: for it was on Brébeuf,
The chieftain of the robes, that hate was centred.
They had the reason why the drums had failed
The hunt, why moose and deer had left the forest,
And why the Manitou who sends the sun
And rain upon the corn, lures to the trap
The beaver, trains the arrow on the goose,
Had not responded to the chants and cries.
The magic of the "breathings" had not cured
The sick and dying. Was it not the prayers
To the new God which cast malignant spells?
The rosary against the amulet?
The Blackrobes with that water-rite performed
Upon the children—with that new sign
Of wood or iron held up before the eyes
Of the stricken? Did the Indian not behold
Death following hard upon the offered Host?
Was not *Echon* Brébeuf the evil one?
Still, all attempts to kill him were forestalled,
For awe and fear had mitigated fury:
His massive stature, courage never questioned,
His steady glance, the firmness of his voice,
And that strange nimbus of authority,
In some dim way related to their gods,
Had kept the bowstrings of the Hurons taut
At the arrow feathers, and the javelin poised
And hesitant. But now cunning might do
What fear forbade. A brace of Huron runners
Were sped to the Neutral country with rich bribes
To put the priests to death. And so Brébeuf
And his companion entered the first town
With famine in their cheeks only to find
Worse than the Petun greetings—corn refused,
Whispers of death and screams of panic, flight
From incarnated plague, and while the chiefs
In closest council on the Huron terms
Voted for life or death, the younger men
Outside drew nearer to the priests, cursed them,
Spat at them while convulsive hands were clutching
At hatchet helves, waiting impatiently

271

The issue of that strident rhetoric
Shaking the cabin bark. The council ended,
The feeling strong for death but ruled by fears,
For if those foreign spirits had the power
To spread the blight upon the land, what could
Their further vengeance not exact? Besides,
What lay behind those regimental colours
And those new drums reported from Quebec?
The older men had qualified the sentence—
The priests at once must leave the Neutral land,
All cabins to be barred against admission,
No food, no shelter, and return immediate.
Defying threats, the Fathers spent four months,
Four winter months, besieging half the towns
In their pursuit of souls, for days their food
Boiled lichens, ground-nuts, star-grass bulbs and roots
Of the wild columbine. Met at the doors
By screams and blows, they would betake themselves
To the evergreens for shelter over-night.
And often, when the body strength was sapped
By the day's toil and there were streaks of blood
Inside the moccasins, when the last lodge
Rejected them as lepers and the welts
Hung on their shoulders, then the Fathers sought
The balm that never failed. Under the stars,
Along an incandescent avenue
The visions trembled, tender, placid, pure,
More beautiful than the doorway of Rheims
And sweeter than the Galilean fields.
For what was hunger and the burn of wounds
In those assuaging, healing moments when
The clearing mists revealed the face of Mary
And the lips of Jesus breathing benedictions?

At dawn they came back to the huts to get
The same rebuff of speech and club. A brave
Repulsed them at the palisade with axe
Uplifted—"*I have had enough,*" he said,
"*Of the dark flesh of my enemies. I mean
To kill and eat the white flesh of the priests.*"
So close to death starvation and assault

Had led them and so meagre of result
Were all their ministrations that they thought
This was the finish of the enterprise.
The winter ended in futility.
And on their journey home the Fathers took
A final blow when March leagued with the natives
Unleashed a northern storm, piled up the snow-drifts,
Broke on the ice the shoulder of Brébeuf,
And stumbled them for weeks before she sent
Them limping through the postern of the fort.
Upon his bed that night Brébeuf related
A vision he had seen—a moving cross,
Its upright beam arising from the south—
The country of the Iroquois: the shape
Advanced along the sky until its arms
Cast shadows on the Huron territory,
"And huge enough to crucify us all".

(THE STORY OF JOGUES)

VII   Bad days had fallen on Huronia.
A blight of harvest, followed by a winter
In which unusual snowfall had thinned out
The hunting and reduced the settlements
To destitution, struck its hardest blow
At Sainte Marie. The last recourse in need,
The fort had been a common granary
And now the bins were empty. Altar-ware,
Vessels, linens, pictures lost or damaged;
Vestments were ragged, writing paper spent.
The Eucharist requiring bread and wine,
Quebec eight hundred miles away, a war
Freshly renewed—the Iroquois (Dutch-armed
And seething with the memories of Champlain)
Arrayed against the French and Huron allies.

1642

The priests assessed the perils of the journey,
And the lot fell on Jogues to lead it. He,
Next to Brébeuf, had borne the heaviest brunt—
The Petun mission, then the following year,

273

The Ojibway where, after a hundred leagues,
Canoe and trail, accompanied by Raymbault,
He reached the shores of Lake Superior,
"And planted a great cross, facing it west".
The soundest of them all in legs, he gathered
A band of Huron traders and set out,
His task made double by the care of Raymbault
Whose health was broken mortally. He reached
Quebec with every day of the five weeks
A miracle of escape. A few days there,
With churches, hospitals, the Indian school
At Sillery, pageant and ritual,
Making their due impression on the minds
Of the Huron guides, Jogues with his band of forty
Packed the canoes and started back. Mohawks,
Enraged that on the east-bound trip the party
Had slipped their hands, awaited them, ambushed
Within the grass and reeds along the shore.

(THE ACCOUNT OF JOGUES' CAPTURE AND ENSLAVEMENT BY THE
MOHAWKS AS TAKEN FROM HIS LETTER TO HIS PROVINCIAL, JEAN
FILLEAU, DATED AUGUST 5, 1643.)

"Unskilled in speech, in knowledge and not knowing
The precious hour of my visitation,
I beg you, if this letter chance to come
Unto your hands that in your charity
You aid me with your Holy Sacrifices
And with the earnest prayers of the whole Province,
As being among a people barbarous
In birth and manners, for I know that when
You will have heard this story you will see
The obligation under which I am
To God and my deep need of spiritual help.
Our business finished at Quebec, the feast
Of Saint Ignatius celebrated, we
Embarked for the Hurons. On the second day
Our men discovered on the shore fresh tracks
Thought by Eustache, experienced in war,
To be the footprints of our enemies.
A mile beyond we met them, twelve canoes

And seventy men. Abandoning the boats,
Most of the Hurons fled to a thick wood,
Leaving but twelve to put up the best front
We could, but seeing further Iroquois
Paddling so swiftly from the other shore,
We ceased from our defence and fled to cover
Of tree and bulrush. Watching from my shelter
The capture of Goupil and Indian converts,
I could not find it in my mind to leave them;
But as I was their comrade on the journey,
And should be made their comrade in the perils,
I gave myself as prisoner to the guard.
Likewise Eustache, always devoted, valiant,
Returned, exclaiming 'I praise God that He
Has granted me my prayer—that I should live
And die with you.' And then Guillaume Couture
Who, young and fleet, having outstripped his foe,
But finding flight intolerable came back
Of his free will, saying 'I cannot leave
My father in the hands of enemies.'
On him the Iroquois let loose their first
Assault for in the skirmish he had slain
A chief. They stripped him naked; with their teeth
They macerated his finger tips, tore off
The nails and pierced his right hand with a spear,
Couture taking the pain without a cry.
Then turning on Goupil and me they beat
Us to the ground under a flurry of fists
And knotted clubs, dragging us up half-dead
To agonize us with the finger torture.
And this was just the foretaste of our trials:
Dividing up as spoils of war our food,
Our clothes and books and vessels for the church,
They led or drove us on our six weeks' journey,
Our wounds festering under the summer sun.
At night we were the objects of their sport—
They mocked us by the plucking of our hair
From head and beard. And on the eighth day meeting
A band of warriors from the tribe on march
To attack the Richelieu fort, they celebrated
By disembarking all the captives, making
Us run the line beneath a rain of clubs.
And following that they placed us on the scaffolds,

Dancing around us hurling jests and insults.
Each one of us attempted to sustain
The other in his courage by no cry
Or sign of our infirmities. Eustache,
His thumbs wrenched off, withstood unconquerably
The probing of a stick which like a skewer
Beginning with the freshness of a wound
On the left hand was pushed up to the elbow.
And yet next day they put us on the route
Again—three days on foot and without food.
Through village after village we were led
In triumph with our backs shedding the skin
Under the sun—by day upon the scaffolds,
By night brought to the cabins where, cord-bound,
We lay on the bare earth while fiery coals
Were thrown upon our bodies. A long time
Indeed and cruelly have the wicked wrought
Upon my back with sticks and iron rods.
But though at times when left alone I wept,
Yet I thanked Him who always giveth strength
To the weary (I will glory in the things
Concerning my infirmity, being made
A spectacle to God and to the angels,
A sport and a contempt to the barbarians)
That I was thus permitted to console
And animate the French and Huron converts,
Placing before their minds the thought of Him
Who bore against Himself the contradiction
Of sinners. Weak through hanging by my wrists
Between two poles, my feet not touching ground,
I managed through His help to reach the stage,
And with the dew from leaves of Turkish corn
Two of the prisoners I baptized. I called
To them that in their torment they should fix
Their eyes on me as I bestowed the sign
Of the last absolution. With the spirit
Of Christ, Eustache then in the fire entreated
His Huron friends to let no thought of vengeance
Arising from this anguish at the stake
Injure the French hope for an Iroquois peace.
Onnonhoaraton, a youthful captive,

They killed—the one who seeing me prepared
For torture interposed, offering himself
A sacrifice for me who had in bonds
Begotten him for Christ. Couture was seized
And dragged off as a slave. René Goupil,
While placing on a child's forehead the sign
Of the Cross was murdered by a sorcerer,
And then, a rope tied to his neck, was dragged
Through the whole village and flung in the River."

(THE LATER ACCOUNT)

A family of the Wolf Clan having lost
A son in battle, Jogues as substitute
Was taken in, half-son, half-slave, his work
The drudgery of the village, bearing water,
Lighting the fires, and clad in tatters made
To join the winter hunt, bear heavy packs
On scarred and naked shoulders in the trade
Between the villages. His readiness
To execute his tasks, unmurmuring,
His courage when he plunged into a river
To save a woman and a child who stumbled
Crossing a bridge made by a fallen tree,
Had softened for a time his master's harshness.
It gained him scattered hours of leisure when
He set his mind to work upon the language
To make concrete the articles of Faith.
At intervals he stole into the woods
To pray and meditate and carve the Name
Upon the bark. Out of the Mohawk spoils
At the first battle he had found and hid
Two books—*The Following of Christ* and one
Of Paul's *Epistles,* and with these when *"weary*
Even of life and pressed beyond all measure
Above his strength" he followed the *"running waters"*
To quench his thirst. But often would the hate
Of the Mohawk foes flame out anew when Jogues
Was on his knees muttering the magic words,
And when a hunting party empty-handed
Returned or some reverse was met in battle,
Here was the victim ready at their door.
Believing that a band of warriors

277

Had been destroyed, they seized the priest and set
His day of death, but at the eleventh hour,
With the arrival of a group of captives,
The larger festival of torture gave
Him momentary reprieve. Yet when he saw
The holocaust and rushed into the flames
To save a child, a heavy weight laid hold
Upon his spirit lasting many days—
"My life wasted with grief, my years with sighs;
Oh wherefore was I born that I should see
The ruin of my people! Woe is me!
But by His favour I shall overcome
Until my change is made and He appear."

This story of enslavement had been brought
To Montmagny, the Governor of Quebec,
And to the outpost of the Dutch, Fort Orange.
Quebec was far away and, short of men,
Could never cope with the massed Iroquois,
Besides, Jogues' letter begged the Governor
That no measures *"to save a single life"*
Should hurt the cause of France. To the Provincial
He wrote—*"Who in my absence would console*
The captives? Who absolve the penitent?
Encourage them in torments? Who baptize
The dying? On this cross to which our Lord
Has nailed me with Himself am I resolved
To live and die."
                         And when the commandant
Of the Dutch fort sent notice that a ship
At anchor in the Hudson would provide
Asylum, Jogues delayed that he might seek
Counsel of God and satisfy his conscience,
Lest some intruding self-preserving thought
Conflict with duty. Death was certain soon.
He knew it—for that mounting tide of hate
Could not be checked: it had engulfed his friends;
'Twould take him next. How close to suicide
Would be refusal? Not as if escape
Meant dereliction: no, his early vows
Were still inviolate—he would return.
He pledged himself to God there on his knees

Before two bark-strips fashioned as a cross
Under the forest trees—his oratory.
And so, one night, the Indians asleep,
Jogues left the house, fumbling his darkened way,
Half-walk, half-crawl, a lacerated leg
Making the journey of one-half a mile
The toil of half a night. By dawn he found
The shore, and, single-handed, pushed a boat,
Stranded by ebb-tide, down the slope of sand
To the river's edge and rowed out to the ship,
Where he was lifted up the side by sailors
Who, fearful of the risk of harbouring
A fugitive, carried him to the hatch
And hid him with the cargo in the hold.
The outcry in the morning could be heard
Aboard the ship as Indians combed the cabins,
Threatened the guards and scoured the neighbouring woods,
And then with strong suspicion of the vessel
Demanded of the officers their captive.
After two days Jogues with his own consent
Was taken to the fort and hid again
Behind the barrels of a store. For weeks
He saw and heard the Mohawks as they passed,
Examining cordage, prying into casks,
At times touching his clothes, but missing him
As he lay crouched in darkness motionless.
With evidence that he was in the fort,
The Dutch abetting the escape, the chiefs
Approached the commandant—"*The prisoner
Is ours. He is not of your race or speech.
The Dutch are friends: the Frenchmen are our foes.
Deliver up this priest into our hands.*"
The cries were countered by the officer—
"*He is like us in blood if not in tongue.
The Frenchman here is under our protection.
He is our guest. We treat him as you treat
The strangers in your cabins, for you feed
And shelter them. That also is our law,
The custom of our nation.*" Argument
Of no avail, a ransom price was offered,
Refused, but running up the bargain scale,
It caught the Mohawks at three hundred livres,
And Jogues at last was safely on the Hudson.

The tale of Jogues' first mission to the Hurons
Ends on a sequel briefly sung but keyed
To the tune of the story, for the stretch
Home was across a wilderness, his bed
A coil of rope on a ship's open deck
Swept by December surge. The voyage closed
At Falmouth where, robbed by a pirate gang,
He wandered destitute until picked up
By a French crew who offered him tramp fare.
He landed on the shore of Brittany
On Christmas Eve, and by New Year he reached
The Jesuit establishment at Rennes.

The trumpets blew once more, and Jogues returned
With the spring expedition to Quebec.
Honoured by Montmagny, he took the post
Of peace ambassador to hostile tribes,
And then the orders came from Lalemant
That he should open up again the cause
Among the Mohawks at Ossernenon.
Jogues knew that he was travelling to his death,
And though each hour of that former mission
Burned at his finger stumps, the wayward flesh
Obeyed the summons. Lalemant as well
Had known the peril—had he not re-named
Ossernenon, the Mission of the Martyrs?
So Jogues, accompanied by his friend Lalande
Departed for the village—his last letter
To his Superior read: *"I will return*
Cost it a thousand lives. I know full well
That I shall not survive, but He who helped
Me by His grace before will never fail me
Now when I go to do His holy will."
And to the final consonant the vow
Was kept, for two days after they had struck
The town, their heads were on the palisades,
And their dragged bodies flung into the Mohawk.

1646

VIII   The western missions waiting Jogues' return
Were held together by a scarlet thread.
The forays of the Iroquois had sent
The fugitive survivors to the fort.
Three years had passed—and where was Jogues? The scant
Supplies of sagamite could never feed
The inflow from the stricken villages.
The sparse reports had filtered to Quebec
And the command was given to Bressani
To lead the rescue band to Sainte Marie.
Leaving Three Rivers in the spring when ice
Was on the current, he was caught like Jogues,
With his six Hurons and a French oblate,
A boy of twelve; transferred to Iroquois'
Canoes and carried up the Richelieu;
Disbarked and driven through the forest trails
To Lake Champlain; across it; and from there
Around the rocks and marshes to the Hudson.
And every time a camp was built and fires
Were laid the torment was renewed; in all
The towns the squaws and children were regaled
With evening festivals upon the scaffolds.
Bressani wrote one day when vigilance
Relaxed and his split hand was partly healed—
"I do not know if your Paternity
Will recognize this writing for the letter
Is soiled. Only one finger of the hand
Is left unburned. The blood has stained the paper.
My writing table is the earth; the ink
Gunpowder mixed with water." And again—
This time to his Superior—*"I could*
Not have believed it to be possible
That a man's body was so hard to kill."
The earlier fate of Jogues was his—enslaved,
But ransomed at Fort Orange by the Dutch;
Restored to partial health; sent to Rochelle
In the autumn, but in April back again
And under orders for the Huron mission,
Where he arrived this time unscathed to take
A loyal welcome from his priestly comrades.

Bressani's presence stimulated faith
Within the souls of priests and neophytes.
The stories burned like fuel of the faggots—
Jogues' capture and his rock stability,
And the no less triumphant stand Eustache
Had made showing the world that native metal
Could take the test as nobly as the French.
And Ragueneau's letter to his General stated—
"Bressani ill-equipped to speak the Huron
Has speech more eloquent to capture souls:
It is his scars, his mutilated hands.
'Only show us,' the neophytes exclaim,
'The wounds, for they teach better than our tongues
Your faith, for you have come again to face
The dangers. Only thus we know that you
Believe the truth and would have us believe it.'"

IX   In those three years since Jogues' departure doubts
Though unexpressed had visited the mission.
For death had come to several in the fold—
Raymbault, Goupil, Eustache, and worse than death
To Jogues, and winter nights were bleaker, darker
Without the company of Brébeuf. Lion
Of limb and heart, he had entrenched the faith,
Was like a triple palisade himself.
But as his broken shoulder had not healed,
And ordered to Quebec by Lalemant,
He took the leave that seven years of work
Deserved. The city hailed him with delight.
For more than any other did he seem
The very incarnation of the age—
Champlain the symbol of exploring France,
Tracking the rivers to their lairs, Brébeuf
The token of a nobler chivalry.
He went the rounds of the stations, saw the gains
The East had made in converts—Sillery
For Indians and Notre Dame des Anges
For the French colonists; convents and schools
Flourished. Why should the West not have the same
Yield for the sowing? It was labourers
They needed with supplies and adequate

Defence. St. Lawrence and the Ottawa
Infested by the Iroquois were traps
Of death. Three bands of Hurons had been caught
That summer. Montmagny had warned the priest
Against the risk of unprotected journeys.
So when the reinforcements came from France,
Brébeuf set out under a guard of soldiers
Taking with him two young recruits—Garreau
And Chabanel—arriving at the fort
In the late fall. The soldiers wintered there
And supervised defensive strategy.
Replaced the forlorn feelings with fresh hopes,
And for two years the mission enterprise
Renewed its lease of life. Rumours of treaties
Between the French and Mohawks stirred belief
That peace was in the air, that other tribes
Inside the Iroquois Confederacy
Might enter—with the Hurons sharing terms.
This was the pipe-dream—was it credible?
The ranks of missionaries were filling up:
At Sainte Marie, Brébeuf and Ragueneau,
Le Mercier, Chastellain and Chabanel;
St. Joseph—Garnier and René Menard;
St. Michel—Chaumonot and Du Peron;
The others—Claude Pijart, Le Moyne, Garreau
And Daniel.
                    What validity the dream
Possessed was given by the seasonal
Uninterrupted visits of the priests
To their loved home, both fort and residence.
Here they discussed their plans, and added up
In smiling rivalry their tolls of converts:
They loitered at the shelves, fondled the books,
Running their fingers down the mellowed pages
As if they were the faces of their friends.
They stood for hours before the saints or knelt
Before the Virgin and the crucifix
In mute transfiguration. These were hours
That put the bandages upon their hurts,
Making their spirits proof against all ills
That had assailed or could assail the flesh,
Turned winter into spring and made return
To their far mission posts an exaltation.

The bell each morning called the neophytes
To Mass, again at evening, and the tones
Lured back the memories across the seas.
And often in the summer hours of twilight
When Norman chimes were ringing, would the priests
Forsake the fort and wander to the shore
To sing the *Gloria* while hermit thrushes
Rivalled the rapture of the nightingales.

The native register was rich in name
And number. Earlier years had shown results
Mainly among the young and sick and aged,
Where little proof was given of the root
Of faith, but now the Fathers told of deeds
That flowered from the stems. Had not Eustache
Bequeathed his record like a Testament?
The sturdiest warriors and chiefs had vied
Among themselves within the martyr ranks:—
Stories of captives led to sacrifice,
Accepting scaffold fires under the rites,
Enduring to the end, had taken grip
Of towns and clans. St. Joseph had its record
For Garnier reported that Totiri,
A native of high rank, while visiting
St. Ignace when a torture was in progress,
Had emulated Jogues by plunging through
The flaming torches that he might apply
The Holy Water to an Iroquois.
Garreau and Pijart added lists of names
From the Algonquins and the Nipissings,
And others told of Pentecostal meetings
In cabins by the Manitoulin shores.

Not only was the faith sustained by hopes
Nourished within the bosom of their home
And by the wish-engendered talk of peace,
But there outside the fort was evidence
Of tenure for the future. Acres rich
In soil extended to the forest fringe.
Each year they felled the trees and burned the stumps,
Pushing the frontier back, clearing the land,
Spading, hoeing. The stomach's noisy protest

At sagamite and wild rice found a rest
With bread from wheat, fresh cabbages and pease,
And squashes which when roasted had the taste
Of Norman apples. Strawberries in July,
October beechnuts, pepper roots for spice,
And at the bottom of a spring that flowed
Into a pond shaded by silver birches
And ringed by marigolds was water-cress
In chilled abundance. So, was this the West?
The Wilderness? That flight of tanagers;
Those linguals from the bobolinks; those beeches,
Roses and water-lilies; at the pools
Those bottle-gentians! For a time the fields
Could hypnotize the mind to scenes of France.
Within five years the change was wrought. The cocks
Were crowing in the yards, and in the pasture
Were sheep and cows and pigs that had been brought
As sucklings that immense eight hundred miles
In sacks—canoed, and portaged on the shoulders.
The traders, like the soldiers, too, had heard
Of a great ocean larger than the Huron.
Was it the western gateway to Cathay?
The Passage? Master-theme of song and ballad;
The *myth* at last resolved into the *fact*!
Along that route, it was believed, French craft
Freighted with jewels, spices, tapestries,
Would sail to swell the coffers of the Bourbons.
Such was the dream though only buffalo roamed
The West and autumn slept upon the prairies.

This dream was at its brightest now, Quebec
Was building up a western citadel
In Sainte Marie. With sixty Frenchmen there,
The eastern capital itself had known
Years less auspicious. Might the fort not be
The bastion to one-half the continent,
New France expanding till the longitudes
Staggered the daring of the navigators?
The priests were breathless with another space
Beyond the measure of the astrolabe—
A different empire built upon the pulses,
Where even the sun and moon and stars revolved
Around a Life and a redemptive Death.

285

They pushed their missions to the north and west
Further into Algonquin territories,
Among the Ottawas at Manitoulin,
And towards the Ojibways at Sault Sainte Marie.
New village groups were organized in stations—
St. Magdalen, St. Jean, and St. Matthias.
Had Chabanel, ecstatic with success,
Not named one fort the Village of Believers?
Brébeuf was writing to his General—
"Peace, union and tranquillity are here
Between the members of our Order. We need
More workers for the apostolic field,
Which more than ever whitens for the harvest."
And to this call came Gabriel Lalemant,
Bonin, Daran, Greslon, besides a score
Of labourers and soldiers. In one year
Twelve hundred converts, churches over-crowded,
With Mass conducted in the open air!

And so the seasons passed. When the wild ducks
Forsook the Huron marshes for the south,
It was the signal for the priests to pack
Their blankets. Not until the juncos came,
And flickers tapped the crevices of bark,
And the bloodroot was pushing through the leaf-mould,
Would they reset their faces towards their home.

X   While Ragueneau's *Relations* were being sent
Homeward, picturing the promise of the west,
The thunder clouds were massing in the east
Under the pounding drums. The treaty signed
Between the Iroquois and Montmagny
Was broken by the murder of Lalande
And Jogues. The news had drifted to the fort—
The prelude only to the heavier blows
And deeper treachery. The Iroquois,
Infesting lake and stream, forest and shore,
Were trapping soldiers, traders, Huron guides:
The whole confederacy was on the march.
Both waterways were blocked, the quicker route—
St. Lawrence, and the arduous Ottawa.

They caught the Hurons at their camps, surprised
Canoe-fleets from the reeds and river bends
And robbed them, killed them on the portages.
So widespread were their forays, they encountered
Bands of Algonquins on the hunt, slew them,
Dispersed them from their villages and sent
Survivors to the northern wilderness.
So keen their lust for slaughter, they enticed
The Huron chieftains under pledge of truce
And closed negotiations with their scalps.

As the months passed the pressure of attack
Moved grimly towards the west, making complete
The isolation of Huronia.
No commerce with Quebec—no traveller
For a whole year came to the Residence.
But constant was the stream of fugitives
From smaller undefended villages,
Fleeing west and ever west. The larger towns,
The deluge breaking down their walls, drove on
The surplus to their neighbours which, in turn,
Urged on the panic herd to Sainte Marie.
This mother of the missions felt the strain
As one by one the buffers were destroyed,
And the flocks came nearer for their pasturage.
There could be only one conclusion when
The priests saw the migration of the missions—
That of St. Jean four times abandoning
Its stations and four times establishing
New centres with a more improved defence;
That of St. Ignace where a double raid
That slaughtered hundreds, lifted bodily
Both town and mission, driving to their last
Refuge the ragged remnants. Yet Ragueneau
Was writing—*"We are here as yet intact
But all determined to shed blood and life
If need be. In this Residence still reigns
The peace and love of Heaven. Here the sick
Will find a hospital, the travellers
A place of rest, the fugitives, asylum.
During the year more than three thousand persons
Have sought and found shelter under our roof.
We have dispensed the Bread of Life to all*

And we have fed their bodies, though our fare
Is down to one food only, crushed corn boiled
And seasoned with the powder of smoked fish."

Despite the perils, Sainte Marie was sending
Her missionaries afield, revisiting
The older sites, establishing the new,
With that same measure of success and failure
Which tested courage or confirmed a faith.
Garreau, sick and expecting death, was brought
By Pijart and a French assistant back
From the Algonquin wastes, for thirteen days
Borne by a canoe and by his comrades' shoulders.
Recovering even after the last rites
Had been administered, he faced the task
Again. Fresh visits to the Petun tribes
Had little yield but cold and starving days,
Unsheltered nights, the same fare at the doors,
Savoured by Jogues and Garnier seven years
Before. And everywhere the labourers worked
Under a double threat—the Iroquois,
And the Huron curse inspired by sorcerers
Who saw black magic in the Jesuit robes
And linked disaster with their ritual.
Between the hammer and the anvil now
Huronia was laid and the first priest
To take the blow was Daniel.
                                                Fourteen years
This priest had laboured at the Huron mission.
Following a week of rest at Sainte Marie
He had returned to his last post, St. Joseph,
Where he had built his church and for the year
Just gone had added to his charge the hundreds
Swarming from villages stormed by the foe.
And now in that inexorable order,
Station by station, town by town, it was
St. Joseph's turn. Aware that the main force
Of Huron warriors had left the town,
The Iroquois had breached the palisade
And, overwhelming the defenders, sacked
And burned the cabins. Mass had just been offered,

When the war yells were heard and Daniel came
Outside. Seeing the panic, fully knowing
Extinction faced the town with this invasion,
And that ten precious minutes of delay
Might give his flock the refuge of the woods,
He faced the vanguard of the Iroquois,
And walked with firm selective dignity
As in the manner of a parley. Fear
And wonder checked the Indians at the sight
Of a single dark-robed, unarmed challenger
Against arrows, muskets, spears and tomahawks.
That momentary pause had saved the lives
Of hundreds as they fled into the forest,
But not the life of Daniel. Though afraid
At first to cross a charmed circumference
To take a struggle hand-to-hand, they drove
Their arrows through him, then in frenzied rush
Mastering their awe, they hurled themselves upon
The body, stripped it of its clothes and flung it
Into the burning church. By noon nothing
Remained but ashes of the town, the fort,
The cabins and their seven hundred dead.

July, 1648

XI   Ragueneau was distraught. He was shepherd-priest.
Daniel was first to die under his care,
And nigh a score of missionaries were lost
In unprotected towns. Besides, he knew
He could not, if he would, resist that mob
That clamoured at the stockades, day by day.
His moral supervision was bound up
With charity that fed and warmed and healed.
And through the winter following Daniel's death
Six thousand Indians sought shelter there.
The season's crops to the last grain were garnered
And shared. *"Through the kind Providence of God,*
We managed, as it were, to draw both oil
And honey from the very stones around us.
The obedience, patience of our missionaries
Excel reward—all with one heart and soul
Infused with the high spirit of our Order;
The servants, boys, and soldiers day and night

Working beyond their strength! Here is the service
Of joy, that we will take whatever God
Ordains for us whether it be life or death."
The challenge was accepted, for the spring
Opened upon the hardest tragic blows
The iron in the human soul could stand.

St. Louis and St. Ignace still remained
The flying buttresses of Sainte Marie.
From them the Residence received reports
Daily of movements of the Iroquois.
Much labour had been spent on their defence.
Ramparts of pine fifteen feet high enclosed
St. Louis. On three sides a steep ravine
Topped by the stakes made nigh impregnable
St. Ignace; then the palisaded fourth,
Subject alone to a surprise assault,
Could rally the main body of defenders.
The Iroquois, alert as eagles, knew
The weakness of the Hurons, the effect
On the morale of unexpected raids
Committing towns to fire and pushing back
The eastern ramparts. Piece by piece, the rim
Was being cracked and fissures driven down
The bowl: and stroke by stroke the strategy
Pointed to Sainte Marie. Were once the fort
Now garrisoned by forty Frenchmen taken,
No power predicted from Quebec could save
The Huron nation from its doom. St. Ignace
Lay in the path but during the eight months
After St. Joseph's fall the enemy
Had leisurely prepared their plans. Their scouts
Reported that one-half of the town's strength
Was lost by flight and that an apathy,
In spite of all the priests could do to stem it,
Had seized the invaded tribes. They knew that when
The warriors were hunting in the forest
This weaker palisade was scalable.
And the day came in March when the whole fate
That overtook St. Joseph in July
Swept on St. Ignace—sudden and complete.

The Mohawks and the Senecas uniting,
A thousand strong, the town bereft of fighters,
Four hundred old and young inside the stakes,
The assault was made two hours before the dawn.
But half-aroused from sleep, many were killed
Within their cabins. Of the four hundred three
Alone managed to reach the woods to scream
The alarm to the drowsed village of St. Louis.

At nine o'clock that morning—such the speed
Of the pursuit—a guard upon the hill
Behind the Residence was watching whiffs
Of smoke to the south, but a league away.
Bush fires? Not with this season's depth of snow.
The Huron bivouacs? The settlements
Too close for that. Camps of the Iroquois?
Not while cunning and stealth controlled their tactics.
The smoke was in the town. The morning air,
Clearing, could leave no doubt of that, and just
As little that the darkening pall could spring
Out of the vent-holes from the cabin roofs.
Ragueneau rushed to the hill at the guard's call;
Summoned Bressani; sheets and tongues of flame
Leaping some fifty feet above the smoke
Meant to their eyes the capture and the torch—
St. Louis with Brébeuf and Lalemant!

Less than two hours it took the Iroquois
To capture, sack and garrison St. Ignace,
And start then for St. Louis. The alarm
Sounded, five hundred of the natives fled
To the mother fort only to be pursued
And massacred in the snow. The eighty braves
That manned the stockades perished at the breaches;
And what was seen by Ragueneau and the guard
Was smoke from the massed fire of cabin bark.

Brébeuf and Lalemant were not numbered
In the five hundred of the fugitives.
They had remained, infusing nerve and will
In the defenders, rushing through the cabins
Baptizing and absolving those who were
Too old, too young, too sick to join the flight.

291

And when, resistance crushed, the Iroquois
Took all they had not slain back to St. Ignace,
The vanguard of the prisoners were the priests.

March 16, 1649

Three miles from town to town over the snow,
Naked, laden with pillage from the lodges,
The captives filed like wounded beasts of burden,
Three hours on the march, and those that fell
Or slowed their steps were killed.
                                        Three days before
Brébeuf had celebrated his last mass.
And he had known it was to be the last.
There was prophetic meaning as he took
The cord and tied the alb around his waist,
Attached the maniple to his left arm
And drew the seamless purple chasuble
With the large cross over his head and shoulders,
Draping his body: every vestment held
An immediate holy symbol as he whispered—
"Upon my head the helmet of Salvation.
So purify my heart and make me white;
With this cincture of purity gird me,
O Lord.
          May I deserve this maniple
Of sorrow and of penance.
                              Unto me
Restore the stole of immortality.
My yoke is sweet, my burden light.
                                  Grant that
I may so bear it as to win Thy grace."

Entering, he knelt before as rude an altar
As ever was reared within a sanctuary,
But hallowed as that chancel where the notes
Of Palestrina's score had often pealed
The *Assumpta est Maria* through Saint Peter's.
For, covered in the centre of the table,
Recessed and sealed, a hollowed stone contained
A relic of a charred or broken body

292

Which perhaps a thousand years ago or more
Was offered as a sacrifice to Him
Whose crucifix stood there between the candles.
And on the morrow would this prayer be answered:—
"Eternal Father, I unite myself
With the affections and the purposes
Of Our Lady of Sorrows on Calvary.
And now I offer Thee the sacrifice
Which Thy Beloved Son made of Himself
Upon the Cross and now renews on this,
His holy altar . . .
                              Graciously receive
My life for His life as he gave His life
For mine . . .
                    This is my body.
                              In like manner . . .
Take ye and drink—the chalice of my blood."

XII No doubt in the mind of Brébeuf that this was the last
Journey—three miles over the snow. He knew
That the margins as thin as they were by which he escaped
From death through the eighteen years of his mission toil
Did not belong to this chapter: not by his pen
Would this be told. He knew his place in the line,
For the blaze of the trail that was cut on the bark by Jogues
Shone still. He had heard the story as told by writ
And word of survivors—of how a captive slave
Of the hunters, the skin of his thighs cracked with the frost,
He would steal from the tents to the birches,
        make a rough cross
From two branches, set it in snow and on the peel
Inscribe his vows and dedicate to the Name
In "litanies of love" what fragments were left
From the wrack of his flesh; of his escape from the tribes;
Of his journey to France where he knocked at the door
        of the College
Of Rennes, was gathered in as a mendicant friar,
Nameless, unknown, till he gave for proof to the priest
His scarred credentials of faith, the nail-less hands
And withered arms—the signs of the Mohawk fury.
Nor yet was the story finished—he had come again
Back to his mission to get the second death.
And the comrades of Jogues—Goupil, Eustache and Couture,

Had been stripped and made to run the double files
And take the blows—one hundred clubs to each line—
And this as the prelude to torture, leisured, minute,
Where thorns on the quick, scallop shells to the joints
    of the thumbs,
Provided the sport for children and squaws till the end.
And adding salt to the blood of Brébeuf was the thought
Of Daniel—was it months or a week ago?
So far, so near, it seemed in time, so close
In leagues—just over there to the south it was
He faced the arrows and died in front of his church.

But winding into the greater artery
Of thought that bore upon the coming passion
Were little tributaries of wayward wish
And reminiscence. Paris with its vespers
Was folded in the mind of Lalemant,
And the soft Gothic lights and traceries
Were shading down the ridges of his vows.
But two years past at Bourges he had walked the cloisters,
Companioned by Saint Augustine and Francis,
And wrapped in quiet holy mists. Brébeuf,
His mind a moment throwing back the curtain
Of eighteen years, could see the orchard lands,
The *cidreries,* the peasants at the Fairs,
The undulating miles of wheat and barley,
Gardens and pastures rolling like a sea
From Lisieux to Le Havre. Just now the surf
Was pounding on the limestone Norman beaches
And on the reefs of Calvados. Had dawn
This very day not flung her surplices
Around the headlands and with golden fire
Consumed the silken argosies that made
For Rouen from the estuary of the Seine?
A moment only for that veil to lift—
A moment only for those bells to die
That rang their matins at Condé-sur-Vire.

By noon St. Ignace! The arrival there
The signal for the battle-cries of triumph,
The gauntlet of the clubs. The stakes were set

And the ordeal of Jogues was re-enacted
Upon the priests—even with wilder fury,
For here at last was trapped their greatest victim,
Echon. The Iroquois had waited long
For this event. Their hatred for the Hurons
Fused with their hatred for the French and priests
Was to be vented on this sacrifice,
And to that camp had come apostate Hurons,
United with their foes in common hate
To settle up their reckoning with *Echon.*

*   *   *   *

Now three o'clock, and capping the height of the passion,
Confusing the sacraments under the pines of the forest,
Under the incense of balsam, under the smoke
Of the pitch, was offered the rite of the font. On the head,
The breast, the loins and the legs, the boiling water!
While the mocking paraphrase of the symbols was hurled
At their faces like shards of flint from the arrow heads—
"We baptize thee with water . . .
                              That thou mayest be led
To Heaven . . .
                        To that end we do anoint thee.
We treat thee as a friend: we are the cause
Of thy happiness; we are thy priests; the more
Thou sufferest, the more thy God will reward thee,
So give us thanks for our kind offices."

The fury of taunt was followed by fury of blow.
Why did not the flesh of Brébeuf cringe to the scourge,
Respond to the heat, for rarely the Iroquois found
A victim that would not cry out in such pain—yet here
The fire was on the wrong fuel. Whenever he spoke,
It was to rally the soul of his friend whose turn
Was to come through the night while the eyes were uplifted
      in prayer,
Imploring the Lady of Sorrows, the mother of Christ,
As pain brimmed over the cup and the will was called
To stand the test of the coals. And sometimes the speech
Of Brébeuf struck out, thundering reproof to his foes,
Half-rebuke, half-defiance, giving them roar for roar.
Was it because the chancel became the arena,
Brébeuf a lion at bay, not a lamb on the altar,

As if the might of a Roman were joined to the cause
Of Judaea? Speech they could stop for they girdled his lips,
But never a moan could they get. Where was the source
Of his strength, the home of his courage that topped the best
Of their braves and even out-fabled the lore of their legends?
In the bunch of his shoulders which often had carried a load
Extorting the envy of guides at an Ottawa portage?
The heat of the hatchets was finding a path to that source.
In the thews of his thighs which had mastered the
        trails of the Neutrals?
They would gash and beribbon those muscles. Was it
        the blood?
They would draw it fresh from its fountain. Was it the heart?
They dug for it, fought for the scraps in the way of the wolves.
But not in these was the valour or stamina lodged;
Nor in the symbol of Richelieu's robes or the seals
Of Mazarin's charters, nor in the stir of the *lilies*
Upon the Imperial folds; nor yet in the words
Loyola wrote on a table of lava-stone
In the cave of Manresa—not in these the source—
But in the sound of invisible trumpets blowing
Around two slabs of board, right-angled, hammered
By Roman nails and hung on a Jewish hill.

The wheel had come full circle with the visions
In France of Brébeuf poured through the mould of St. Ignace.
Lalemant died in the morning at nine, in the flame
Of the pitch belts. Flushed with the sight of the bodies, the foes
Gathered their clans and moved back to the north and west
To join in the fight against the tribes of the Petuns.
There was nothing now that could stem the Iroquois blast.
However undaunted the souls of the priests who were left,
However fierce the sporadic counter attacks
Of the Hurons striking in roving bands from the ambush,
Or smashing out at their foes in garrison raids,
The villages fell before a blizzard of axes
And arrows and spears, and then were put to the torch.

The days were dark at the fort and heavier grew
The burdens on Ragueneau's shoulders. Decision was his.
No word from the east could arrive in time to shape
The step he must take. To and fro—from altar to hill,

From hill to altar, he walked and prayed and watched.
As governing priest of the Mission he felt the pride
Of his Order whipping his pulse, for was not St. Ignace
The highest test of the Faith? And all that torture
And death could do to the body was done. The Will
And the Cause in their triumph survived.

     Loyola's mountains,
Sublime at their summits, were scaled to the uttermost peak.
Ragueneau, the Shepherd, now looked on a battered fold.
In a whirlwind of fire St. Jean, like St. Joseph, crashed
Under the Iroquois impact. Firm at his post,
Garnier suffered the fate of Daniel. And now
Chabanel, last in the roll of the martyrs, entrapped
On his knees in the woods met death at apostate hands.

The drama was drawing close to its end. It fell
To Ragueneau's lot to perform a final rite—
To offer the fort in sacrificial fire!
He applied the torch himself. *"Inside an hour,"*
He wrote, *"we saw the fruit of ten years' labour*
Ascend in smoke,—then looked our last at the fields,
Put altar-vessels and food on a raft of logs,
And made our way to the island of St. Joseph."
But even from there was the old tale retold—
Of hunger and the search for roots and acorns;
Of cold and persecution unto death
By the Iroquois; of Jesuit will and courage
As the shepherd-priest with Chaumonot led back
The remnant of a nation to Quebec.

THE MARTYRS' SHRINE

Three hundred years have passed, and the winds of God
Which blew over France are blowing once more through
    the pines
That bulwark the shores of the great Fresh Water Sea.
Over the wastes abandoned by human tread,
Where only the bittern's cry was heard at dusk;
Over the lakes where the wild ducks built their nests,
The skies that had banked their fires are shining again
With the stars that guided the feet of Jogues and Brébeuf.
The years as they turned have ripened the martyrs' seed,
And the ashes of St. Ignace are glowing afresh.

297

The trails, having frayed the threads of the cassocks, sank
Under the mould of the centuries, under fern
And brier and fungus—there in due time to blossom
Into the highways that lead to the crest of the hill
Which havened both shepherd and flock in the days of their
    trial.
For out of the torch of Ragueneau's ruins the candles
Are burning today in the chancel of Sainte Marie.
The Mission sites have returned to the fold of the Order.
Near to the ground where the cross broke under the hatchet,
And went with it into the soil to come back at the turn
Of the spade with the carbon and calcium char of the bodies,
The shrines and altars are built anew; the *Aves*
And prayers ascend, and the Holy Bread is broken.

DUNKIRK

(1941)

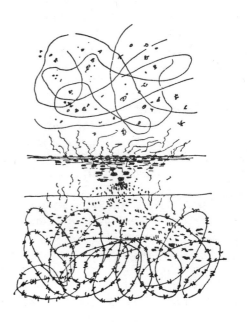

DUNKIRK

The English May was slipping into June
With heralds that the spring had never known.
Black cavalry were astride the air;
The Downs awoke to find their faces slashed;
There was blood on the hawthorn,
And song had died in the nightingales' throats.

Appeasement is in its grave: it sleeps well.
The mace had spiked the parchment seals
And pulverized the hedging *ifs* and *wherefores,*
The wheezy adverbs, the gutted modifiers.
Churchill and Bevin have the floor,
Whipping snarling nouns and action-verbs
Out of their lairs in the lexicon,
Bull-necked *adversatives* that bit and clawed,
An age before gentility was cubbed.

A call came in from the Channel
Like the wash of surf on sand,
Borne in by the winds against the chalk escarpments,
Into the harbours, up the rivers, along the estuaries,
And but one word in the call.

Three hundred thousand on the beaches,
Their spirit-level vision training West!
A vast patience in their eyes,
They had fought pig-iron, manganese, tungsten, cobalt;
And their struggle with hunger, thirst,
And the drug of sleep,
Had multiplied the famine in their cheeks
For England,
By forty miles divided from her brood.

Seven millions on the roads in France,
Set to a pattern of chaos
Fashioned through years for this hour.
Inside the brain of the planner
No tolerance befogged the reason—
The *reason* with its clear-swept halls,
Its brilliant corridors,
Where no recesses with their healing dusk
Offered asylum for a fugitive.

The straightedge ruled out errors,
The tremors in the sensory nerves,
Pity and the wayward impulses,
The liberal imbecilities.
The reason reckoned that the allied guns
Would not be turned upon the roads
To clear the path for the retreat.
It reasoned well.

REGATTA AND CREW

Millenniums it had taken to make their stock.
Piltdown hung on the frontals of their fathers.
They had lain as sacrifices
Upon the mortuary slabs of Stonehenge.
Their souls had come to birth out of their racial myths.
The sea was their school; the storm, their friend.
Foot by foot and hand to hand
They had met the legions
On the beaches and in the surf.
Great names had been delivered unto them;
Caractacus,
Taking his toll of the invaders
In his retreat to the fens and hills;
Boadicea,
The storming of Londinium and Verulamium,
And the annihilation of the Roman *ninth*;
Alban, Alfred, Athelney, Edington!
And in the march of their survival
They had fought the poll-tax and burned
The manor rolls under Ball and Tyler.
They had led the riots against the Enclosures.
They had sung ballads to the rhythms of the gibbets.
The welts had been around their necks and ankles.
They had swept the Main with Hawkins and Drake.
Morgan-mouthed vocabularians,
Lovers of the beef of language,
They had carved with curse and cutlass
Castilian grandees in the Caribbean.
They had signed up with Frobisher,
Had stifled cries in the cockpits of Trafalgar.
They had emptied their veins into the Marne.
Freedom to them was like the diver's lust for air.

301

DUNKIRK

Children of oaths and madrigals,
They had shambled out of caves
To write the clauses of the Charters,
To paint the Channel mists,
To stand hushed before the Canterbury tapers.

THE RACE ON THE CHANNEL

The Royal Yacht squadrons of the Thames and Cowes,
Those slim and rakish models of the *wave-line theory*,
Flying the ensign with their Club devices—
Grand-daughters of *Genesta* and the *Galatea*
Whose racing spinnakers
Outsilvered and outflew the sea-gulls off the Isle of Wight.
Cutters, the pride of Folkestone and Sheerness
With their press balloon-jibs,
Their billows of flax and hemp
Smothering their single masts
And straight-running bowsprits.

Excursion paddlers—
Last of the family known as the *fleet of the butterflies*,
Purveyors of moonlight sonatas and Sunday siestas.

The fireboats from the London Fire Brigade.
Luggers with four-sided sails bent to the yards
And slung obliquely to the masts,
Smelling of the wharves of Deal.
Smacks that built the Grimsby name.
Yawls with their handy mizzen-sails—
The Jacks-of-all-trades on the English coast.
Barges spritsail-rigged with jigger booms.
Bluff-bowed billyboys and Norfolk wherries,
Skiffs that stank of herring roes and Yarmouth.
Dutch scoots and square-stemmed bawleys rank
With kelp, fish-scales and the slime of eels.
And with them all, the merchantmen,
Three-funnel liners turbine-driven,
Cabin cruisers, with whaleboats, rafts and dories
Tied to the grimy tails of barges drawn by tugs.

A Collingwood came from Newcastle-on-Tyne,
Trelawney and Grenville of the Cornish Line,
And Raleigh and Gilbert from the Devon Seas
With a Somerset Blake. They met at the quays—
McCluskey, Gallagher, Joe Millard,
Three riveters red from Dumbarton Yard,
And Peebles of Paisley, a notary clerk,
Two joiners from Belfast, Mahaffy and Burke,
Blackstone and Coke of Lincoln's Inn,
A butcher from Smithfield, Toby Quinn,
Jonathan Wells, a Sheffield bricklayer,
Tim Thomas of Swansea, a borough surveyor,
Jack Wesley, a stoker, by way of South Shields,
And Snodgrass and Tuttle from Giles-in-the-Fields,
Young Bill of Old Bill with Hancock and Reid,
Two sons of a bishop from Berwick-on-Tweed,
A landscape gardener of Tunbridge, Kent,
Povey, a draper from Stoke-on-Trent,
Arthur Cholmondeley Bennington-Grubbe
With Benbow of the Boodles Club,
A Ralph Abercrombie, a Fetherstonehaugh
With Smith, and Ibbs, and Jones, and Buggs—
They met on the liners, yachts and tugs:
The *Princess Maud,* the *Massy Shaw,*
The *Crested Eagle,* the *Nicholas Drew,*
The *Gurgling Jean* and the *Saucy Sue.*

Two prefects from Harrow—Dudley and Fraser
Fresh in their grey flannel trousers and blazer,
Helping two tanners, Muggins and Day,
To rig up a sail at a mizzen stay,
Were hailed by a Cambridge stroke—*"Ahoy!*
Will you let me go on your billyboy?"

A curate from Cardiff, the Reverend Evans,
Inspired with zeal by a speech of Bevin's,
Called on a Rochester verger named Burchall,
Likewise inflamed by a speech from Churchill—
Together they went to a Greenwich jetty
And boarded a lighter—the *Bouncing Betty.*

Meadows, the valet, tapped at the door
Of Colonel Ramsbottom, late of Lahore:
'Twas dawn, and the Colonel was sick with a head;

"The Dean and his lordship, the Bishop, are here,
And your sloop, sir, is ready down at the pier,
And may I go with you?" Meadows said—
"No," roared the Colonel, as he creaked out of bed,
Blasting out damns with a spot of saliva,
Yet the four of them boarded the *Lady Godiva.*

A Captain with a Cape Horn face,
Being down on his luck without a ship,
Had spent ten years in his own disgrace
As skipper of a river ferry—
To-night he was taking his finest trip
As master of a Norfolk wherry.

The Junior partner, Davie Scott,
Of MacTavish, MacEachren, MacGregor, and Scott,
Conspired with Murdoch, MacNutt and MacPhail
To go to Gravesend that evening and sail
For the Beach in Mr. MacTavish's yacht. ·

HEARD ON THE COLLIERS

"I've been in a bit of a muss, mesen,
With my game left leg," said Eddie Glen,
"And every night my faintin' spells,
Contracted in the Dardanelles."

"My floatin' kidney keeps me 'ome,
My shoulder too 'as never 'ealed."
Quoth Rufus Stirk of 'Uddersfield,
Cracked with shrapnel at Bapaume.

"Ow, wot's a kidney, look at me,
A bleedin' boulder in my lung,"
Said 'Umphrey 'Iggins of Bermondsey;
"A 'Igh Explosive 'ad me strung
On the top of a ruddy poplar tree
For thirty hours at Armenteers,
'Aven't spit straight nigh twenty years."

"Now, my old woman," said Solomon Pike,
"Says 'Itler's such a fidget like;
'E steals the cows and 'ens from the Danes,

'*E rummages France, 'e chases the Poles,*
And comes over 'ere with 'is blinkin' planes
To drive us to the 'Yde Park 'oles
Where there's nary a roof that isn't leakin',
Swipin' the pillows right under our 'eads,
Shooin' us out from our 'umble beds."
" 'E's a mug, I says, in a manner o' speakin'."

"How lang d'ye ken it'll take to get through it?"
Said a cautious drover, Angus Bain.
"It'll take a bit o' doin' to do it,
The blighters are dropping bombs like rain,"
Said the costermonger from Petticoat Lane.

    ＊   ＊   ＊   ＊

Out on the Channel—laughter died.
Casual understatement
Was driven back from its London haunts
To its clinical nakedness
Along the banks of the Ilissus.
In front of the crew were rolling mountains of smoke
Spilling fire from their Vesuvian rims;
The swaying fringes of Borealis blue;
The crimson stabs through the curtains;
The tracers' fiery parabolas,
The falling pendants of green from the Very lights;
The mad colours of the murals of Dunkirk.

Space, time, water, bread, sleep,
Above all—sleep;
Commodities beyond the purchase of the Rand.
Space—a thousand pounds per foot! Not up for sale
In the cabin suites or on the floors of the lighters.
The single Mole was crammed with human termites,
Stumbling, falling on the decks of the destroyers,
Sleeping, dying on the decks of the transports
Strung along the seaward end.
The solid black queues on the sand waited their turn
To file along the bridgehead jetties
Improvised from the army lorries,
Or waded out to swim
Or clutch at drifting gangplanks, rafts and life-belts.
Time—Days, weeks of the balance of life
Offered in exchange for minutes now.

305

DUNKIRK

Stuff of the world's sagas in the heavens!
Spitfires were chasing Heinkels, one to twenty.
The nation's debt unpaid, unpayable,
Was climbing up its pyramid,
As the Hurricanes took on the Messerschmitts.

THE MULTIPEDES ON THE ROADS

Born on the blueprints,
They are fed by fire.
They grow their skin from carburized steel.
They are put together by cranes.
Their hearts are engines that do not know fatigue
In the perfection of their valves,
In the might of their systolic thrusts.
Their blood is petrol: Oil bathes their joints.
Their nerves are wire.
From the assembly lines they are put on inspection.
They pass tests,
Are pronounced fit by the drill-sergeants.
They go on parade and are the pride of the High Command.
They take, understand and obey orders.
They climb hills, straddle craters and the barbed barricades.
They defy bullets and shells.
Faster than Genghis' cavalry they speed,
Crueller than the hordes of Tamburlaine,
Yet unknowing and uncaring.
It is these that the rearguards are facing—
Creatures of conveyer belts,
Of precision tools and schedules.
They breathe through carburetted lungs;
If pierced, they do not feel the cut,
And if they die, they do not suffer death.
And Dunkirk stands between the rearguards and the sea.

*   *   *   *

Motor launches from the Port of London,
Life-boats from the liners,
Whale-boats, bottoms of shallow draught,
Rammed their noses into the silt,

Packed their loads and ferried them to scoots and drifters.
Blood and oil smut on their faces,
The wounded, dying and dead were hauled up
Over the rails of the hospital carriers
In the nets and cargo slings.

IN THE SKIES

The world believed the trap was sprung,
And no Geneva words or signatures of mercy
Availed the quarry on the sands.
The bird's right to dodge the barrels on the wing,
The start for the hare,
The chance for the fox to cross his scent,
For the teeth to snap at the end of the chase,
Did not belong to this tally-ho.
The proffered sword disclaimed by the victor,
The high salute at the burial of a foe
Wrapped in the folds of his flag,
The wreath from the skies,
Were far romantic memories.
As little chivalry here
As in the peregrines chasing the carriers,
As in the sniff of the jackals about a carcass!
Here over the dunes
The last civil rag was torn from the body of war—
The decencies had perished with the Stukas.

*   *   *   *

From Dover to Dunkirk,
From Dunkirk to Ramsgate,
And back to the dunes.
Power boats of the enemy
Were driving torpedoes into transports and colliers,
Lifting the engines clear from their beds,
Blowing the boilers, sheering the sterns,
And the jettisoned loads gathered up from the sea
Were transferred to other decks
And piled in steep confusion
On the twisted steel of the listed destroyers,
On the rough planks of the barges,
Into the hatches of the freighters,

Jammed against bulkheads and riddled ventilators,
On the coils of the cables,
On quarterdecks and in the fo'c'sles,
On the mess-tables and under them.
"Was that roar in the North from the 'Rodney'?
We hope to God it was."
Drip of the leadlines on the bows—
"Two fathoms, sir, four feet, three and a half."
"Wake up, you dead end. You're not on the feathers now.
Make room for this 'ere bloke."
"Stiff as cement 'e is." "Git a gait on,
Or the Stukas 'll be raisin' boils on your necks."
"Ahoy, skipper, a can of petrol."
"Compass out of gear—Give us the line to Ramsgate."
"Follow the scoots."

The great birds, carrying under their wings
The black distorted crosses,
Plunged, straightened out.
Laid their eggs in air,
Hatched them in fountains of water,
In craters of sand,
To the leap of flame,
To the roar of avalanche.

And in those hours,
When Death was sweating at his lathe,
When heads and legs and arms were blown from their trunks,
When the seventh day on the dunes became the eighth,
And the eighth slumped into the dawn of the ninth,
When the sand's crunch and suck under the feet
Were sounds less to be endured than the crash of bombs
In that coma and apathy of horror—
It was then that the feel of a deck,
The touch of a spar or a halyard,
Was like a hold on the latch of the heart of God.
It's the Navy's job!
It's their turn now,
From the Beach to the ports.
Let the Stukas break their bloody necks on the Mole;
Let the fires scorch the stars—
For now, whether on the burnished oak of the cabins,

Or on the floor-boards of the punts,
Or in the cuddies of the skiffs,
Sleep at last has an even game with Death.

The blessed fog—
Ever before this day the enemy,
Leagued with the quicksands and the breakers—
Now mercifully masking the periscope lenses,
Smearing the hair-lines of the bomb-sights,
Hiding the flushed coveys.
And with it the calm on the Channel,
The power that drew the teeth from the storm,
The peace that passed understanding,
Soothing the surf, allaying the lop on the swell.
Out of the range of the guns of Nieuport,
Away from the immolating blasts of the oil-tanks,
The flotillas of ships were met by flotillas of gulls
Whiter than the cliffs of Foreland;
Between the lines of the Medway buoys
They steamed and sailed and rowed,
Back to the roadsteads, back to the piers
Inside the vigilant booms,
Back to the harbours,
Back to the River of London, to England,
Saved once again by the tread of her keels.

BEHIND THE LOG

(1947)

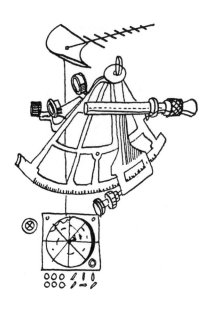

BEHIND THE LOG

There is a language in a naval log
That rams the grammar down a layman's throat,
Where words unreel in paragraphs, and lines
In chapters. Volumes lie in graphs and codes,
Recording with an algebraic care
The idiom of storms, their lairs and paths;
Or, in the self-same bloodless manner, sorting
The mongrel litters of a battle signal
In victories or defeats or bare survivals,
Flags at half-mast, salutes and guards of honour,
Distinguished crosses, burials at sea.

Our navigators trained their astrolabes
And sextants on the skies in lucky weather,
Or added guesses to dead reckoning,
Hauled up their lead, examined mud or shell
Or gravel on the arming—fifty fathoms,
Now forty, thirty, twenty-five, shallowing
Quickly! *"Engines astern, reefs, keep your lead
Going. Have plenty of water under you."*
They did not wait till miracles of science
Unstopped the naked ears for supersonics,
Or lifted cataracts from finite vision
To make night and its darkness visible.
How long ago was it since sailors blew
Their sirens at the cliffs while nearing land,
Traversing channels, cocked their ears and waited?
"Where did you hear that echo, mate?"
                              *"Right off
The starboard quarter, Captain. Took ten seconds."*
"That's Gull Rock there a mile away. Where now?"
"Two seconds for the echo from port bow."
"That's Porpoise Head I reckon—Hard a-port!"
With echoes everywhere, stand out to sea.
But when the winds deafened their ears or cloud
And rain blinded their eyes, they were shoved back
Upon their mother wit which either had
To find the exits to the runs and round
The Capes or pile their ships upon the reefs.

And of that lineage are the men today.
They still are calling to the rocks: they get

Their answers in the same hard terms: they call
To steel gliding beneath the sea: they pierce
Horizons for the surface hulls: they ping
The sky for the plane's fuselage: even
The moon acknowledged from her crater sills.
But though the radio bursts and vacuum tubes
And electronic beams were miracles
Of yesterday, dismissing cloud and rain
And darkness as illusions of the sense,
Yet always there to watch the colours, note
The V-break in the beam's straight line, to hear
The echoes, feel the pain, are eyes, ears, nerves:
Always remains the guess within the judgment
To jump the fine perfection of the physics
And smell mortality behind the log.

As weird a game of ping-pong ever played
Was on the sea—the place, off Cape Farewell,
With the back-curtain of the Greenland ice-cap:
Time—'41 autumnal equinox.
The crisis was the imminence of famine
And the cutting of the ganglia and veins
That vitalized the sinews, fed the cells
Of lungs demanding oxygen in air.
The wicks were guttering from want of oil,
And without oil, the bread went with the light,
And without bread, the will could not sustain
The fight, piping its courage to the heart.

Grey predatory fish had pedigreed
With tiger sharks and brought a speed and power
The sharks had never known, for they had been
Committed to the sea under a charter
Born of a mania of mind and will
And nurtured by a Messianic slogan.
They were not bounded by the parallels.
They found their habitats wherever there
Was open sea and keels to ride upon it.
Off the North Cape they had outsped the narwhals,
The sawfish off the Rios and the Horn.
They did not kill for food: they killed that food
Should not be used as food. They were the true
Expendables—the flower of their type.
They left their mothers for self-immolation,

The penalty the same for being on
Or off the target—for the first to join
Their own combustion to that of the ships,
And for the second, just to go the way
Their victims went—a drunken headlong spiral,
Shunted from an exhausted radius
Down fifteen thousand feet or more of sea,
Engines, propellers, gyros, rudders, dead.

The S.C. 42 was being groomed
To match a new suspected strategy.
The sleuths till now had surfaced, stabbed and dived
In lone attack. This convoy had to face
The risk of concentrated ambush, meet it
By leaving beaten sea-lanes, east and west,
And in the ambiguity of the wastes
To seek the harsh alliance of the ice
And fog, where Arctic currents were more friendly,
And long nights blanketed the periscopes.

THE CONVOY CONFERENCE

In the Conference room the language dripped with brine.
Veterans, who nearly half a century
Ago had flown their flags on battle cruisers,
Were busy grafting some new sprouts of Gaelic
And Newfie-Irish on an English stump.
They had saluted Fisher as cadets,
Heard *Open Fire* under Jellicoe,
Outridden typhoons off the Solomons
And at the Falklands cancelled Coronel.
'Twas time they had a spell of garden peace,
A time to trim their briers and colour Meerschaums.
Those old days were the real days—now, by God
They had to tread the decks of merchantmen,
From flagships to dry cargo-ships and tankers.

THE NAVAL CONTROL SERVICE OFFICER ADDRESSES THE MASTERS:

*"Good morning, gentlemen. It is a pleasure
To see familiar faces here today.
To such of you who have commanded ships*

In earlier convoys what I have to say
Will be just dishing up the old instructions.
But since to many it is the first adventure,
I know you'll pardon me if I should cover
With some precision the important points.
Let me begin by saying that your convoy
Has, in its Commodore, one of the most
Renowned men in the Service. It is not
For me to talk at length about his fine
And honourable record. It is known
To all of you. He has of his free choice
Issued from his well-earned retirement
To place at the disposal of the Allies
His knowledge, skill, and practical seamanship.
Here at this table, gentlemen: Rear-Admiral
Sir Francis Horatio Trelawney-Camperdown!

"The Senior Naval Officer will have
Escort and convoy under his command.
An able and distinguished officer,
He is through long and personal experience
Well-versed in enemy tactics, and your safety
Will be the escort's first consideration.

N.C.S.O. THUMBING THE PAGES OF "GENERAL INSTRUCTIONS"

"Being in all respects ready for sea,
The ships will have steam up and hoist pennants
At daybreak. Note—The Commodore will sound
A prolonged blast. The ships will leave anchorage
In single column and at intervals
Of three minutes, and in the following order,
The Commodore leading . . .
                                You will shorten cables
XX minutes before you heave up. Note—
You will be making seaward on the ebb.
You start two columns after dropping pilots.
Notice in Form A1 all the instructions
Governing matters of sequence, columns and speed.

"May I now draw your most thorough attention
To that important fire page, section B
Of General Instructions (a voice—'regular page
of bumph');   *that* COMPLETE

315

BLACKOUT AT NIGHT. *Only last week reports*
Came in of a ship sunk because she showed
A light, and that despite the most emphatic
Warnings at the conference prior to the sailing.
Remember—have deadlights and scuttles closed,
The blackout curtains checked, no cigarettes
Or pipes lighted on deck and every measure
To conceal the convoy put into effect.

"And likewise of the first significance,
Page 3 at section D concerning 'Smoke'.
Advice is being received of ships making
Black smoke which with good visibility
May be observed for many miles at sea,
And I may add for hours after a convoy
Has passed a given point. I must repeat
This warning—Do not make black smoke in daylight!

"Again. Your route has with the greatest care
Been chosen by the Admiralty experts.
But may I point out that such care and judgment
Could be offset by so simple a matter
As refuse-dumping over rails. Do not—
(Voices—'Wrap it around the bully beef.'
'No, put it in the soup to give it body.'
'God, that tomato soup needs body and flavour.'
'I'd put it in the kye to take the stink out.')
Do NOT throw garbage in the sea in day time.
That's a dead give-away. A crate or carton
Floating astern a convoy might betray
The existence and position of the ships.
That practice must at all cost be avoided.
And most important for internal safety
Of convoy lines is that of station-keeping.
A ship that's not in station is out of control;
The turns in moments of emergency
Cannot successfully be executed,
Unless this measure strictly is observed.
I do not need to emphasize this maxim.

"These measures are of front-line urgency.
W/T silence must always be maintained

Along the route. Occasionally it's broken,
Not wilfully indeed but carelessly,
By operators fresh from the radio school,
Whose fingers have not lost the itch to tap
The keys to break the tedium by listening
To crackle on 500 kilocycles.
A random da da dit dit dit might be
An invitation to the U-boats ready
To accept it. They are ever listening
In on our frequencies and you know well
The manner the Direction Finder Loop
On a surfaced U-boat will follow a signal.
It's like a human ear alerted, which
Will turn to the source of a sound to get a bearing.
You must remember that the enemy
Will not relax his efforts to pick up
Those waves, that German D/F stations even
As far away as Occupied Europe
Are taking bearings, plotting out our ships.

"Now, gentlemen: here is the Commodore."

SIR FRANCIS HORATIO:
"Gentlemen: I shall be very brief and I hope
To be as brief after we get to sea.
I shall keep my signals to a minimum,
But when a hoist DOES *go up I shall*
Expect immediate acknowledgment.
Many of us have sailed together already,
And gone through several trying situations.
But our success, such as it is, has sprung
From absolute obedience to instructions
And from endurance which must be assumed.
While it is true that for the navigation
Of his own ship each master must be held
Responsible, there is but little room
For rugged individualists. Elsewhere
Perhaps the Nelson touch may be applied,
And a captain's intuitions exercised,
But not within the stations of a convoy.
(Chuckles amongst the older masters.)

"The N.C.S.O. has referred to the matter
Of showing lights. A match, lit on deck, has

317

Been spotted by an escort at two miles,
And last crossing, a thoughtless biped left
A port open and failed to notice the signal
From a destroyer. It required a burst
From a machine-gun to close it. I am sure
We shall require no such emphasis
In this convoy but I should urge each master
To make the business of lights a top concern,
Particularly at the change of Watch.
Men dropping in to a stuffy galley to make
A mug of tea before going below
Are the principal offenders.

                      "Do not wait
Till you are deep in fog before you stream
Your fog-buoys. That is generally too late.
Your next astern by that time has lost touch.
Good seamanship and team-play should prevent
Avoidable collisions in thick fog.

"If you are new to convoy you may be
Tempted to flash on at full brilliancy
Your navigation lights when another ship
Closes you. DON'T. *You are as visible*
To him as he to you. Keep closed up. Keep
Lights dimmed except in an emergency.

"I shall say little here about the stragglers.
The record of the losses says it much
More clearly, and the escort cannot help
You if you leave the family. They are good;
They can work wonders but not miracles.

"And now if you're uncertain of anything—
Emergency turns, for instance—come and have
A chin with me at the close of the conference.
And to repeat, we're in this business all
Together, and in it up to the neck:
For my part, I am bloody proud of it.
Good morning, gentlemen, and a good voyage."

N.C.S.O.:
"Questions?"

CHORUS: *"Plenty."*

HARVEY BUTT: *"I'm in the wrong position.*
Too far astern. I have a 12-knot ship.
I want a place in first or second line
To save me bumpin' into 6-knot tramps."

JIM BURDOCK:
"This convoy got no tramps."

BUTT: *"Well, all I know*
The last one had 'em, and I knocked the sterns
Off three of them, and I was always goin'
Full speed astern to save my goddam neck."

"JOHN KNOX" O'FLAHERTY:
"I could make 8 knots if I didn't have
Such lousy coal. The bloody stuff won't steam.
A half of it is gravel—wouldn't boil
A kettle: looks like salvage from a wreck
Picked up from sweepings left on Sable Island."

CHARLIE SHIPSIDE:
"And I don't like my place—gummed up between
A couple of tankers. God, if I'm not fished
I'll be run down."

JACK DOUCETTE: *"Why should I be back there?*
Never did like the stern of columns. Suppose
I'm in there just for picking up survivors.
What do you take me for—an ambulance?"

JERRY PAYNE:
"8 knots would tear the guts out of my tub.
I haven't had a refit for three years.
Can't execute a turn of forty-five degrees.
We'll be colliding every fifteen seconds."

ROBERT FITZSIMMONS:
"My pumps were out of gear when she was built;
Still out of gear; complained a hundred times,
But can't get any action."

319

MICHAEL SALTAWAY: *"I have this*
To say. I only got one boiler workin';
And that one's on half-time—the other half
Is restin'—and I've only half a crew."

NORWEGIAN CAPTAIN, LEANING HEAVILY ON NATIVE SPEECH:
"I kan ikke forstaa fordommt ord.
How in helvete tink dey dat I kan
Faa 8 knots ut of my old vaskelbalja.
Har ikke hatt fullt mannskap for two year.
I lar mig fan ikke fortelle what I
Skal do. You go helvete alle mann."

N.C.S.O.:
"What did he say?"

'ARRY STUBBINS: *" 'E says the bleedin' hinstructions*
Are fine and quite clear to 'is hunderstandin'."

ROBIN MACALLISTER:
"Nae, nae, he canna' thole thae English turrms.
He'd ken a' richt, gin you gae him the Gaelic.
I wad respeckfully suggest the wurrds
O' the Genneral Instructions be convairted
Into a ceevilized tongue so that a chiel
Micht hae nae doots. Noo, let me spik mi thochts."

(Voices: "Now, what did HE *say?" "Noo's the day*
and noo's the hour." "Is this St. Andrew's Night?"
"Pipe in the haggis.")

A DANISH CAPTAIN:
"No, no. He sess he do not IKKE *know*
One word. His vaskelbalja—tub-tub, washtub,
Das iss he mean his ship, can't make 8 knots.
No crew MANNSKAP *full up for long long time.*
Ship had no refit since she left Bergen
In 1894. He tol' me dat
Himself. He not quite clear. He sess ve can

All go to hella. Don't care damn.
                                    I got
Complaints ALSO. *Want get dem off my chest.*
Goddam nuisance, I seh, dose para-a-vanes.
Muss up de vurks. Crew don't like dem damn bit.
Dey seh put hex on ship—a buncha Jonahs.
And more ALSO *I seh. No compass checks.*
Dose D/G coils play hell wid compasses.
De gear get loose on deck. Dey come adrift."

CYRUS BUMSTEAD:
"I don't want anyone to tell me how
To run my ship—been in the Services,
Merchant and Navy, nigh come forty years.
I was a Master when the most of them
Were spottin' patterns on their diapers."

MARK KNEE TO CYRUS:
"I squeezed the Atlantic from my mitts before
Those Juniors had their birthday buttons on."

CAPTAIN, THE HONOURABLE GUY BRIMBLECOMBE:
"Well, sir, you needn't worry about MY *ship.*
She went through this before: she'll go again.
She's in good trim. I have a splendid crew.
Signals will be acknowledged to the letter,
And in the sea tradition, I assure you."

N.C.S.O.:
"Now, gentlemen, since it is quite apparent
That we are all in utmost harmony
On the main grounds, it is just left for me
To wish 'good-luck'. Never have I attended
A Conference where there was such fine feeling
Combined with insight and rare technical grasp
Of the problems of a convoy operation.
Let me congratulate you. May I now
Invite you, on behalf of a great friend
Of the R.C.N., to the Periwinkle Club
At Lobster Point where you may hoist a couple
To take the chill from the September fog."

*   *   *   *

In a few hours from the time the blinds
Were drawn upon the jags and the last lisp
Against the universe and things marine
Was but a reminiscence lapsed in rum,
Those men were on the Bridge peering through fog
And moving towards their ordered rendezvous.

*   *   *   *

One half a million tons were in the holds,
Cramming to the last precious cubic inch
The slow-keeled merchantmen—the sixty-six.
No longer were those ships an industry
Run for peacetime returns upon investment.
They took their line positions for defence.
Against them mainly was the warfare waged—
Bulk cargo carriers with box-like sections,
Ship side to ship side and the main deck to keel,
Carrying their gross of ore and coal and grain;
The ships with 'tween decks running the full length;
Tankers equipped with special pumps for oil;
Refrigeration ships, holds insulated
For storage of the perishable goods;
And hybrid types that had their bellies full
Of oranges, aluminum and lint.

How desperate the strait which would commit
A treasure of this price to such a journey!
Where find a steward who would risk his name
To close the page of such accountancy
When every mile along the ocean highway
Was calling for protection, and in calling
Demanded life and life's expenditure?
And here the call was answered with a guard
Whose substitute for numbers was its courage—
Four terriers slipped from the Canadian kennel:
But one destroyer, *Skeena*; three corvettes,
Kenogami, *Orillia* and *Alberni*.
Upon their vigil hung the life of all,
Of ships and men. Of sleeker, faster breed,
The *Skeena* ranged a far periphery
At thirty knots, now out of sight and now

Closing the convoy as her nose tried out
The dubious scents in narrowing ellipses.
The slower guards kept closer to their broods,
Pushing their way within the column lanes,
Emerged to pace the port and starboard flanks
Or nuzzled with a deep strategic caution
The hulls of those whose tardy engine beats
Brought down the knots of faster ships and made
The gravest risk and worry for the fleet.
They kept a special watch upon the tankers.
No ships, no aeroplanes, no jeeps could stir
Without this source of power and lubrication.
Even the merchantmen must flank these ships,
Herded like buffalo young inside the ring.

*   *   *   *

COMMODORE TO SIGNALMAN:
"Signal to pennants 73, relay
To pennants 103, Stop Pouring Smoke!"

INTERNAL MURMURINGS:
"Look at it tossin' like a Texas twister.
That smoke is blacker than an Afghan's whiskers.
I'd like to tell that Captain of the Heads
He should have stayed at home with the kind of job
That suited him—housebreakin' his Angoras."

OFFICIAL:
"And pennants 114 is out of station."

UNOFFICIAL:
"That flappin' penguin from the Auckland Islands
Has been a week on route, yet needs more time
To get rid of that Newfie-Crowsnest screech.
He'll lose it when he's doused. Get back in station,
For if you don't, the canaries will stop singin'."

THE MASTER'S THOUGHTS:
"I told those sculpins at the conference
I couldn't make that eight—a half a knot
Above a six would blow my stinkin' boilers.
I haven't had a cleanin' for a year,

And there's a beach of sand inside the gears,
And yet that bargee yells—GET BACK IN STATION!"

COMMODORE:
"And pennants 74 by the Diet of Worms!
He's waddlin' like an old barnyard merganser.
Another hour by the way he's goin'
He'll be out on the flanks duckin' his feathers,
Or lost in fog and stragglin' back to Sydney.
Keep pumpin' Morse into his ruddy blinkers."

THE MASTER IN QUESTION:
"I've got a twisted rudder—like a corkscrew,
And if that poopin' punk there on that flagship
Imagines he's Paul Bunyan or the devil,
Tell him put on his shorts and straighten it."

P.O. TO GALLEY-BOY:
"Gallagher, did your mother tell you nothin'
On the way home? Stop pitchin' gash in daytime.
Handin' the convoy on a platter to the subs.
As bad as smoke to give the trail away.
Just one more bad tomato over there,
And all the ships will quit this lovely Service,
And you'll go with the galley, do you hear?"

GALLAGHER:
"Why won't that windpipe slitter tell me what
I got to do with all that mouldy gash?
'Twas gash when it was brought aboard, 'twas gash
When it was crated; now it's maggoty.
Can't eat it and can't burn it and can't dump it.
I'd like to foul his beak in those tomatoes."

North of the sixtieth, they had, it seemed,
Found refuge in a sea-berth where the foe,
Finding the chill enter his crop, might seek
More southern fodder. Least of all the hazards
Were winds and waves: for these the ships were built.
Their bows could bull the heavier seas head-on.
Their hulls could stand the shock beam-to. The keels

Had learned the way to bite into the troughs:
Such was their native element. The acts
Of God were taken as their daily fare
Received alike with prayers or curses. These
Were as the dice fell—whether luck of devil
Or luck of God spilled on a shifting floor
Close to the steady fringe of the Arctic Circle.

For seven days and nights without attack!
The asdic operator in his hut
Had sent his ultra-sounds out and reported
Echoes, but only such as might return
As the dull, soft reverberation notes
From seaweed or low forms of ocean life
Or from a school of porpoises or whales.
His hearing was as vital to the ship
As was the roving sight in a crowsnest.

His ear was as the prism is to light,
Unravelling meanings from a skein of tone.
Each sound might hold a threat, a Bremen slur,
An overture to a dementia
Of guns and rockets and torpedo hits
Competing with the orders from the Bridge.
He had to know that threat and not mistake it.
For that his body was a sounding-board.
Even his knees must feel it and his face
Become a score for undetermined notes,
As if a baton in his cortex played
Wry movements on his neurones fiddle-taut,
Twitched his reflexes into spasms, narrowed
His pupils, kicked his heart into his throat.

He had an instrument in his control
Attested by the highest signatures of science.
The echoes had traversed wide spans of time:—
Helmholtz and Doppler tapping to each other
Through laboratory walls, and there was Rayleigh
Calling to Langevin, he to Fresnel,
The three hymning Pindarics to Laplace,
And all vibrating from their resonators
Salutes to Robert Boyle, halloos to Newton.
And here, his head-phones on, this operator,
Sleeve-rolled mechanic to the theorists,

Was holding in his personal trust, come life,
Come death, their cumulative handiwork.
Occasionally a higher note might hit
The ear-drum like a drill, bristle the chin,
Involving everything from brain to kidneys,
Only to be dismissed as issuing
From the submerged foundations of an iceberg,
Or classified as "mutual interference".

The hopes were running higher the farther north
The convoy steamed. Would this one get its break?
The Arctic pressed into the human service,
The Circle which had caught the navigators—
The hardiest in the annals of The Search,
Willoughby, Chancelor, Hudson, Bering, Franklin—
Impounded them, twisted and broken them,
Their ships and crews upon its icy spokes:
This time through the ironic quirk of War
Changed to an allied *cordon sanitaire*.

The evening of the eighth day and a moon,
High-sailing and impersonal, picked out
The seventy ships, deriding the constrained
Hush of the blackout. Was the latitude
Itself not adequate watch? The sea was calm,
Although with a beam swell the wallowing rate
Was but five knots. The moon illuminated
The *Empire Hudson,* leader of port wing,
Loaded with grain, the *Gypsum Queen* with sulphur,
The *Winterswyck,* the *Garm,* the *Scania,*
Muneric (iron ore—sink like a rock
She would if hit), *Bretwalda, Baron Ramsay,*
Gullpool, the *Empire Panther* and *Macgregor,*
The *Lorient, Arosa, Hampton Lodge,*
And others with the same high names and pennants,
Carrying at the load-water line their freight—
Twelve columns of them in their blueprint stations.
A half an hour to dusk the bo'sun's mate
Had piped his strictest order—*Darken Ship.*

Thousands of sailors under decks were sealed
As in vast envelopes. They ate and worked
And slept within a world self-quarantined
Against the pestilence of light by bolts,
Bulkheads and battened portholes, for each cell
Was like a tumoured brain, danger within,
Danger without, divided from the world
By an integument of iron bone.
What chance for life the moment when a shell
Trepanned the skull? What would release the pressure
Of that stampede to reach the for'ard hatch—
That burial hole in the deckhead—and come up
When the plates buckled in the lower mess?
Danger within? Could not the magazines
By a raffle flirt of fate be made to turn
Against the convoy, striking through the escort,
With final undeliberated measure,
When the oil tanks would join the magazines
To the last ton, to the last gram of blunder?
The fires that warmed the galleys could cremate:
For oil and fulminate of mercury,
Nitrated cellulose and T.N.T.
And the constituents of our daily bread,
Fresh water and fresh air, could by a shift,
Sudden and freakish in the molecules,
Be transubstantiated into death.

Added to this might come the blows where friend
Struck friend with utmost shoulder energy—
Blows just as murderous as torpedo hits
Where in the darkness, executing turns,
Or in the fog, the convoy ships would find
Their plates as vulnerable as cellophane:
Or from excess of their protective zeal
The fighting units with their double rate
Of convoy speed might plough their sinuous way
Up through the narrow lanes and turn too sharp,
Presenting their full beams across the bows
Of leading merchantmen. Lucky they were
If they escaped with nothing but a blast
Of roaring basso from the Commodore's lungs—
"Those lousy, noisy, nattering sons o' badgers,
Where do they think they're going—to Miami,
Harpooning porpoises or flying fish?"

The Silent Service never won its name
With fairer title than it did this night.
Evening at half-past nine and a fresh sound,
An instant octave lift to treble pitch
From the dull datum of "reverbs" startled
The ear. *"An echo bearing* GREEN FOUR-O,
Range 1500."
              "Hold and classify."
The *ping-g-g* with its death's head identity!

C.O. TO OFFICER-OF-WATCH:
"Increase speed 250 revolutions."

(Officer-of-the-Watch repeats, calls down voice-pipe to coxswain who sets engine-room telegraph to speed. The Engineer Officer-of-Watch acknowledges. His chief E.R.A. swings wheel-throttle-valve open to make required revolutions. Engine-room telegraph confirms to wheelhouse and coxswain calls up voice-pipe—*"Wheelhouse-Bridge: 250 revolutions on, sir."* Bridge Officer-of-Watch repeats to captain.)

The *Skeena* heeled to port on *"starboard ten"*
To keep the target on the bow. *"Steady
On* TWO-FOUR-SEVEN." (Harry one at the dip.)
"Left cut on TWO-FOUR-SIX. . . . *Right cut
On* TWO-FIVE-THREE." (Reporting Doppler)
"Echo high and inclination closing."
The range 1200. *"Target moving right:
Centre bearing,* TWO-FIVE-FIVE."
One thousand yards: *"extent of target—ten."*

Not ice this time but moving steel submerged—
Two hundred feet of longitudinal plate,
Forged at the Krupp's and tested in the Baltic,
Were answering the taps.
                    "Stand by depth-charges."

CAPTAIN TO CHIEF YEOMAN:
*"Take an emergency report to shore:
'In contact with classified submarine'."*

(Chief Yeoman repeats to W.T. office.)
A crackle of Morse, and in bare space of seconds
The warning goes to Admiralty, from there
To allied ships in threatened area,
And on the walls in *Operations,* where
The swastikas and shadows of the U-boats
Follow in replica the Atlantic movements,
A red peg moves along the chart to plot
The first of the disease spots that would pock
The body of the S.C. 42.

Whatever doubt the eye might have imposed
Upon the ear soon vanished with the signals.
Jedmore reported two torpedoes passed
Ahead. *Muneric,* fourth ship in port column,
Attacked, dragged instantly, sank with her iron.
The Commodore—*"Saw U-boat on port bow."*
Kenogami in contact with another,
A third, a fourth. Suspicions which had wormed
Their way along the vine were proved. The first
Wolf-pack engagement of the Atlantic War
Was on! A fifth . . . a seventh! They had trailed
The ships to Greenland waters. Moonlight full,
Without the mercy of clouds, had turned
A traitor to the convoy, cancelling
The northern length of nights. Like teal not yet
Surprised to wing, the silhouetted ships
Awaited leisured barrels from the hunters,
And the warheads drilled them as from open sights.

Orillia, detailed to sweep astern,
Picked up the few survivors, took in tow
The S.S. *Tachee,* badly hit but still
Afloat: rockets were seen in midst of convoy:
A signal from the flagship—" *'Empire Hudson'*
Torpedoed on port side." The triple task—
To screen the convoy, counter-attack, and then,
The humane third of rescuing the sailors,
Seemed far beyond the escort's hope or effort.
To save to kill, to kill to save, were means
And ends closely and bloodily allied.
Hundreds of sailors un-lifejacketed
Clawed at the jetsam in the oil and water.
Captains and Commodore were well aware

Of how a lame one in a chase could spatter
With blood the entire herd. High strategy
Demanded of the brain an execution
Protested by the tactics of the heart.
And there was only half an inch or less
Of a steel skin upon the escort's hulls—
Not for self-safety were those ships designed.
Just here the log with its raw elements
Enshrined a saga in a phrase of action.
"The 'Empire Hudson' listing badly, crew
And officers were disembarked. Someone
Reported—'Secret papers have not been
Destroyed, mersigs, swept-channels, convoy route,
And codes, the CODES!' And as there was a chance
The steamer might not sink, 'Kenogami'
Was ordered to embark an officer,
Return him to the listed deck to find
And sink the weighted papers—which was done."
This stark undecorated phrase was just
An interlinear item in the drama,
Three words spelling a deed unadvertised,
When ships announced their wounds by rockets, **wrote**
Their own obituaries in flame that soared
Two hundred feet and stabbed the Arctic night
Like some neurotic and untimely sunrise.
Exploding tankers turned the sky to canvas,
Soaked it in orange fire, kindled the sea,
Then carpeted their graves with wreaths of soot.
The sea would tidy up its floor in time,
But not just now,—gaskegs and rafts and mops,
Oilskins, sou'westers, sea-boots, duffel coats
Drifted above the night's burnt offerings.
Only the names remained uncharred—*Muneric,*
Ulysses, Baron Pentland, Sally Maersk,
The *Empire Crossbill, Empire Hudson, Stargard*—
Merely heroic memories by morning.
The early hours of daylight drove the subs
To cover though the escort knew that eyes,
As sleepless as their own but unobserved
Behind the grey-green mesh of swell and lop,
Were following the convoy's desperate plunge.

All knew that no restrictive rules would hedge
This fight: to the last ship, to the last shot,
To the last man, for fair was foul and foul
Was fair in that *mêlée* of strength and cunning.
Tirpitz and Fisher thirty years before
Had scanned the riddles in each other's eyes.
What was the argument about the belt
That drained the sophistry of principles
Inside a ring? *"Hit first, hit hard, hit fast!"*
Tirpitz had trumped him with—*"Hit anywhere."*
And here today only one point was certain—
Sailors above the sea, sailors below,
Drew equally upon a fund of courage.
No one might gamble on the other's fear
Or waning will, Commander Schmidt might flood
His tanks and dive when something on his mirror
Called for discretion, but in his own shrewd time
He could be reckoned on to blow the ballast
And frame that picture on the glass again.
He would come up with Botterschult and Rickert,
Von Braundorff, Niebergall, Schippmann and Fritzsche.
They knew their crews would never fail the switches
Or rush the conning towers before the orders,
Though the depth-charges pounded the blood vessels,
Though combing rams just missed them overhead.
In what proportions did the elements
Combine to move those individual pawns
Of power in their massed flesh-and-nerve formation
Across a board? Grit human; bruinine;
Habits that would not heckle a command,
Obedience that sealed the breach of fear,
A frenzy that would spurn the slopes of Reason
Under a rhetoric of Will which placed
Before the *herrenvolk* historic choices—
To scramble up a cliff and vandalize
The sunlight or else perish on the ledges.

These were the enemies the convoy fronted:
Metal to metal, though in this arena
The odds lay heavily with the pursuers,
Even by day—for what were periscopes
At distance of three thousand yards, that reared
Their tiny heads curved like swamp moccasins?
What was their smothered wake compared with that

Propeller wash, that height and drift of smoke,
Those lines of funnels with their sixty hulls?
And so it was a safe bet on the sub
When at high noon one left her nest and sped
Her charge right at the S.S. *Thistleglen,*
Dead at the waterline and full amidships.
It took three minutes for the merchantman
To dock her pigiron on the ocean floor.

"There, there he is!"
                     Seven cables from the spot
Where suction swirled above the foundering,
The periscope light-grey—one minute only!
The *Skeena* carried out a pounce attack
Of ten depth-charges fired with shallow settings.
The asdic trailed the sub proceeding north
At three-knot speed. *Kenogami* confirmed
Echoes. Depth-charges with deep settings dropped,
The echoes ceased, and a great patch of oil
Surfaced, and a huge bubble like a blister
Broke, close to the position of explosions.
"This time for keeps we pinged his bloody hide, sir:
We've sent him down to join the 'Thistleglen'."

With this by day, what could another night
Not call forth from the cupboard? Afternoon
Wore on till dusk with that dramatic lull
Which acted like narcotics on the heart,
Yet put high-tension circuits in the brain.

"The 'Sally Maersk' went down with bread enough
To feed an army for a month."
                            "But what
A job the corvettes did in rescuing
Them all—the fifty-four under that fire."
"Most of the 'Baron Pentland' too."
                            "Her back
Was broken though her lumber kept her floating."

Could the same chance be taken the next night?

An hour after nightfall and the convoy
Had pierced the sixty-second parallel.
Twelve shortened columns tightened up their gaps,
All ships under instructions— (You will not—repetition—
Not break W.T. silence without deep suspicion of
U-boat presence.)   Owing to moon
Rear ships of the port column were instructed
To drop smoke floats should enemy appear
On the port side. Each minute passed, each mile
Northward were credit items on a ledger.
And now quickening the heart, two friendly shadows,
Corvettes, steamed into shape—*Moose Jaw, Chambly*—
Two added to the four. But still the hope
Was on evasion—on the North—to kick
Them with their wounded heels and merge the spoors
Within the Greenland-Iceland ocean tundras.
And so the last night's vigil was repeated,
Although more ominous the silences:
More broken, too, the sleep as the ears buzzed
Still with the dental burr of the point-fives,
And the yellow cordite from the four-point-sevens
Kept up its smart under exhausted eyelids.
The average rate was lowered by three knots.
The *Tachee* was in tow of the *Orillia*,
Fumbling her rudder. From the *Chambly*'s deck,
Two miles away, the ships seemed fated targets.
Silent and slow and dark as, clothed with crape,
They journeyed on like mourners, having left
The Saxon burial of their sister ships,
And bearing on themselves the same contagion.
The air was breathing out its prophecy.
So was the water. There was mockery
Within the sea's caress—the way a wave
Would clamber up the bow of the *Moose Jaw*, scout
Around the shadows of the foc's'le,
Tattoo the face of the Bridge and lazily
Slither along the deck and then hiss through
The hawse-pipes as the corvette dipped her nose
To the slow anaesthetic of the swell.
Mockery it was on face and lips and fingers,
For, after her reconnaissance, the sea,
As urging death with a forensic fury,
Would shed her velvet syllables, return

With loaded fists to thunder at the gun-shields,
Trying to crack defence before the battle
Was joined between the "patterns" and the "tubes".

Eleven-thirty, and the navigator,
His coat and boots on in his bunk, completes
A nightmare with a steady mumbling curse.
He thought the order was *Abandon Ship*—
It was an O.D. calling Middle Watch.
He wakes, turns over, and again turns over,
Yawns, stretches and turns out, proceeds to Bridge,
Peers through the blackout curtains, and in dim
Blue battle-light he squints and notes night orders,
The toughest order of the toughest Watch
(Maintain tail sweep from two to four thousand yards).

He focuses binoculars to range
The horizon arcs. *"A lot of whales about
Tonight."* The echoes picked them up. Four hours!
He has to fight that Middle Watch fatigue,
And as the minutes crawl he sucks life-savers,
Or cracks one on his teeth for company.
A line of spray leaps up above the dodger
And like rawhide cuts him across the face.
Then, too, that phosphorescence on the sea
Is easily mistaken in its darts,
Flashes and curves for what the lookout fears.
Two hours are gone: another two to go.
(That wrist-watch ticks off hours instead of seconds.)
His eyelids blink to ease the strain that falls
Like mist upon a telescopic lens.
A starboard lookout yell jerks back his senses—
"Torpedo bearing green-four-O." Lookout
Recoils from an expected blow that does
Not strike. *"Damn porpoises: they always home
In on the bow."*
*(The navigating officer wipes the sweat from his forehead with
his sleeve, tells the sub-lieutenant to take over for a few minutes
as he wants to go to Heads. Then he calls to a stand-by.)*
                        *"Say, Spinney, what about
A mug of kye?"*
                        "Yes, Sir."

                                                      Spinney had not
Yet found his legs. Less than six months before
He had been learning Latin and the class-
Room smell had not been kippered from his system.
To him the ocean was a place of travel,
A blue-green oriental boulevard
Round unknown continents—up to this year;
And even to last night the illusion stayed,
When for his benefit the Borealis
Staged a rehearsal of the Merry Dancers
Before the blood-red footlights till it paled
The myth upon a tracery of starshell.
He now goes to the galley, fills a jug
With kye, picks up a half a dozen mugs,
Stumbles, skates, splashes half of it on deck.
Some drops of rain and sea-foam tincture it.
Along the way a leading-hand of the Watch
And a rheumatic coder cadge a drink,
And by the time that Spinney finds his balance
On the bridge only a soapy seawash greets
The navigator's throat. *"What in the name*
Of all buck goats is this? Where did you get
This swill?" (He hands it to the sub to drink.)
                    "Go back and fill her up again,
And keep her clean."
                    Spinney steps down from bridge,
Staggers, makes for the ladder, cracks the jug
Against the signal-box before he slides,
Reaches the galley and returns, tries hard
To wean his legs from the quadrangle walk,
Does a Blue Danube on the deck, and then
Revokes his quondam heroes (what a bunch
Of fools those ancients were to travel,
Aeneas was the biggest ass on earth!)
And flinging out his last accusative
At what is limned on the horizon, he
Remeasures his Virgilian cadences
In terms of stresses gliding queasily
Along the black ramps of the North Atlantic.

At ten to four Lieutenant Snell takes over,
And the two victims of the Watch slope down
With brains of fog and eyes of fractured glass.

335

Their legs go aft by instinct to their bunks,
Their minds well in advance entering a coma
Beyond gun-cotton shock or Gabriel's horn.

'Twas only in a stupor that O'Leary
Recalled his reprimand. When did it happen?
"Yeoman, you dropped no markers with that pattern.
That's standing orders now—smoke-floats to mark
Areas attacked. Ever heard it? Don't you know
Your drill? You'll be in my report in the morning."
O'Leary gagged upon his chewing quid,
Hiccupped, sending a spurt of nicotine
And hydrochloric acid on the sea.
"He said to me, said he, 'O'Leary, don't
You know your drill?'—Say, how the hell would I know?
Nobody tells me nothing in this Navy."

A bo'sun caught the Peggy with a fag.
"Cripes, do you want to bitch this midnight show?
That lighted butt is visible for miles,
And on the starboard wing, too. Don't you know
The one and only moral law of Moses
Is never light a fag on deck at night?
A law you got to learn while in the Service.
A light can be machine-gunned by the escort.
They'd ping your fag and teeth at the same time."

PEGGY, OUT OF EARSHOT:
"I didn't light it on the deck. I cupped
My hands and took three drags and that was all.
That jockey groomed for donkeys thinks he's got
The whole world by the tail in a down pull.
When I get back to Civvy Street, I'll call him."

O'Meara, Steele and Casey had a lot
To say. They'd gab it when the day came round—
The day the *Stargard* reached her port—but somehow
The water and the salt got in their throats
The moment when the *Stargard* took them under.

The dark was sedative and irritant.
How easy was it for an interval

To muffle the senses with a hushed blackout,
And the diminuendo of the run
Could well delude the reason. This was not
The rate that marked the fever of pursuit,
And nothing from the decks was visible
To show the way the trimmest escort unit
Could be in shackles to a lubber keel,
And have to be replaced in precious moments;
Nothing to show how gyros and magnetics
Could be ungeared by submarine explosions.
For this was information undiffused
Among the crew or countered by illusions,
Or by resumption of the normal tasks.
No one from the *Ulysses* lived to cite
The witness of the E.R.A.s and firemen,
Pounding the steel rungs in that inner trap
When the torpedo struck her gas and oil.

The drama of the night before was over.
No headlines would record as news the toil,
As stokers every hour took temperatures
Of bearings, scribbled them on pads, transferred
Them to the logs and then resumed their rounds
To watch for popping valves, to check the flow
By turning wheels when the full head of steam
Was hitting the square inches of the boilers.
There was no spotlight on the items when
A leading seaman of the watch reported
*"The temperature of the sea forty degrees,
The lowering falls are clear, boats off the pins,
The watertight compartments are all closed."*
No one would mould the linotype for such
A mass that might survive or not survive
Their tedium of watches in the holds—
The men with surnames blotted by their jobs
Into a scrawl of anonymity.
A body blow at the boilers would untype
All differentiations in the blood
Of pumpmen, wipers, messmen, galley boys
Who had become incorporate with the cogs
On ships that carried pulp and scrap to Europe.

Desire invoking for the memory
Amnesia for the nightmare that had passed,

It might have been a run in peaceful times.
The sounds seemed casual enough—lookouts
Reporting to the officers on watch,
Got back the usual laconic answers.
The turbine notes ran up from C to G
And down according to the scale of speed.
The scraps of speech from duffel-coated forms,
Huddled beneath the after-canopy,
Had by tacit agreement in the eyes
Nothing to do with present urgencies.
A rating "in the rattle" salved his mind
By giving his opinion of a buffer,
Casting suspicion on the buffer's birth
And pedigree. His *b*'s and *g*'s and *s*'s,
Delivered through his teeth in confidence
To the high winds and seas from A-gun deck,
Had all the symptoms of a normal trip.
Only the action-station gongs could jar
That gentle wishful thinking—and they did.

Horse-power to the limit on the engines,
Levied for scout assault and close defence,
Was routed quickly to defence, for short
Beyond believing was the interval
Between the echoes and torpedo hits,
Between them and the spotted periscopes.
The Commodore reported, " '*Gypsum Queen*'
Torpedoed and sunk." *Alberni* gets an echo,
Five hundred yards, *Kenogami* confirming.
Chambly and *Moose Jaw* get a definite kill
With prisoners, and then a "probable".
The peril of the night before was doubled.
This time the subs had dived within the convoy,
"*Attacking from within the lines*"—the fear
Above all fears, for, out to sea, the lairs
Might be discerned and the protective screens
Be interposed between them and the convoy.
But now the hazards of the fight were weighted
In favour of the foe. Seven or eight

Out of the estimated twelve were there
Inside or hanging on to flank or rear.
Even blindly they could not miss—on port
And starboard bow, amidships, on the quarter.

Upon the *Skeena's* Bridge the judgment fought
With chaos. Blindness, deafness visited
The brain. Through a wild paradox of sight
And sound, the asdic echoes would not fall
Within their ribbon-tidy categories.
They bounded in confusion from the hulls
Of tankers and corvettes: the ash-can sounds
Were like those of explosions from torpedoes.
Wake-echoes and reverbs, and *quenching* caused
By pitch and roll of a heavy following sea,
Had blended with the sharper pings from steel
To give the effect of a babel and a brawl.

But blindness was the worst. To find the foe
By starshell served indeed to spot the target,
But carved in white the escort's silhouette.
The need called for the risk. A megaphone
Informed the *Skeena* that a sub was seen
Between the columns seven and eight, its course
Marked by a steady hail of tracer bullets.
The *Skeena* tried to ram; the sub escaped
To an adjacent lane and turned right angles
In opposite direction to destroyer.
The shelter of the dark was now a threat
Holding collision as the convoy ships
Made their sharp turn of forty-five degrees.
Her fighting and her navigating lights
Were switched on to identify the *Skeena,*
Scratching the paint upon the merchant hulls,
As orders pelted down the voice-pipe, helm
And engines answering—*"Full speed ahead . . .
Starboard twenty . . . Stop both . . . Half-ahead port . . .
Half-astern starboard . . . Stop starboard . . .
Half-ahead starboard . . . Full ahead both . . ."*

This was infighting at its grisly worst.
The issue grew more leaden as the night
Advanced, and what relief could daylight offer

Against the weary arithmetic count?
The *Winterswyck* blown up, sunk with her phosphate;
Stonepool torpedoed on both sides, gone down
With general cargo and a fleet of trucks.
And matching the confusion on the decks
Was the confusion in the ether, ships
Torpedoed, burning, sinking, hammering out
Their cryptocodes. What listeners could sort them,
Solve those recurring decimals of dots
And those long dashes when the operators
Screwed down the keys—their last official acts—
To give the drowning wails of instruments?
What rescuers could hurry to position?
Only the fighting ships—and they were fighting.

"Which one was that?"
                              "A tanker bad enough,
But not as bad as that; a flame that would
Frizzle a glacier."
                              "Aviation gas?"

"It could create that light but not that roar,
'Twould cause stokehold concussion miles away,
And wake up Julianehaab."
                              "'Twas ammunition."

The *Garm* and *Scania* with their lumber lost!
Rockets observed from *Randa* and *Benury*—
The signals ceased—both missing in the morning!

The fourteen sunk and others just afloat,
The remnant staggered on still north-by-east.

*   *   *   *

Last night, the second night, and must there come
A third? The ratio of loss had climbed
Beyond all normal fears. The logs themselves
Might not be legible on that third morning.
So far the tale was grim enough—but six
Saved of the *Jedmore*'s crew; eight from the *Stonepool*;
Less than half from the *Garm*; six from the *Stargard*;
Two from the *Winterswyck*; and a great blank—
The fate of crew unknown—was logged for *Scania*,
The *Empire Springbuck, Crossbill, Thistleglen*,

Muneric and *Ulysses*. The third night
To come! Those hammerheads were off there still,
Hiding, biding. How many? How those freighters
Foundered! How fast? Minutes or seconds?

                                         "Did

You see the way the 'Crossbill' took her dive?
Her cargo steel, she went down like a gannet."

"The 'Muneric' beat her to it. A life-belt
Would have no chances in that suction-hole,
Say nothing of a man. I saw her blades
Rise, edge themselves against the 'Alberni' gunfire."

Why should those phobias of speed, colour
And shape belonging to the night alone
Return to plague the mind in open daylight?
Would those fires start again? A chemistry
That would incinerate its own retort
Raged round the *Stonepool* when she sank. Water
And fire, water and oil, blood, fire and salt
Had agonized their journey through nerve-endings
To char themselves upon a graphite-grey
Precipitate. Survivors from the *Stargard*,
Who would for life carry their facial grafts,
Told of the scramble from the boiler rooms,
Up canted ladders and the reeling catwalks,
Only to find their exit was the sea,
And there to find their only exit from
Its cauldron surface was its drowning depth.
Where find the straws to grasp at in this sea?
Where was the cause which once had made a man
Disclaim the sting of death? What ecstasy
Could neutralize this salt and quench this heat
Or open up in victory this grave?
But oil and blood were prices paid for blood
And oil. However variable the time,
The commerce ever was in barter. Oil
Propelled the ships. It blew them up. The men
Died oil-anointed as it choked the *"Christ!"*
That stuttered on their lips before the sea
Paraded them as crisps upon her salver.
This was the payment for the oil designed
To sleek the gears and punch the pistons in
And over Alamein and Normandy.

And blood mixed with the sea-foam was the cost
Of plasma safely carried in the holds
Across an ocean to a continent,
There to unblanch the faces on the fields,
There to revein the vines for fresher fruits
In a new harvest on a hoped tomorrow;
And over all, the purchase of the blood
Was that an old dishonoured postulate,
Scrubbed of its rust, might shine again—*Granted*
That what the mind may think, the tongue may utter.

*   *   *   *

Three morning hours were gone and no attack.
Were the U-boats destroyed or shaken off
Or still awaiting night? What mattered it?
What mattered the rotation of the earth?
The clock had struck in seasons those two nights,
And Time was but a fiddler off his key,
Treading the youth through middle age towards death.

From the lookout a signal—*Smoke ahead!*
Was it a surface raider? This would mean
Extinction, still another word for sleep.
The smoke took shape—five funnels pouring it.
Binoculars from the crowsnests and bridges
Of all the ships, escort and convoy, swept
The horizon: dots turned into lines, the lines
To hulls and decks and guns and turrets—five
British destroyers making thirty knots.
This was the restoration for the hearts
Of fifty ships—the maimed, the blind, the whole.
Around them raced the fighters, plotting out
Suspicious zones whenever asdic sweeps
Reported doubtful contacts, searching far
Afield, then closing to resume position
On screen. And so the S.C. 42,
With mutilated but with fashioned columns,
Covered the lap across the Denmark Strait
With that same chivalry of knots which meant
Rescue for hundreds in the Greenland battle.
For with the battered *Tachee* still in tow

Of the *Orillia*, they reached the two
Most northern outposts of the Old World havens,
Rock-armoured Hvalfjord and Reykjavik,
Then took their southern stretch until the convoy
Sighted Inishtrahull and there dispersed.
And the fighting ships, miraculously unscathed,
Proceeded to Moville, to Lishahally,
'Thence up the winding Foyle to seek their berths
Around the crowded docks of Londonderry.

TOWARDS THE LAST SPIKE
(1952)

To Victoria College
and all its happy associations

TOWARDS THE LAST SPIKE

It was the same world then as now—the same,
Except for little differences of speed
And power, and means to treat myopia
To show an axe-blade infinitely sharp
Splitting things infinitely small, or else
Provide the telescopic sight to roam
Through curved dominions never found in fables.
The same, but for new particles of speech—
Those algebraic substitutes for nouns
That sky cartographers would hang like signboards
Along the trespass of our thoughts to stop
The stutters of our tongues with their equations.

As now, so then, blood kept its ancient colour,
And smoothly, roughly, paced its banks; in calm
Preserving them, in riot rupturing them.
Wounds needed bandages and stomachs food:
The hands outstretched had joined the lips in prayer—
"Give us our daily bread, give us our pay."
The past flushed in the present and tomorrow
Would dawn upon today: only the rate
To sensitize or numb a nerve would change;
Only the quickening of a measuring skill
To gauge the onset of a birth or death
With the precision of micrometers.
Men spoke of acres then and miles and masses,
Velocity and steam, cables that moored
Not ships but continents, world granaries,
The east-west cousinship, a nation's rise,
Hail of identity, a world expanding,
If not the universe: the feel of it
Was in the air—*"Union required the Line."*
The theme was current at the banquet tables,
And arguments profane and sacred rent
God-fearing families into partisans.
Pulpit, platform and floor were sounding-boards;
Cushions beneath the pounding fists assumed
The hues of western sunsets; nostrils sniffed
The prairie tang; the tongue rolled over texts:
Even St. Paul was being invoked to wring
The neck of Thomas in this war of faith

With unbelief. Was ever an adventure
Without its cost? Analogies were found
On every page of history or science.
A nation, like the world, could not stand still.
What was the use of records but to break them?
The tougher armour followed the new shell;
The newer shell the armour; lighthouse rockets
Sprinkled their stars over the wake of wrecks.
Were not the engineers at work to close
The lag between the pressures and the valves?
The same world then as now thirsting for power
To crack those records open, extra pounds
Upon the inches, extra miles per hour.
The mildewed static schedules which before
Had like asbestos been immune to wood
Now curled and blackened in the furnace coal.
This power lay in the custody of men
From down-and-outers needing roofs, whose hands
Were moulded by their fists, whose skins could feel
At home incorporate with dolomite,
To men who with the marshal instincts in them,
Deriving their authority from wallets,
Directed their battalions from the trestles.

THE GATHERING

*("Oats—a grain which in England is generally
given to horses, but in Scotland supports the
people."—Dr. Samuel Johnson. "True, but where
will you find such horses, where such men?"—
Lord Elibank's reply as recorded by Sir Walter
Scott.)*

Oatmeal was in their blood and in their names.
Thrift was the title of their catechism.
It governed all things but their mess of porridge
Which, when it struck the hydrochloric acid
With treacle and skim-milk, became a mash.
Entering the duodenum, it broke up
Into amino acids: then the liver
Took on its natural job as carpenter:
Foreheads grew into cliffs, jaws into juts.
The meal, so changed, engaged the follicles:
Eyebrows came out as gorse, the beards as thistles,

347

And the chest-hair the fell of Grampian rams.
It stretched and vulcanized the human span:
Nonagenarians worked and thrived upon it.
Out of such chemistry run through by genes,
The food released its fearsome racial products:—
The power to strike a bargain like a foe,
To win an argument upon a burr,
Invest the language with a Bannockburn,
Culloden or the warnings of Lochiel,
Weave loyalties and rivalries in tartans,
Present for the amazement of the world
Kilts and the civilized barbaric Fling,
And pipes which, when they acted on the mash,
Fermented lullabies to *Scots wha hae*.

Their names were like a battle-muster—Angus
(He of the Shops) and Fleming (of the Transit),
Hector (of the *Kicking Horse*), Dawson,
"Cromarty" Ross, and Beatty (Ulster Scot),
Bruce, Allan, Galt and Douglas, and the "twa"—
Stephen (Craigellachie)* and Smith (Strathcona)—
Who would one day climb from their Gaelic hide-outs,
Take off their plaids and wrap them round the mountains.
And then the everlasting tread of the Macs,
Vanguard, centre and rear, their roving eyes
On summits, rivers, contracts, beaver, ledgers;
Their ears cocked to the skirl of Sir John A.,
The general of the patronymic march.

(*Sir John revolving round the Terms of Union with
British Columbia. Time, late at night.*)

Insomnia had ripped the bed-sheets from him
Night after night. How long was this to last?
Confederation had not played this kind
Of trickery on him. That was rough indeed,
So gravelled, that a man might call for rest
And take it for a life accomplishment.
It was his laurel though some of the leaves

* *"Stand Fast, Craigellachie,"* the war-cry of the Clan
Grant, named after a rock in the Spey Valley, and used
as a cable message from Stephen in London to the
Directors in Montreal.

Had dried. But this would be a longer tug
Of war which needed for his team thick wrists
And calloused fingers, heavy heels to dig
Into the earth and hold—men with bull's beef
Upon their ribs. Had he himself the wind,
The anchor-waist to peg at the rope's end?
'Twas had enough to have these questions hit
The waking mind: 'twas much worse when he dozed;
For goblins had a way of pinching him,
Slapping a nightmare on to dwindling snoozes.
They put him and his team into a tug
More real than life. He heard a judge call out—
"Teams settle on the rope and take the strain!"
And with the coaches' *heave*, the running welts
Reddened his palms, and then the gruelling *backlock*
Inscribed its indentations on his shoulders.
This kind of burn he knew he had to stand;
It was the game's routine; the other fire
Was what he feared the most for it could bake him—
That white dividing rag tied to the rope
Above the centre pole had with each heave
Wavered with chances equal. With the backlock,
Despite the legs of Tupper and Cartier,
The western anchor dragged; the other side
Remorselessly was gaining, holding, gaining.
No sleep could stand this strain and, with the nightmare
Delivered of its colt, Macdonald woke.

Tired with the midnight toss, lock-jawed with yawns,
He left the bed and, shuffling to the window,
He opened it. The air would cool him off
And soothe his shoulder burns. He felt his ribs:
Strange, nothing broken—how those crazy drowses
Had made the fictions tangle with the facts!
He must unscramble them with steady hands.
Those Ranges pirouetting in his dreams
Had their own knack of standing still in light,
Revealing peaks whose known triangulation
Had to be read in prose severity.
Seizing a telescope, he swept the skies,
The north-south drift, a self-illumined chart.
Under Polaris was the Arctic Sea
And the sub-Arctic gates well stocked with names:

Hudson, Davis, Baffin, Frobisher;
And in his own day Franklin, Ross and Parry
Of the Canadian Archipelago;
Kellett, McClure, McClintock, of *The Search.*
Those straits and bays had long been kicked by keels,
And flags had fluttered on the Capes that fired
His youth, making familiar the unknown.
What though the odds were nine to one against,
And the Dead March was undertoning trumpets,
There was enough of strychnine in the names
To make him flip a penny for the risk,
Though he had palmed the coin reflectively
Before he threw and watched it come down *heads.*
That stellar path looked too much like a road map
Upon his wall—the roads all led to market—
The north-south route. He lit a candle, held
It to a second map full of blank spaces
And arrows pointing west. Disturbed, he turned
The lens up to the zenith, followed the course
Tracked by a cloud of stars that would not keep
Their posts—Capella, Perseus, were reeling;
Low in the north-west, Cassiopeia
Was qualmish, leaning on her starboard arm-rest,
And Aries was chasing, butting Cygnus,
Just diving. Doubts and hopes struck at each other.
Why did those constellations look so much
Like blizzards? And what lay beyond the blizzards?

'Twas chilly at the window. He returned
To bed and savoured soporific terms:
Superior, the *Red River, Selkirk, Prairie,*
Port Moody and *Pacific.* Chewing them,
He spat out *Rocky* grit before he swallowed.
Selkirk! This had the sweetest taste. Ten years
Before, the Highland crofters had subscribed
Their names in a memorial for the Rails.
Sir John reviewed the story of the struggle,
That four months' journey from their native land—
The Atlantic through the Straits to Hudson Bay,
Then the Hayes River to Lake Winnipeg
Up to the Forks of the Assiniboine.

He could make use of that—just what he needed,
A Western version of the Arctic daring,
Romance and realism, double dose.
How long ago? Why, this is '71.
Those fellows came the time Napoleon
Was on the steppes. For sixty years they fought
The seasons, 'hoppers, drought, hail, wind and snow;
Survived the massacre at Seven Oaks,
The "Pemmican War" and the Red River floods.
They wanted now the Road—those pioneers
Who lived by spades instead of beaver traps.
Most excellent word that, pioneers! Sir John
Snuggled himself into his sheets, rolling
The word around his tongue, a theme for song,
Or for a peroration to a speech.

THE HANGOVER AT DAWN

He knew the points that had their own appeal.
These did not bother him: the patriot touch,
The Flag, the magnetism of explorers,
The national unity. These could burn up
The phlegm in most of the provincial throats.
But there was one tale central to his plan
(The focus of his headache at this moment),
Which would demand the limit of his art—
The ballad of his courtship in the West:
Better reveal it soon without reserve.

THE LADY OF BRITISH COLUMBIA

Port Moody and Pacific! He had pledged
His word the Line should run from sea to sea.
"From sea to sea", a hallowed phrase. Music
Was in that text if the right key were struck,
And he must strike it first, for, as he fingered
The clauses of the pledge, rough notes were rasping—
"No Road, No Union", and the converse true.
East-west against the north-south run of trade,
For California like a sailor-lover
Was wooing over-time. He knew the ports.
His speech was as persuasive as his arms,
As sinuous as Spanish arias—
Tamales, Cazadero, Mendecino,

351

Curling their baritones around the Lady.
Then Santa Rosa, Santa Monica,
Held absolution in their syllables.
But when he saw her stock of British temper
Starch at ironic sainthood in the whispers—
*"Rio de nuestra señora de buena guia,"**
He had the tact to gutturalize the liquids,
Steeping the tunes to drinking songs, then take
Her on a holiday where she could watch
A roving sea-born Californian pound
A downy chest and swear by San Diego.

Sir John, wise to the tricks, was studying hard
A fresh proposal for a marriage contract.
He knew a game was in the ceremony.
That southern fellow had a healthy bronze
Complexion, had a vast estate, was slick
Of manner. In his ardour he could tether
Sea-roses to the blossoms of his orchards,
And for his confidence he had the prime
Advantage of his rival—*he was there.*

THE LONG-DISTANCE PROPOSAL

A game it was, and the Pacific lass
Had poker wisdom on her face. Her name
Was rich in values—*British*; this alone
Could raise Macdonald's temperature: so could
Columbia with a different kind of fever,
And in between the two, *Victoria.*
So the *Pacific* with its wash of letters
Could push the Fahrenheit another notch.
She watched for bluff on those Disraeli features,
Impassive but for arrowy chipmunk eyes,
Engaged in fathoming a contract time.
With such a dowry she could well afford
To take the risk of tightening the terms—
"Begin the Road in two years, end in ten"—
Sir John, a moment letting down his guard,
Frowned at the Rocky skyline, but agreed.

"River of Our Lady of Safe Conduct."

(The Terms ratified by Parliament, British Columbia enters Confederation July, 1871, Sandford Fleming being appointed engineer-in-chief of the proposed Railway, Walter Moberly to cooperate with him in the location of routes. "Of course, I don't know how many millions you have, but it is going to cost you money to get through those canyons."—Moberly to Macdonald.)

THE PACIFIC SCANDAL

(Huntingdon's charges of political corruption based on correspondence and telegrams rifled from the offices of the solicitor of Sir Hugh Allan, Head of the Canada Pacific Company; Sir John's defence; and the appearance of the Honourable Edward Blake who rises to reply to Sir John at 2 a.m.)

BLAKE IN MOOD

Of all the subjects for debate here was
His element. His soul as clean as surf,
No one could equal him in probing cupboards
Or sweeping floors and dusting shelves, finding
A skeleton inside an overcoat;
Or shaking golden eagles from a pocket
To show the copper plugs within the coins.
Rumours he heard had gangrened into facts—
Gifts nuzzling at two-hundred-thousand dollars,
Elections on, and with a contract pending.
The odour of the bills had blown his gorge.
His appetite, edged by a moral hone,
Could surfeit only on the Verities.

November 3, 1873

A Fury rode him to the House. He took
His seat, and with a stoic gloom he heard
The Chieftain's great defence and noted well
The punctuation of the cheers. He needed all

The balance of his mind to counterpoise
The movements of Macdonald as he flung
Himself upon the House, upon the Country,
Upon posterity, upon his conscience.
That plunging played the devil with Blake's tiller,
Threatened the set of his sail. To save the course,
To save himself, in that five hours of gale,
He had to jettison his meditation,
His brooding on the follies of mankind,
Clean out the wadding from his tortured ears:
That roaring mob before him could be quelled
Only by action; so when the last round
Of the applause following the peroration
Was over, slowly, weightily, Blake rose.

A statesman-chancellor now held the Floor.
He told the sniffing Commons that a sense
Keener than smell or taste must be invoked
To get the odour. Leading them from facts
Like telegrams and stolen private letters,
He soared into the realm of principles
To find his scourge; and then the men involved,
Robed like the Knights of Malta, Blake undressed,
Their cloaks inverted to reveal the shoddy,
The tattered lining and bare-threaded seams.
He ripped the last stitch from them—by the time
Recess was called, he had them in the dock
As brigands in the Ministry of Smells,
Naked before the majesty of Heaven.

For Blake recesses were but sandwiches
Provided merely for cerebral luncheons—
No time to spread the legs under the table,
To chat and chaff a while, to let the mind
Roam, like a goblet up before the light
To bask in natural colour, or by whim
Of its own choice to sway luxuriously
In tantalizing arcs before the nostrils.
A meal was meant by Nature for nutrition—
A sorry farinaceous business scaled
Exactly to caloric grains and grams
Designed for intellectual combustion,

For energy directed into words
Towards proof. Abuse was overweight. He saw
No need for it; no need for caricature,
And if a villainous word had to be used,
'Twas for a villain—keen upon the target.
Irrelevance was like a moral lesion
No less within a speech than in a statute.
What mattered it who opened up the files,
Sold for a bid the damning correspondence—
That Montreal-Chicago understanding?
A dirty dodge, so let it be conceded.
But *here* the method was irrelevant.
Whether by legal process or by theft,
The evidence was there unalterable.
So with the House assembled, he resumed
Imperial indictment of the bandits.
The logic left no loopholes in the facts.
Figures that ran into the hundred-thousands
Were counted up in pennies, each one shown
To bear the superscription of debasement.

Again recess, again the sandwiches,
Again the invocation of the gods:
Each word, each phrase, each clause went to position,
Each sentence regimented like a lockstep.
The only thing that would not pace was time;
The hours dragged by until the thrushes woke—
Two days, two nights—someone opened a window,
And members of the House who still were conscious
Uncreaked their necks to note that even Sir John
Himself had put his fingers to his nose.

(*The appeal to the country: Macdonald defeat-
ed: Mackenzie assumes power, 1874.*)

A change of air, a drop in temperature!
The House had rarely known sobriety
Like this. No longer clanged the *"Westward Ho!"*
And quiet were the horns upon the hills.
Hard times ahead. The years were rendering up
Their fat. Measured and rationed was the language
Directed to the stringency of pockets.
The eye must be convinced before the *vision.*
"But one step at a time," exclaimed the feet.

355

It was the story of the hen or egg;
Which came before the other? *"'Twas the hen,"*
Cried one; *"undoubtedly the hen must lay*
The egg, hatch it and mother it." "Not so,"
Another shouted, *"'Twas the egg or whence*
The hen?" For every one who cleared his throat
And called across the House with Scriptural passion—
"The Line is meant to bring the loaves and fishes,"
A voting three had countered with the question—
"Where are the multitudes that thirst and hunger?"
Passion became displaced by argument.
Till now the axles justified their grease,
Taught coal a lesson in economy.
All doubts here could be blanketed with facts,
With phrases smooth as actuarial velvet.

For forty years in towns and cities men
Had watched the Lines baptized with charters, seen
Them grow, marry and bring forth children.
Parades and powder had their uses then
For gala days; and bands announced arrivals,
Betrothals, weddings and again arrivals.
Champagne brimmed in the font as they were named
With titles drawn from the explorers' routes,
From Saints and Governors, from space and seas
And compass-points—Saints Andrew, Lawrence, Thomas,
Louis and John; Champlain, Simcoe; Grand Trunk,
Intercolonial, the Canadian Southern,
Dominion-Atlantic, the Great Western—names
That caught a continental note and tried
To answer it. Half-gambles though they were,
Directors built those Roads and heard them run
To the sweet silver jingle in their minds.

The airs had long been mastered like old songs
The feet could tap to in the galleries.
But would they tap to a new rhapsody,
A harder one to learn and left unfinished?
What ear could be assured of absolute pitch
To catch this kind of music in the West?
The far West? Men had used this flattering name
For East or but encroachment on the West.

And was not Lake Superior still the East,
A natural highway which ice-ages left,
An unappropriated legacy?
There was no discord in the piston-throbs
Along this Road. This was old music too.
That northern spine of rock, those western mountains,
Were barriers built of God and cursed of Blake.
Mild in his oaths, Mackenzie would avoid them.
He would let contracts for the south and west,
Push out from settlement to settlement.
This was economy, just plain horse-sense.
The Western Lines were there—American.
He would link up with them, could reach the Coast.
The Eagle and the Lion were good friends:
At least the two could meet on sovereign terms
Without a sign of fur and feathers flying.
As yet, but who could tell? So far, so good.
Spikes had been driven at the boundary line,
From Emerson across the Red to Selkirk,
And then to Thunder Bay—to Lake Superior;
Across the prairies in God's own good time,
His plodding, patient, planetary time.

Five years' delay: surveys without construction;
Short lines suspended, discord in the Party.
The West defrauded of its glittering peaks,
The public blood was stirring and protesting
At this continuous dusk upon the mountains.
The old conductor off the podium,
The orchestra disbanded at the time
The daring symphony was on the score,
The audience cupped their ears to catch a strain:
They heard a plaintive thinning oboe-A
That kept on thinning while slow feeble steps
Approached the stand. Was this the substitute
For what the auditorium once knew—
The maestro who with tread of stallion hoofs
Came forward shaking platforms and the rafters,
And followed up the concert pitch with sound
Of drums and trumpets and the organ blasts
That had the power to toll out apathy
And make snow peaks ring like Cathedral steeples?
Besides, accompanying those bars of music,

There was an image men had not forgotten,
The shaggy chieftain standing at his desk,
That last-ditch fight when he was overthrown,
That desperate five hours. At least they knew
His personal pockets were not lined with pelf,
Whatever loot the others grabbed. The words
British, the West instead of South, the Nation,
The all-Canadian route—these terms were singing
Fresher than ever while the grating tones
Under the stress of argument had faded
Within the shroud of their monotony.

*(Sir John returns to power in 1878 with a
National Policy of Protective Tariff and the
Transcontinental.)*

Two years of tuning up: it needed that
To counterpoint Blake's eloquence or lift
Mackenzie's non-adventurous common sense
To the ignition of an enterprise.
The pace had to be slow at first, a tempo
Cautious, simple to follow. Sections strewn
Like amputated limbs along the route
Were sutured. This appealed to sanity.
No argument could work itself to sweat
Against a prudent case, for the terrain
Looked easy from the Lake to the Red River.
To stop with those suspensions was a waste
Of cash and time. But the huge task announced
Ten years before had now to start afresh—
The moulding of men's minds was harder far
Than moulding of the steel and prior to it.
It was the battle of ideas and words
And kindred images called by the same name,
Like brothers who with temperamental blood
Went to it with their fists. Canyons and cliffs
Were precipices down which men were hurled,
Or something to be bridged and sheared and scaled.
Likewise the Pass had its ambiguous meaning.
The leaders of the factions in the House
And through the country spelled the word the same:
The way they got their tongue around the word

Was different, for some could make it hiss
With sound of blizzards screaming over ramparts:
The Pass—the Yellowhead, the Kicking Horse—
Or jam it with *coureur-de-bois* romance,
Or join it to the empyrean. Eagles,
In flight banking their wings above a fish-stream,
Had guided the explorers to a route
And given the Pass the title of their wings.
The stories lured men's minds up to the mountains
And down along the sandbars of the rivers.
Rivalling the *"brown and barren"* on the maps,
Officially *"not fit for human life"*,
Were vivid yellows flashing in the news—
"Gold in the Cariboo," "Gold in the Fraser."
The swish of gravel in the placer-cradles
Would soon be followed by the spluttering fuses,
By thunder echoing thunder; for one month
After Blake's Ottawa roar would Onderdonk
Roar back from Yale by ripping canyon walls
To crash the tons by millions in the gorges.

The farther off, as by a paradox
Of magnets, was the golden lure the stronger:
Two thousand miles away, imagined peaks
Had the vacation pull of mountaineering,
But with the closer vision would the legs
Follow the mind? 'Twas Blake who raised the question
And answered it. Though with his natural eyes
Up to this time he had not sighted mountains,
He was an expert with the telescope.

THE ATTACK

Sir John was worried. The first hour of Blake
Was dangerous, granted the theme. Eight years
Before, he had the theme combined with language.
Impeachment—word with an historic ring,
Reserved for the High Courts of Parliament,
Uttered only when men were breathing hard
And when the vertebrae were musket-stiff:
High ground was that for his artillery,
And *there*, despite the hours the salvos lasted.

359

But *here* this was a theme less vulnerable
To fire, Macdonald thought, to Blake's gunfire,
And yet he wondered what the orator
Might spring in that first hour, what strategy
Was on the Bench. He did not mind the close
Mosaic of the words—too intricate,
Too massive in design. Men might admire
The speech and talk about it, then forget it.
But few possessed the patience or the mind
To tread the mazes of the labyrinth.
Once in a while, however, would Blake's logic
Stumble upon stray figures that would leap
Over the walls of other folds and catch
The herdsmen in their growing somnolence.
The waking sound was not—*"It can't be done"*;
That was a dogma, anyone might say it.
It was the following burning corollary:
"To build a Road over that sea of mountains."
This carried more than argument. It was
A flash of fire which might with proper kindling
Consume its way into the public mind.
The House clicked to the ready and Sir John,
Burying his finger-nails into his palms,
Muttered—*"God send us no more metaphors
Like that—except from Tory factories."*

Had Blake the lift of Chatham as he had
Burke's wind and almost that sierra span
Of mind, he might have carried the whole House
With him and posted it upon that sea
Of mountains with sub-zeros on their scalps,
Their glacial ribs waiting for warmth of season
To spring an avalanche. Such similes
Might easily glue the members to their seats
With frost in preparation for their ride.
Sir John's *"from sea to sea"* was Biblical;
It had the stamp of reverent approval;
But Blake's was pagan, frightening, congealing.
The chieftain's lips continued as in prayer,
A fiercely secular and torrid prayer—
"May Heaven intervene to stop the flow

Of such unnatural images and send
The rhetorician back to decimals,
Back to his tessellated subtleties."
The prayer was answered for High Heaven did it.
The second hour entered and passed by,
A third, a fourth. Sir John looked round the House,
Noticed the growing shuffle of the feet,
The agony of legs, the yawn's contagion.
Was that a snore? Who was it that went out?
He glanced at the Press Gallery. The pens
Were scratching through the languor of the ink
To match the words with shorthand and were failing.
He hoped the speech would last another hour,
And still another. Well within the law,
This homicidal master of the opiates
Loosened the hinges of the Opposition:
The minds went first; the bodies sagged; the necks
Curved on the benches and the legs sprawled out.
And when the Fundy Tide had ebbed, Sir John,
Smiling, watched the debris upon the banks,
For what were yesterday grey human brains
Had with decomposition taken on
The texture and complexion of red clay.

*(In 1880 Tupper lets contract to Onderdonk for
survey and construction through the Pacific Section of the mountains. Sir John, Tupper, Pope,
and McIntyre go to London to interest capital
but return without a penny.)*

Failing to make a dent in London dams,
Sir John set out to plumb a reservoir
Closer in reach. He knew its area,
Its ownership, the thickness of its banks,
Its conduits—if he could get his hands
Upon the local stopcocks, could he turn them?
The reservoir was deep. Two centuries
Ago it started filling when a king
Had in a furry moment scratched a quill
Across the bottom of His Royal Charter—
*"Granting the Governor and His Company
Of Gentlemen Adventurers the right
Exclusive to one-third a continent."*
Was it so easy then? A scratch, a seal,

361

A pinch of snuff tickling the sacred nostrils,
A puff of powder and the ink was dry.
Sir John twisted his lips: he thought of London.
Empire and wealth were in that signature
For royal, princely, ducal absentees,
For courtiers to whom the parallels
Were nothing but chalk scratches on a slate.
For them wild animals were held in game
Preserves, foxes as quarry in a chase,
And hills were hedges, river banks were fences,
And cataracts but fountains in a garden
Tumbling their bubbles into marble basins.
Where was this place called Hudson Bay? Some place
In the Antipodes? Explorers, traders,
Would bring their revenues over that signet.
Two centuries—the new empire advanced,
Was broken, reunited, torn again.
The *fleur-de-lis* went to half-mast, the *Jack*
To the mast-head, but fresher rivalries
Broke out—Nor'-Westers at the Hudson's throat
Over the pelts, over the pemmican;
No matter what—the dividends flowed in
As rum flowed out like the Saskatchewan.

The twist left Sir John's lips and he was smiling.
Though English in ambition and design,
This reservoir, he saw there in control
Upon the floodgates not a Londoner
In riding breeches but, red-flannel-shirted,
Trousered in homespun, streaked and blobbed with seal-oil,
A Scot with smoke of peat fire on his breath—
Smith? Yes: but christened Donald Alexander
And loined through issue from the Grants and Stuarts.

To smite the rock and bring forth living water,
Take lead or tin and transmute both to silver,
Copper to gold, betray a piece of glass
To diamonds, fabulize a continent,
Were wonders once believed, scrapped and revived;
For Moses, Marco Polo, Paracelsus,
Fell in the same retort and came out *Smith*.
A miracle on legs, the lad had left

Forres and Aberdeen, gone to Lachine—
"Tell Mr. Smith to count and sort the rat-skins."
Thence Tadoussac and Posts off Anticosti;
From there to Rigolet in Labrador,
A thousand miles by foot, snowshoe and dog-sled.
He fought the climate like a weathered yak,
And conquered it, ripping the stalactites
From his red beard, thawing his feet, and wringing
Salt water from his mitts; but most of all
He learned the art of making change. Blankets,
Ribbons and beads, tobacco, guns and knives,
Were swapped for muskrat, marten, fox and beaver.
And when the fur trade thinned, he trapped the salmon,
Canned it; hunted the seal, traded its oil
And fertilized the gardens with the carcass.
Even the melons grew in Labrador.
What could resist this touch? Water from rock!
Why not? No more a myth than pelts should be
Thus fabricated into bricks of gold.

If rat-skins, why not tweeds? If looms could take
Raw wool and twill it into selling shape,
They could under the draper's weaving mind
Be patterning gold braid:
                    So thought George Stephen.

His legs less sturdy than his cousin Donald's,
His eyes were just as furiously alert.
His line of vision ran from the north-west
To the Dutch-held St. Paul-Pacific Railway.
Allied with Smith, Kitson and Kennedy,
Angus, Jim Hill and Duncan McIntyre,
Could he buy up this semi-bankrupt Road
And turn the northern traffic into it?
Chief bricklayer of all the Scotian clans,
And foremost as a banking metallurgist,
He took the parchments at their lowest level
And mineralized them, roasted them to shape,
Then mortared them into the pyramid,
Till with the trowel-stretching exercise
He grew so Atlas-strong that he could carry
A mountain like a namesake on his shoulders.

(The Charter granted to The Canadian Pacific
Railway, February 17, 1881, with George Stephen
as first President . . . One William Cornelius
Van Horne arrives in Winnipeg, December 31,
1881, and there late at night, forty below zero,
gives vent to a soliloquy.)

Stephen had laid his raw han!ds on Van Horne,
Pulled him across the border, sent him up
To get the feel of northern temperatures.
He knew through Hill the story of his life
And found him made to order. Nothing less
Than geologic space his field of work,
He had in Illinois explored the creeks
And valleys, brooded on the rocks and quarries.
Using slate fragments, he became a draughtsman,
Bringing to life a landscape or a cloud,
Turning a tree into a beard, a cliff
Into a jaw, a creek into a mouth
With banks for lips. He loved to work on shadows.
Just now the man was forcing the boy's stature,
The while the youth tickled the man within.
Companioned by the shade of Agassiz,
He would come home, his pockets stuffed with fossils—
Crinoids and fish-teeth—and his tongue jabbering
Of the earth's crust before the birth of life,
Prophetic of the days when he would dig
Into Laurentian rock. The morse-key tick
And tape were things mesmeric—space and time
Had found a junction. Electricity
And rock, one novel to the coiling hand,
The other frozen in the lap of age,
Were playthings for the boy, work for the man.
As man he was the State's first operator;
As boy he played a trick upon his boss
Who, cramped with current, fired him on the instant;
As man at school, escaping Latin grammar,
He tore the fly-leaf from the text to draw
The contour of a hill; as boy he sketched
The principal, gave him flapdoodle ears,
Bristled his hair, turned eyebrows into quills,

His whiskers into flying buttresses,
His eye-tusks into rusted railroad spikes,
And made a truss between his nose and chin.
Expelled again, he went back to the keys,
To bush and rock and found companionship
With quarry-men, stokers and station-masters,
Switchmen and locomotive engineers.

Now he was transferred to Winnipeg.
Of all the places in an unknown land
Chosen by Stephen for Van Horne, this was
The pivot on which he could turn his mind.
Here he could clap the future on the shoulder
And order Fate about as his lieutenant,
For he would take no nonsense from a thing
Called Destiny—the stars had to be with him.
He spent the first night in soliloquy,
Like Sir John A. but with a difference.
Sir John wanted to sleep but couldn't do it:
Van Horne could sleep but never wanted to.
It was a waste of time, his bed a place
Only to think or dream with eyes awake.
Opening a jack-knife, he went to the window,
Scraped off the frost. Great treks ran through his mind,
East-west. Two centuries and a half gone by,
One trek had started from the Zuyder Zee
To the new Amsterdam. 'Twas smooth by now,
Too smooth. His line of grandsires and their cousins
Had built a city from Manhattan dirt.
Another trek to Illinois; it too
Was smooth, but this new one it was his job
To lead, then build a highway which men claimed
Could not be built. Statesmen and engineers
Had blown their faces blue with their denials:
The men who thought so were asylum cases
Whose monomanias harmless up to now
Had not swept into cells. His bearded chin
Pressed to the pane, his eyes roved through the west.
He saw the illusion at its worst—the frost,
The steel precision of the studded heavens,
Relentless mirror of a covered earth.
His breath froze on the scrape: he cut again
And glanced at the direction west-by-south.

365

That westward trek was the American,
Union-Pacific—easy so he thought,
Their forty million stacked against his four.
Lonely and desolate this. He stocked his mind
With items of his task: the simplest first,
Though hard enough, the Prairies, then the Shore
North of the Lake—a quantity half-guessed.
Mackenzie like a balky horse had shied
And stopped at this. Van Horne knew well the reason,
But it was vital for the all-land route.
He peered through at the South. Down there Jim Hill
Was whipping up his horses on a road
Already paved. The stations offered rest
With food and warmth, and their well-rounded names
Were tossed like apples to the public taste.

He made a mental note of his three items.
He underlined the Prairies, double-lined
The Shore and triple-lined *Beyond the Prairies,*
Began counting the Ranges—first the Rockies;
The Kicking Horse ran through them, this he knew;
The Selkirks? Not so sure. Some years before
Had Moberly and Perry tagged a route
Across the lariat loop of the Columbia.
Now Rogers was traversing it on foot,
Reading an aneroid and compass, chewing
Sea-biscuit and tobacco. Would the steel
Follow this trail? Van Horne looked farther west.
There was the Gold Range, there the Coastal Mountains.
He stopped, putting a period to the note,
As rivers troubled nocturnes in his ears.
His plans must not seep into introspection—
Call it a night, for morning was at hand,
And every hour of daylight was for work.

(Van Horne goes to Montreal to meet the Directors.)

He had agenda staggering enough
To bring the sweat even from Stephen's face.
As daring as his plans, so daring were
His promises. To build five hundred miles

Upon the prairies in one season: this
Was but a cushion for the jars ahead.
The Shore—he had to argue, stamp and fight
For this. The watercourses had been favoured,
The nation schooled to that economy.
He saw that Stephen, after wiping beads
From face and forehead, had put both his hands
Deep in his pockets—just a habit merely
Of fingering change—but still Van Horne went on
To clinch his case: the north shore could avoid
The over-border route—a national point
If ever there was one. He promised this
As soon as he was through with buffalo-grass.
And then the little matter of the Rockies:
This must be swallowed without argument,
As obvious as space, clear as a charter.
But why the change in Fleming's survey? Why
The Kicking Horse and not the Yellowhead?
The national point again. The Kicking Horse
Was shorter, closer to the boundary line;
No rival road would build between the two.
He did not dwell upon the other Passes.
He promised all with surety of schedule,
And with a self-imposed serenity
That dried the sweat upon the Board Room faces.

NUMBER ONE

Oak Lake to Calgary. Van Horne took off
His coat. The North must wait, for that would mean
His shirt as well. First and immediate
This prairie pledge—five hundred miles, and it
Was winter. Failure of this trial promise
Would mean—no, it must not be there for meaning.
An order from him carried no repeal:
It was as final as an execution.
A cable started rolling mills in Europe:
A tap of Morse sent hundreds to the bush,
Where axes swung on spruce and the saws sang,
Changing the timber into pyramids
Of poles and sleepers. Clicks, despatches, words,
Like lanterns in a night conductor's hands,
Signalled the wheels: a nod put Shaughnessy
In Montreal: supplies moved on the minute.

Thousands of men and mules and horses slipped
Into their togs and harness night and day.
The grass that fed the buffalo was turned over,
The black alluvial mould laid bare, the bed
Levelled and scraped. As individuals
The men lost their identity; as groups,
As gangs, they massed, divided, subdivided,
Like numerals only—sub-contractors, gangs
Of engineers, and shovel gangs for bridges,
Culverts, gangs of mechanics stringing wires,
Loading, unloading and reloading gangs,
Gangs for the fish-plates and the spiking gangs,
Putting a silver polish on the nails.
But neither men nor horses ganged like mules:
Wiser than both they learned to unionize.
Some instinct in their racial nether regions
Had taught them how to sniff the five-hour stretch
Down to the fine arithmetic of seconds.
They tired out their rivals and they knew it.
They'd stand for overwork, not overtime.
Faster than workmen could fling down their shovels,
They could unhinge their joints, unhitch their tendons;
Jumping the foreman's call, they brayed *"Unhook"*
With a defiant, corporate instancy.
The promise which looked first without redemption
Was being redeemed. From three to seven miles
A day the parallels were being laid,
Though Eastern throats were hoarse with the old question—
Where are the settlements? And whence the gift
Of tongues which could pronounce place-names that purred
Like cats in relaxation after kittens?
Was it a part of the same pledge to turn
A shack into a bank for notes renewed;
To call a site a city when men saw
Only a water-tank? This was an act
Of faith indeed—substance of things unseen—
Which would convert preachers to miracles,
Lure teachers into lean-to's for their classes.
And yet it happened that while labourers
Were swearing at their blisters in the evening
And straightening out their spinal kinks at dawn,
The tracks joined up Oak Lake to Calgary.

On the North Shore a reptile lay asleep—
A hybrid that the myths might have conceived,
But not delivered, as progenitor
Of crawling, gliding things upon the earth.
She lay snug in the folds of a huge boa
Whose tail had covered Labrador and swished
Atlantic tides, whose body coiled itself
Around the Hudson Bay, then curled up north
Through Manitoba and Saskatchewan
To Great Slave Lake. In continental reach
The neck went past the Great Bear Lake until
Its head was hidden in the Arctic Seas.
This folded reptile was asleep or dead:
So motionless, she seemed stone dead—just seemed:
She was too old for death, too old for life,
For as if jealous of all living forms
She had lain there before bivalves began
To catacomb their shells on western mountains.
Somewhere within this life-death zone she sprawled,
Torpid upon a rock-and-mineral mattress.
Ice-ages had passed by and over her,
But these, for all their motion, had but sheared
Her spotty carboniferous hair or made
Her ridges stand out like the spikes of molochs.
Her back grown stronger every million years,
She had shed water by the longer rivers
To Hudson Bay and by the shorter streams
To the great basins to the south, had filled
Them up, would keep them filled until the end
Of Time.

   Was this the thing Van Horne set out
To conquer? When Superior lay there
With its inviting levels? Blake, Mackenzie,
Offered this water like a postulate.
"Why those twelve thousand men sent to the North?
Nonsense and waste with utter bankruptcy."
And the Laurentian monster at the first
Was undisturbed, presenting but her bulk
To the invasion. All she had to do
Was lie there neither yielding nor resisting.

Top-heavy with accumulated power
And overgrown survival without function,
She changed her spots as though brute rudiments
Of feeling foreign to her native hour
Surprised her with a sense of violation
From an existence other than her own—
Or why take notice of this unknown breed,
This horde of bipeds that could toil like ants,
Could wake her up and keep her irritated?
They tickled her with shovels, dug pickaxes
Into her scales and got under her skin,
And potted holes in her with drills and filled
Them up with what looked like fine grains of sand,
Black sand. It wasn't noise that bothered her,
For thunder she was used to from her cradle—
The head-push and nose-blowing of the ice,
The height and pressure of its body: these
Like winds native to clime and habitat
Had served only to lull her drowsing coils.
It was not size or numbers that concerned her.
It was their foreign build, their gait of movement.
They did not crawl—nor were they born with wings.
They stood upright and walked, shouted and sang;
They needed air—that much was true—their mouths
Were open but the tongue was alien.
The sounds were not the voice of winds and waters,
Nor that of any beasts upon the earth.
She took them first with lethargy, suffered
The rubbing of her back—those little jabs
Of steel were like the burrowing of ticks
In an elk's hide needing an antler point,
Or else left in a numb monotony.
These she could stand but when the breed
Advanced west on her higher vertebrae,
Kicking most insolently at her ribs,
Pouring black powder in her cavities,
And making not the clouds but her insides
The home of fire and thunder, then she gave
Them trial of her strength: the trestles tottered;
Abutments, bridges broke; her rivers flooded:
She summoned snow and ice, and then fell back

On the last weapon in her armoury—
The first and last—her passive corporal bulk,
To stay or wreck the schedule of Van Horne.

NUMBER THREE

The big one was the mountains—seas indeed!
With crests whiter than foam: they poured like seas,
Fluting the green banks of the pines and spruces.
An eagle-flight above they hid themselves
In clouds. They carried space upon their ledges.
Could these be overridden frontally,
Or like typhoons outsmarted on the flanks?
And what were on the flanks? The troughs and canyons,
Passes more dangerous to the navigator
Than to Magellan when he tried to read
The barbarous language of his Strait by calling
For echoes from the rocky hieroglyphs
Playing their pranks of hide-and-seek in fog:
As stubborn too as the old North-West Passage,
More difficult, for ice-packs could break up;
And as for bergs, what polar architect
Could stretch his compass points to draught such peaks
As kept on rising there beyond the foothills?
And should the bastions of the Rockies yield
To this new human and unnatural foe,
Would not the Selkirks stand? This was a range
That looked like some strange dread outside a door
Which gave its name but would not show its features,
Leaving them to the mind to guess at. This
Meant tunnels—would there be no end to boring?
There must be some day. Fleming and his men
Had nosed their paths like hounds; but paths and trails,
Measured in every inch by chain and transit,
Looked easy and seductive on a chart.
The rivers out there did not flow: they tumbled.
The cataracts were fed by glaciers;
Eddies were thought as whirlpools in the Gorges,
And gradients had paws that tore up tracks.

Terror and beauty like twin signal flags
Flew on the peaks for men to keep their distance.
The two combined as in a storm at sea—

"Stay on the shore and take your fill of breathing,
But come not to the decks and climb the rigging."
The Ranges could put cramps in hands and feet
Merely by the suggestion of the venture.
They needed miles to render up their beauty,
As if the gods in high aesthetic moments,
Resenting the profanity of touch,
Chiselled this sculpture for the eye alone.

(Van Horne in momentary meditation at the Foothills.)

His name was now a legend. The North Shore,
Though not yet conquered, yet had proved that he
Could straighten crooked roads by pulling at them,
Shear down a hill and drain a bog or fill
A valley overnight. Fast as a bobcat,
He'd climb and run across the shakiest trestle
Or, with a locomotive short of coal,
He could supply the head of steam himself.
He breakfasted on bridges, lunched on ties;
Drinking from gallon pails, he dined on moose.
He could tire out the lumberjacks; beat hell
From workers but no more than from himself.
Only the devil or Paul Bunyan shared
With him the secret of perpetual motion,
And when he moved among his men they looked
For shoulder sprouts upon the Flying Dutchman.

But would his legend crack upon the mountains?
There must be no retreat: his bugles knew
Only one call—the summons to advance
Against two fortresses: the mind, the rock.
To prove the first defence was vulnerable,
To tap the treasury at home and then
Untie the purse-strings of the Londoners,
As hard to loosen as salt-water knots—
That job was Stephen's, Smith's, Tupper's, Macdonald's.
He knew its weight: had heard, as well as they,
Blake pumping at his pulmonary bellows,
And if the speeches made the House shock-proof
Before they ended, they could still peal forth
From print more durable than spoken tones.

Blake had returned to the attack and given
Sir John the ague with another phrase
As round and as melodious as the first:
"*The Country's wealth, its millions after millions
Squandered*—LOST IN THE GORGES OF THE FRASER":
A beautiful but ruinous piece of music
That could only be drowned with drums and fifes.
Tupper, fighting with fists and nails and toes,
Had taken the word *scandal* which had cut
His master's ballots, and had turned the edge
With his word *slander*, but Blake's *sea*, how turn
That edge? Now this last devastating phrase!
But let Sir John and Stephen answer this
Their way. Van Horne must answer it in his.

INTERNECINE STRIFE

The men were fighting foes which had themselves
Waged elemental civil wars and still
Were hammering one another at this moment.
The peaks and ranges flung from ocean beds
Had wakened up one geologic morning
To find their scalps raked off, their lips punched in,
The colour of their skins charged with new dyes.
Some of them did not wake or but half-woke;
Prone or recumbent with the eerie shapes
Of creatures that would follow them. Weather
Had acted on their spines and frozen them
To stegosaurs or, taking longer cycles,
Divining human features, had blown back
Their hair and, pressing on their cheeks and temples,
Bestowed on them the gravity of mummies.
But there was life and power which belied
The tombs. Guerrilla evergreens were climbing
In military order: at the base
The *ponderosa* pine; the fir backed up
The spruce; and it the Stoney Indian lodge-poles;
And these the white-barks; then, deciduous,
The outpost suicidal Lyell larches
Aiming at summits, digging scraggy roots
Around the boulders in the thinning soil,
Till they were stopped dead at the timber limit—
Rock *versus* forest with the rock prevailing.

Or with the summer warmth it was the ice,
In treaty with the rock to hold a line
As stubborn as a Balkan boundary,
That left its caves to score the Douglases,
And smother them with half a mile of dirt,
And making snow-sheds, covering the camps,
Futile as parasols in polar storms.
One enemy alone had battled rock
And triumphed: searching levels like lost broods,
Keen on their ocean scent, the rivers cut
The quartzite, licked the slate and softened it,
Till mud solidified was mud again,
And then, digesting it like earthworms, squirmed
Along the furrows with one steering urge—
To navigate the mountains in due time
Back to their home in worm-casts on the tides.

Into this scrimmage came the fighting men,
And all but rivers were their enemies.
Whether alive or dead the bush resisted:
Alive, it must be slain with axe and saw,
If dead, it was in tangle at their feet.
The ice could hit men as it hit the spruces.
Even the rivers had betraying tricks,
Watched like professed allies across a border.
They smiled from fertile plains and easy runs
Of valley gradients: their eyes got narrow,
Full of suspicion at the gorges where
They leaped and put the rickets in the trestles.
Though natively in conflict with the rock,
Both leagued against invasion. At Hell's Gate
A mountain laboured and brought forth a bull
Which, stranded in mid-stream, was fighting back
The river, and the fight turned on the men,
Demanding from this route their bread and steel.
And there below the Gate was the Black Canyon
With twenty-miles-an-hour burst of speed.

(ONDERDONK BUILDS THE "SKUZZY" TO FORCE THE PASSAGE.)

'Twas more than navigation: only eagles
Might follow up this run; the spawning salmon

Gulled by the mill-race had returned to rot
Their upturned bellies in the canyon eddies.
Two engines at the stern, a forrard winch,
Steam-powered, failed to stem the cataract.
The last resource was shoulders, arms and hands.
Fifteen men at the capstan, creaking hawsers,
Two hundred Chinese tugging at shore ropes
To keep her bow-on from the broadside drift,
The *Skuzzy* under steam and muscle took
The shoals and rapids, and warped through the Gate,
Until she reached the navigable water—
The adventure was not sailing: it was climbing.

As hard a challenge were the precipices
Worn water-smooth and sheer a thousand feet.
Surveyors from the edges looked for footholds,
But, finding none, they tried marine manoeuvres.
Out of a hundred men they drafted sailors
Whose toes as supple as their fingers knew
The wash of reeling decks, whose knees were hardened
Through tying gaskets at the royal yards:
They lowered them with knotted ropes and drew them
Along the face until the lines were strung
Between the juts. Barefooted, dynamite
Strapped to their waists, the sappers followed, treading
The spider films and chipping holes for blasts,
Until the cliffs delivered up their features
Under the civil discipline of roads.

RING, RING THE BELLS

Ring, ring the bells, but not the engine bells:
Today only the ritual of the steeple
Chanted to the dull tempo of the toll.
Sorrow is stalking through the camps, speaking
A common mother-tongue. 'Twill leave tomorrow
To turn that language on a Blackfoot tepee,
Then take its leisurely Pacific time
To tap its fingers on a coolie's door.
Ring, ring the bells but not the engine bells:
Today only that universal toll,
For granite, mixing dust with human lime,
Had so compounded bodies into boulders

As to untype the blood, and, then, the Fraser,
Catching the fragments from the dynamite,
Had bleached all birthmarks from her swirling dead.

Tomorrow and the engine bells again!

THE LAKE OF MONEY

(*The appeal to the Government for a loan of*
twenty-two-and-a-half million, 1883.)

Sir John began to muse on his excuses.
Was there no bottom to this lake? One mile
Along that northern strip had cost—how much?
Eleven dollars to the inch. The Road
In all would measure up to ninety millions,
And diverse hands were plucking at his elbow.
The Irish and the Dutch he could outface,
Outquip. He knew Van Horne and Shaughnessy
Had little time for speeches—one was busy
In grinding out two thousand miles; the other
Was working wizardry on creditors,
Pulling rabbits from hats, gold coins from sleeves
In Montreal. As for his foes like Blake,
He thanked his household gods the Irishman
Could claim only a viscous brand of humour,
Heavy, impenetrable till the hour
To laugh had taken on a chestnut colour.
But Stephen was his friend, hard to resist.
And there was Smith. He knew that both had pledged
Their private fortunes as security
For the construction of the Road. But that
Was not enough. Sir John had yet to dip
And scrape farther into the public pocket,
Explore its linings: his, the greater task;
His, to commit a nation to the risk.
How could he face the House with pauper hands?
He had to deal with Stephen first—a man
Laconic, nailing points and clinching them.
Oratory, the weapon of the massed assemblies
Was not the weapon here—Scot meeting Scot.
The burr was hard to take; and Stephen had

A Banffshire-cradled *r*. Drilling the ear,
It paralysed the nerves, hit the red cells.
The logic in the sound, escaping print,
Would seep through channels and befog the cortex.

Sir John counted the exits of discretion:
Disguise himself? A tailor might do much;
A barber might trim down his mane, brush back
The forelock, but no artist of massage,
Kneading that face from brow to nasal tip,
Could change a chunk of granite into talc.
His rheumatism? Yet he still could walk.
Neuralgia did not interfere with speech.
The bronchial tubing needed softer air?
Vacations could not cancel all appointments.
Men saw him in the flesh at Ottawa.
He had to speak this week, wheedling committees,
Much easier than to face a draper's clerk,
Tongue-trained on Aberdonian bargain-counters.
He raised his closed left hand to straighten out
His fingers one by one—four million people.
He had to pull a trifle on that fourth,
Not so resilient as the other three.
Only a wrench could stir the little finger
Which answered with a vicious backward jerk.

The dollar fringes of one hundred million
Were smirching up the blackboard of his mind.
But curving round and through them was the thought
He could not sponge away. Had he not fathered
The Union? Prodigy indeed it was
From Coast to Coast. Was not the Line essential?
What was this fungus sprouting from his rind
That left him at the root less clear a growth
Than this Dutch immigrant, William Van Horne?
The name suggested artificial land
Rescued from swamp by bulging dikes and ditches;
And added now to that were bogs and sloughs
And that most cursèd diabase which God
Had left from the explosions of his wrath.
And yet this man was challenging his pride.
North-Sea ancestral moisture on his beard,
Van Horne was now the spokesman for the West,
The champion of an all-Canadian route,

The Yankee who had come straight over, linked
His name and life with the Canadian nation.
Besides, he had infected the whole camp.
Whether acquired or natural, the stamp
Of faith had never left his face. Was it
The artist's instinct which had made the Rockies
And thence the Selkirks, scenes of tourist lure,
As easy for the passage of an engine
As for the flight of eagles? Miracles
Became his thought: the others took their cue
From him. They read the lines upon his lips.
But miracles did not spring out of air.
Under the driving will and sweltering flesh
They came from pay-cars loaded with the cash.
So that was why Stephen had called so often—
Money—that lake of money, bonds, more bonds.

*(The Bill authorizing the loan stubbornly carries
the House.)*

DYNAMITE ON THE NORTH SHORE

The lizard was in sanguinary mood.
She had been waked again: she felt her sleep
Had lasted a few seconds of her time.
The insects had come back—the ants, if ants
They were—dragging *those* trees, *those* logs athwart
Her levels, driving in *those* spikes; and how
The long grey snakes unknown within her region
Wormed from the east, unstriped, sunning themselves
Uncoiled upon the logs and then moved on,
Growing each day, ever keeping abreast!
She watched them, waiting for a bloody moment,
Until the borers halted at a spot,
The most invulnerable of her whole column,
Drove in that iron, wrenched it in the holes,
Hitting, digging, twisting. Why that spot?
Not this the former itch. That sharp proboscis
Was out for more than self-sufficing blood
About the cuticle: 'twas out for business
In the deep layers and the arteries.

And this consistent punching at her belly
With fire and thunder slapped her like an insult,
As with the blasts the caches of her broods
Broke—nickel, copper, silver and fool's gold,
Burst from their immemorial dormitories
To sprawl indecent in the light of day.
Another warning—this time different.

Westward above her webs she had a trap—
A thing called muskeg, easy on the eyes
Stung with the dust of gravel. Cotton grass,
Its white spires blending with the orchids,
Peeked through green table-cloths of sphagnum moss.
Carnivorous bladder-wort studded the acres,
Passing the water-fleas through their digestion.
Sweet-gale and sundew edged the dwarf black spruce;
And herds of cariboo had left their hoof-marks,
Betraying visual solidity,
But like the thousands of the pitcher plants,
Their downward-pointing hairs alluring insects,
Deceptive—and the men were moving west!
Now was her time. She took three engines, sank them
With seven tracks down through the hidden lake
To the rock bed, then over them she spread
A counterpane of leather-leaf and slime.
A warning, that was all for now. 'Twas sleep
She wanted, sleep, for drowsing was her pastime
And waiting through eternities of seasons.
As for intruders bred for skeletons—
Some day perhaps when ice began to move,
Or some convulsion ran fires through her tombs,
She might stir in her sleep and far below
The reach of steel and blast of dynamite,
She'd claim their bones as her possessive right
And wrap them cold in her pre-Cambrian folds.

THREATS OF SECESSION

The Lady's face was flushed. Thirteen years now
Since that engagement ring adorned her finger!
Adorned? Betrayed. She often took it off
And flung it angrily upon the dresser,
Then took excursions with her sailor-lover.

Had that man with a throat like Ottawa,
That tailored suitor in a cut-away,
Presumed compliance on her part? High time
To snub him for delay—for was not time
The marrow of agreement? At the mirror
She tried to cream a wrinkle from her forehead,
Toyed with the ring, replaced it and removed it.
Harder, she thought, to get it on and off—
This like the wrinkle meant but one thing, age.
So not too fast; play safe. Perhaps the man
Was not the master of his choice. Someone
Within the family group might well contest
Exotic marriage. Still, her plumes were ruffled
By Blake's two-nights' address before the Commons:
Three lines inside the twenty-thousand words
Had maddened her. She searched for hidden meanings—
"Should she insist on those preposterous terms
And threaten to secede, then let her go,
Better than ruin the country." "Let her go,"
And *"ruin"*—language this to shake her bodice.
Was this indictment of her character,
Or worse, her charm? Or was it just plain dowry?
For this last one at least she had an answer.
Pay now or separation—this the threat.
Dipping the ring into a soapy lather,
She pushed it to the second knuckle, twirled
It past. Although the diamond was off-colour,
She would await its partner ring of gold—
The finest carat; yes, by San Francisco!

BACK TO THE MOUNTAINS

As grim an enemy as rock was time.
The little men from five-to-six feet high,
From three-to-four score years in lease of breath,
Were flung in double-front against them both
In years a billion strong; so long was it
Since brachiapods in mollusc habitats
Were clamping shells on weed in ocean mud.
Now only yesterday had Fleming's men,
Searching for toeholds on the sides of cliffs,

Five thousand feet above sea-level, set
A tripod's leg upon a trilobite.
And age meant pressure, density. Sullen
With aeons, mountains would not stand aside;
Just block the path—morose but without anger,
No feeling in the menace of their frowns,
Immobile for they had no need of motion;
Their veins possessed no blood—they carried quartzite.
Frontal assault! To go through them direct
Seemed just as inconceivable as ride
Over their peaks. But go through them the men
Were ordered and their weapons were their hands
And backs, pickaxes, shovels, hammers, drills
And dynamite—against the rock and time;
For here the labour must be counted up
In months subject to clauses of a contract
Distinguished from the mortgage-run an age
Conceded to the trickle of the rain
In building river-homes. The men bored in,
The mesozoic rock arguing the inches.

This was a kind of surgery unknown
To mountains or the mothers of the myths.
These had a chloroform in leisured time,
Squeezing a swollen handful of light-seconds,
When water like a wriggling casuist
Had probed and found the areas for incision.
Now time was rushing labour—inches grew
To feet, to yards: the drills—the single jacks,
The double jacks—drove in and down; the holes
Gave way to excavations, these to tunnels,
Till men sodden with mud and roof-drip steamed
From sunlight through the tar-black to the sunlight.

HOLLOW ECHOES FROM THE TREASURY VAULT

Sir John was tired as to the point of death.
His chin was anchored to his chest. Was Blake
Right after all? And was Mackenzie right?
Superior could be travelled on. Besides,
It had a bottom, but those northern bogs
Like quicksands could go down to the earth's core.
Compared with them, quagmires of ancient legend

Were backyard puddles for old ducks. To sink
Those added millions down that wallowing hole!
He thought now through his feet. Many a time
When argument cemented opposition,
And hopeless seemed his case, he could think up
A tale to laugh the benches to accord.
No one knew better, when a point had failed
The brain, how to divert it through the ribs.
But now his stock of stories had run out.
This was exhaustion at its coma level.
Or was he sick? Never had spots like these
Assailed his eyes. He could not rub them out—
Those shifting images—was it the sunset
Refracted through the bevelled window edges?
He shambled over and drew down the blind;
Returned and slumped; it was no use; the spots
Were there. No light could ever shoot this kind
Of orange through a prism, or this blue,
And what a green! The spectrum was ruled out;
Its bands were too inviolate. He rubbed
The lids again—a brilliant gold appeared
Upon a silken backdrop of pure white,
And in the centre, red—a scarlet red,
A dancing, rampant and rebellious red
That like a stain spread outward covering
The vision field. He closed his eyes and listened:
Why, what was that? 'Twas bad enough that light
Should play such pranks upon him, but must sound
Crash the Satanic game, reverberate
A shot fifteen years after it was fired,
And culminate its echoes with the thud
Of marching choruses outside his window:

"We'll hang Riel up the Red River,
And he'll roast in hell forever,
We'll hang him up the River
With a yah-yah-yah."

The noose was for the shot: 'twas blood for blood;
The death of Riel for the death of Scott.
What could not Blake do with that on the Floor,
Or that young, tall, bilingual advocate

Who with the carriage of his syllables
Could bid an audience like an orchestra
Answer his body swaying like a reed?
Colours and sounds made riot of his mind—
White horses in July processional prance,
The blackrobe's swish, the Métis' sullen tread,
And out there in the rear the treaty-wise
Full-breeds with buffalo wallows on their foreheads.

This he could stand no longer, sick indeed:
Send for his doctor, the first thought, then No;
The doctor would advise an oculist,
The oculist return him to the doctor,
The doctor would see-saw him to another—
A specialist on tumours of the brain,
And he might recommend close-guarded rest
In some asylum—Devil take them all,
He had his work to do. He glanced about
And spied his medicine upon the sideboard;
Amber it was, distilled from Highland springs,
That often had translated age to youth
And boiled his blood on a victorious rostrum.
Conviction seized him as he stood, for here
At least he was not cut for compromise,
Nor curried to his nickname Old Tomorrow.
Deliberation in his open stance,
He trenched a deep one, gurgled and sat down.
What were those paltry millions after all?
They stood between completion of the Road
And bankruptcy of both Road and Nation.
Those north-shore gaps must be closed in by steel.
It did not need exhilarated judgment
To see the sense of that. To send the men
Hop-skip-and-jump upon lake ice to board
The flatcars was a revelry for imps.
And all that cutting through the mountain rock,
Four years of it and more, and all for nothing,
Unless those gaps were spanned, bedded and railed.
To quit the Road, to have the Union broken
Was irredeemable. He rose, this time
Invincibility carved on his features,
Hoisted a second, then drew up the blind.
He never saw a sunset just like this.

383

He lingered in the posture of devotion:
That sun for sure was in the west, or was it?
Soon it would be upholstering the clouds
Upon the Prairies, Rockies and the Coast:
He turned and sailed back under double-reef,
Cabined himself inside an armchair, stretched
His legs to their full length under the table.
Something miraculous had changed the air—
A chemistry that knew how to extract
The iron from the will: the spots had vanished
And in their place an unterrestrial nimbus
Circled his hair: the jerks had left his nerves:
The millions kept on shrinking or were running
From right to left: the fourth arthritic digit
Was straight, and yes, by heaven, the little fifth
Which up to now was just a calcium hook
Was suppling in the Hebridean warmth.
A blessèd peace fell like a dew upon him,
And soon, in trance, drenched in conciliation,
He hiccuped gently—"*Now let S-S-Stephen come!*"

(*The Government grants the Directors the right
to issue $35,000,000, guarantees $20,000,000, the
rest to be issued by the Railway Directors.
Stephen goes to London, and Lord Revelstoke,
speaking for the House of Baring, takes over the
issue.*)

SUSPENSE IN THE MONTREAL BOARD ROOM

Evening had settled hours before its time
Within the Room and on the face of Angus.
Dejection overlaid his social fur,
Rumpled his side-burns, left moustache untrimmed.
The vision of his Bank, his future Shops,
Was like his outlook for the London visit.
Van Horne was fronting him with a like visage
Except for two spots glowing on his cheeks—
Dismay and anger at those empty pay-cars.
His mutterings were indistinct but final
As though he were reciting to himself

The Athanasian damnatory clauses.
He felt the Receiver's breath upon his neck:
To come so near the end, and then this hurdle!

Only one thing could penetrate that murk—
A cable pledge from London, would it come?
Till now refusal or indifference
Had met the overtures. Would Stephen turn
The trick?
                    A door-knock and a telegram
With Stephen's signature! Van Horne ripped it
Apart. Articulation failed his tongue,
But Angus got the meaning from his face
And from a noisy sequence of deductions:—
An inkstand coasted through the office window,
Followed by shredded maps and blotting-pads,
Fluttering like shad-flies in a summer gale;
A bookshelf smitten by a fist collapsed;
Two chairs flew to the ceiling—one retired,
The other roosted on the chandelier.
Some thirty years erased like blackboard chalk,
Van Horne was in a school at Illinois.
Triumphant over his two-hundred weight,
He leaped and turned a cartwheel on the table,
Driving heel sparables into the oak,
Came down to teach his partner a Dutch dance;
And in the presence of the messenger,
Who stared immobilized at what he thought
New colours in the managerial picture,
Van Horne took hold of Angus bodily,
Tore off his tie and collar, mauled his shirt,
And stuffed a Grand Trunk folder down his breeches.

(*The last gap in the mountains—between the
Selkirks and Savona's Ferry—is closed.*)

The Road itself was like a stream that men
Had coaxed and teased or bullied out of Nature.
As if watching for weak spots in her codes,
It sought for levels like the watercourses.
It sinuously took the bends, rejoiced
In plains and easy grades, found gaps, poured through them,
But hating steep descents avoided them.
Unlike the rivers which in full rebellion

Against the canyons' hydrophobic slaver
Went to the limit of their argument:
Unlike again, the stream of steel had found
A way to climb, became a mountaineer.
From the Alberta plains it reached the Summit,
And where it could not climb, it cut and curved,
Till from the Rockies to the Coastal Range
It had accomplished what the Rivers had,
Making a hundred clean Caesarian cuts,
And bringing to delivery in their time
Their smoky, lusty-screaming locomotives.

THE SPIKE

Silver or gold? Van Horne had rumbled *"Iron"*.
No flags or bands announced this ceremony,
No Morse in circulation through the world,
And though the vital words like Eagle Pass,
Craigellachie, were trembling in their belfries,
No hands were at the ropes. The air was taut
With silences as rigid as the spruces
Forming the background in November mist.
More casual than camera-wise, the men
Could have been properties upon a stage,
Except for road maps furrowing their faces.

Rogers, his both feet planted on a tie,
Stood motionless as ballast. In the rear,
Covering the scene with spirit-level eyes,
Predestination on his chin, was Fleming.
The only one groomed for the ritual
From smooth silk hat and well-cut square-rig **beard**
Down through his Caledonian longitude,
He was outstaturing others by a foot,
And upright as the mainmast of a brig.
Beside him, barely reaching to his waist,
A water-boy had wormed his way in front
To touch this last rail with his foot, his face
Upturned to see the cheek-bone crags of Rogers.
The other side of Fleming, hands in pockets,
Eyes leaden-lidded under square-crowned hat,

And puncheon-bellied under overcoat,
Unsmiling at the focused lens—Van Horne.
Whatever ecstasy played round that rail
Did not leap to his face. Five years had passed,
Less than five years—so well within the pledge.

The job was done. Was this the slouch of rest?
Not to the men he drove through walls of granite.
The embers from the past were in his soul,
Banked for the moment at the rail and smoking,
Just waiting for the future to be blown.

At last the spike and Donald with the hammer!
His hair like frozen moss from Labrador
Poked out under his hat, ran down his face
To merge with streaks of rust in a white cloud.
What made him fumble the first stroke? Not age:
The snow belied his middle sixties. Was
It lapse of caution or his sense of thrift,
That elemental stuff which through his life
Never pockmarked his daring but had made
The man the canniest trader of his time,
Who never missed a rat-count, never failed
To gauge the size and texture of a pelt?
Now here he was caught by the camera,
Back bent, head bowed, and staring at a sledge,
Outwitted by an idiotic nail.
Though from the crowd no laughter, yet the spike
With its slewed neck was grinning up at Smith.
Wrenched out, it was replaced. This time the hammer
Gave a first tap as with apology,
Another one, another, till the spike
Was safely stationed in the tie and then
The Scot, invoking his ancestral clan,
Using the hammer like a battle-axe,
His eyes bloodshot with memories of Flodden,
Descended on it, rammed it to its home.

        *   *   *   *

The stroke released a trigger for a burst
Of sound that stretched the gamut of the air.
The shouts of engineers and dynamiters,
Of locomotive-workers and explorers,

Flanking the rails, were but a tuning-up
For a massed continental chorus. Led
By Moberly (of the Eagles and *this* Pass)
And Rogers (of *his own*), followed by Wilson,
And Ross (charged with the Rocky Mountain Section),
By Egan (general of the Western Lines),
Cambie and Marcus Smith, Harris of Boston,
The roar was deepened by the bass of Fleming,
And heightened by the laryngeal fifes
Of Dug McKenzie and John H. McTavish.
It ended when Van Horne spat out some phlegm
To ratify the tumult with *"Well Done"*
Tied in a knot of monosyllables.

Merely the tuning up! For on the morrow
The last blow on the spike would stir the mould
Under the drumming of the prairie wheels,
And make the whistles from the steam out-crow
The Fraser. Like a gavel it would close
Debate, making Macdonald's *"sea to sea"*
Pour through two oceanic megaphones—
Three thousand miles of *Hail* from port to port;
And somewhere in the middle of the line
Of steel, even the lizard heard the stroke.
The breed had triumphed after all. To drown
The traffic chorus, she must blend the sound
With those inaugural, narcotic notes
Of storm and thunder which would send her back
Deeper than ever in Laurentian sleep.

388

INDEX OF TITLES

391

INDEX OF FIRST LINES